Innovation and Tradition

in the

Writings of

The Venerable Bede

Medieval European Studies VI
Patrick W. Conner, Series Editor

Other Titles in the Series:

Innovation and Tradition
in the Writings of
The Venerable Bede

Edited by

Scott DeGregorio

West Virginia University Press
Morgantown 2006

West Virginia University Press, Morgantown 26506
© 2006 by West Virginia University Press

First edition published 2006 by West Virginia University Press
Printed in the United States of America

13 12 11 10 09 08 07 06   9 8 7 6 5 4 3 2 1

ISBN 1-933202-09-2 (alk. paper)

Library of Congress Cataloguing-in-Publication Data

Innovation and Tradition in the Writings of the Venerable Bede / edited
by Scott DeGregorio.
p. cm. – (Medieval European Studies ; 7)
1. Bede, the Venerable, Saint, 673-735. 2. Church history–Middle Ages,
600-1500. 3. Northumbria (England : Region)–Church history. I. Title.
II. DeGregorio, Scott. III. Series.

IN PROCESS

Library of Congress Control Number: 2005937639

Cover image: Bede writing the *De temporum ratione*, after an initial in a
12th-century version of *De temporum ratione*, Glasgow University Library
Hunter T.4.2, fol. 35r (Durham Cathedral Priory S.XII[1]).

To a great student of Bede,

Patrick Wormald,

whose camaraderie and wisdom

on all things Bedan

are sadly missed,

this volume is dedicated

Contents

Contents

Acknowledgments

THIS VOLUME HAS BEEN a long time in the making, and as its editor I wish to thank the contributors for their unflagging patience and good will as the process crept along. I wish to thank them too for their diligence in meeting various deadlines, often with too little notice. I am also grateful to the contributors as well as to Allen Frantzen, Celia Chazelle, and Paul Kershaw and for their helpful comments on the Introduction, and to the anonymous readers from West Virginia University Press for their meticulous reading of the entire manuscript and suggestions for revision. Thanks are due as well to Thomas N. Hall for his invitation to run a series of sessions on Bede as part of the "Sources of Anglo-Saxon Literary Culture" sessions at the Kalamazoo International Medieval Congress, which provided a most fertile soil out of which grew most of the contributions to this volume. The contributors also wish to thank Pat Conner and the staff at West Virginia University Press. They were indefatigable in dispensing assistance every step of the way, and we owe them a huge debt of gratitude for making this a better book. Finally, to the Humanities Department at the University of Michigan-Dearborn I am thankful for release-time granted during the Winter 2005 semester, which allowed me to focus on bringing this project finally to completion.

Abbreviations

Bede   CPE = *Collectio Bedae presbyteri ex opusculis sancti Augustini in Epistolae Pauli Apostoli*, still unprinted

DAM = *De arte metrica, ed.* Kendall, CCSL 123A

De oct. quest. = *De octo quaestionibus,* PL 93

De tab. = *De tabernaculo,* ed. Hurst, CCSL 119A

De templ. = *De templo,* ed. Hurst, CCSL 119A

DNR = *De natura rerum liber,* ed. Hurst CCSL 123A

DST = *De schematibus et tropis,* ed. Kendall, CCSL 123A

DT = *De temporibus,* ed. Jones, CCSL 123C

DTR = *De temporum ratione,* ed. Jones, CCSL 123B

Epist. Cath. = *In epistolas VII catholicas,* ed. Hurst, CCSL 121

Epist. Ecg. = *Epistola ad Ecgbertum Episcopum,* ed. Plummer, *Baedae opera historica*

Epist. Pleg. = *Epistola ad Plegwin,* ed. Jones, CCSL 123C

Epist. Wicht. = *Epistola ad Wichthedum,* ed. Jones, CCSL 123C

Exp. Apoc. = *Expositio Apocalypseos,* ed. Gryson, CCSL 121A

Exp. Act. = *Expositio Actuum Apostolorum,* ed. Laistner, CCSL 121

HA = *Historia abbatum auctore Baeda,* ed. Plummer, *Baedae opera historica*

HE = *Historia eccelesiastica gentis Anglorum,* ed. Colgrave and Mynors

Hom. = *Homiliae euangelii,* ed. Hurst CCSL 122

In Cant. = *In Cantica Canticorum,* ed. Hurst, CCSL 119B

In Ezram = *In Ezram et Neemiam,* ed. Hurst, CCSL 119A

In Gen. = *In principium Genesis,* ed. Jones, CCSL 118

In Hab. = *In Habacuc,* ed. Hudson, CCSL 119B

In Lucam = *In Lucam euangelium expositio,* ed. Hurst, CCSL 120

In Marcum = *In Marcum euangelium expositio,* ed. Hurst, CCSL 120

In prou. Sal. = *In prouerbia Salomonis,* ed. Hurst CCSL 119B

In Regum = *In Regum librum XXX quaestiones,* ed. Hurst, CCSL 119

In Sam. = *In primam partem Samuhelis,* ed. Hurst CCSL 119

In Tob. = *In Tobiam,* ed. Hurst, CCSL 119B

Retract. Act. = *Retractatio in Actus Apostolorum,* ed. Laistner, CCSL 121

VCP = *Vita sancti Cuthberti,* ed. Colgrave, *Two Lives of Saint Cuthbert*

CSEL	Corpus scriptorum ecclesiasticorum latinorum
CCSL	Corpus Christianorum, Series Latina
CPL	Clavis patrum latinorum
GCS	Die griechischen christlichen Schriftstellar der ersten drei Jahrhunderte
LCL	Loeb Classical Library
MGH	Monumenta Germaniae Historica
PG	Patrologia Graeca
PL	Patrologia Latina
SC	Sources chrétiennes

Introduction: The New Bede

Scott DeGregorio

F OR THE QUANTITY, VARIETY, AND BRILLIANCE of his work, it is likely that Bede would have stood out in any age.[1] The recent
increase in collective interpretations of his writings has done
much to remind us of that and, in itself, provides a clear sign of
the vitality currently animating the study of Bede and his world.[2]
Innovation and Tradition in the Writings of the Venerable Bede, which
had its origin in a series of sessions held between 1998 and 2003

---

[1] Good accounts of Bede's life are available in George Hardin Brown, *Bede
the Venerable,* (Boston, 1987), pp. 1–23; and Benedicta Ward, *The Venerable
Bede* (London, 1990), pp. 1–18.

[2] See the essay collections by L. A. J. R. Houwen and A. A. MacDonald, eds.,
Beda Venerabilis: Historian, Monk and Northumbrian (Groningen, 1996) and
Stéphane Lebecq, Michel Perrin, and Olivier Szerwiniack, eds., *Bède le
Vénérable: entre tradition et postérité* (Lille, 2005); earlier volumes include
*Bede: His Life, Times, and Writings: Essays in Commemoration of the Twelfth
Centenary of his Death,* ed. A. Hamilton Thompson (Oxford, 1935);
*Famulus Christi: Essays in Commemoration of the Thirteenth Centenary of the
Birth of the Venerable Bede,* ed. Gerald Bonner (London, 1976); and *Bede
and Anglo-Saxon England: Papers in Honour of the 1300th Anniversary of the
Birth of Bede, given at Cornell University in 1973 and 1974,* ed. Robert T.
Farrell, British Archaeological Reports 46 (London, 1978). In addition,
see *Northumbria's Golden Age,* ed. Jane Hawkes and Susan Mills (Stroud,
1999), which contains six papers on Bede; and the annual Jarrow Lecture,
the first thirty-six of which are now gathered in *Bede and His World: The
Jarrow Lectures,* ed. Michael Lapidge, 2 vols. (Aldershot, 1994).

at the International Medieval Congress,[3] continues this development but differs from its predecessors in showing how Bedan scholarship has shifted its emphasis in recent years. The studies gathered here attest to three developments in particular.

The first and perhaps most significant of these—insofar as it makes way for the other two—is the ground that has been gained in the study of Bede's *opera exegetica*. The importance of his *opera historica* notwithstanding, the exegesis of Scripture was undeniably his life work. Evident not only from the sheer bulk of his output, it is a point Bede himself wished to make in his autobiographical note at the end of the *Historia ecclesiastica.* "I have spent all my life in this monastery," he would write, "applying myself entirely to the study of Scripture."[4] Earlier scholars were not deaf to his words; in her 1946 study of Bede's spiritual teachings, Carroll noted the "particular irony" of Bede's modern celebrity as a historian: "When renown first attached to his name, it was as a 'Candle of the Church,' as an 'authority' in ecclesiastical doctrine, as the composer of precious volumes of biblical commentaries and homilies that he was known."[5] Still, as late as 1973, Gerald Bonner had no choice but to conclude his

---

[3] The only exceptions are Goffart's essay, which originated from the "Bede as Writer and Thinker" conference held at the University of Minnesota in April of 1998; and DeGregorio's essay, which was composed for this volume.

[4] *HE* 5.24 (p. 566). The full passage reads as follows: "cunctumque . . . uitae in eiusdem monasterii habitatione peragens, omnem meditandis scripturis operam dedi, atque inter obseruantiam disciplinae regularis, et cotidianam cantandi in ecclesia curam, semper aut discere aut docere aut scribere dulce habui. . . . Ex quo tempore accepti presbyteratus usque ad annum aetatis meae LVIIII haec in Scripturam sanctam meae meorumque necessitati ex opusculis uenerabilium patrum breuiter adnotare, siue etiam ad formam sensus et interpretationis eorum superadicere curaui."

[5] Sister Mary Thomas Aquinas Carroll, *Bede: Spiritual Teachings: His Spiritual Teachings,* Catholic University of America Studies in Medieval History 9 (Washington, D.C., 1946), p. vii. Cf. Claude Jenkins, "Bede as Exegete and Theologian," in *Bede: His Life, Times, and Writings,* p. 152.

2

appraisal of the state of Bedan studies on a low note, forced as he was to characterize biblical exegesis as the one area "most in need of investigation in contemporary Bedan studies."[6] "Thirty years ago," Bonner went on to explain in poignant lines:

> in his great history, *Anglo-Saxon England,* Sir Frank Stenton pointed out that Bede would himself have wished to be remembered by these works of exposition, and the Middle Ages undoubtedly thought of him first and foremost as an exegete, standing in the patristic tradition. Yet in spite of this Bede has been little studied in modern times as an interpreter of Scripture. Yet it is here, perhaps, that he is most himself and speaks to the reader heart to heart; for to Bede the elucidation of Holy Scripture was the goal to which all learning and study was ultimately directed. Let us end, then, with a plea for scholars with a taste for ecclesiastical Latin to take the hint and give Bede the attention in this field which he undoubtedly deserved."[7]

It would take some time still, but the kind of intensive study of Bede's exegesis for which Bonner longed has at last come into its own. The advances that have been made since Bonner drafted his appraisal are impressive by any standards. Today we possess not only a nearly-complete run of critical editions of Bede's eighteen commentaries, little more than a desideratum for an earlier generation of scholars.[8] All but a handful of these are now readily available in outstanding English translations as

---

[6] Gerald Bonner, "Bedan Studies in 1973," *The Clergy Review* 53 (1973): 695.

[7] Bonner, "Bedan Studies in 1973," pp. 695–6.

[8] See, for example, Laistner's regret over the dearth of proper editions: "Bede as a Classical and Patristic Scholar," *Transactions of the Royal Historical Society,* 4th Series 16 (1933): 79–80; also Paul Meyvaert, *Bede and Gregory the Great* (Jarrow Lecture, 1966), pp. 14–15. Bede's commentaries are now printed in CCSL 118–121A; these have replaced the nineteenth-century editions by J. A. Giles that are reprinted in PL 91–93. See Michael Gorman, "The Canon of Bede's Works and the World of Ps-Bede," *Revue*

well, while work on translating many of the remaining volumes is either underway or projected.[9] Obviously of value for opening up Bede's exegetical corpus to wider audiences unable to penetrate his challenging Latin, these English translations have in addition helped specialists to arrive at new insights on the works themselves and, beyond that, on Bede's wider merits as a commentator. The trend is well evidenced by five of the essays dealing with his exegesis in the present volume (Kendall, Brown, DeGregorio, Holder, and Martin), as they all are the work of scholars who have translated the text under discussion.[10]

The intensification of interest in Bede's exegesis has helped

---

Bénédictine 111 (2001): 399–445, for a superb overview of the earlier print history. To date, CCSL contains all but two of Bede's commentaries, *De octo quaestionibus* and the Collectaneum on the Pauline Epistles, which still lies in manuscript. On a less positive note, some of the CCSL volumes are scarcely ideal: see Paul Meyvaert, "Bede the Scholar," in *Famulus Christi*, p. 44, and Michael Gorman, "Source Marks and Chapter Divisions in Bede's Commentary on Luke," *Revue Bénédictine* 112 (2002): 256–8.

[9] Those now available in translation include the commentaries on 1) the Apocalypse; 2) the Seven Catholic Epistles; 3) the Acts of the Apostles; 4) the Tabernacle; 5) the Temple; 6) portions of Kings; 7) Ezra-Nehemiah; 8) Habakkuk; 9) Tobit; and 10) the Pauline Epistles; there is also a translation of the fifty gospel homilies: see Bibliography for complete details. Additionally, *Bede: A Biblical Miscellany*, trans. W. Trent Foley and Arthur G. Holder, Translated Texts for Historians 28 (Liverpool, 1999), contains translations of *De octo quaestionibus, De locis sanctis, De mansionibus filiorum Israel*, and *De eo quod ait Isaias*, which may be described as four shorter biblical works. Translations currently in progress include *In primam partem Samuhelis* by George Hardin Brown, *In Canticum* by Arthur Holder, *In Genesim* by Calvin Kendall, and a new translation of *Expositio Apocalypseos* by Faith Wallis.

[10] See the previous note for translations now in progress. For other important recent studies of the commentaries, see the entries in the Bibliography under Gorman, Holder, and DeGregorio.

to pave the way for the maturation of the second development. I say "maturation" because at issue is not so much a brand new insight, as one that has only recently gained wider support from scholars. I refer here to an appreciation of the inter-textual dimension of Bede's writings, to the recognition that they can and should be studied in full concert with each other rather than in isolation.

Earlier Bedan scholarship was more often than not content with studying Bede strictly as an historian, an exegete, a hagiographer, or a scientist, without bringing these discourses into contact as he develops them.[11] To be sure, such approaches have their value; they are employed by some of the contributors to this volume. Already in the latter part of the last century, however, Roger Ray for one was keen to recognize that an integrated mode of approach has its purchase too. Writing specifically about the commentaries, he argued "that exegesis was the driving force of all Bede's learning and that strong ties link the commentaries to his other writings."[12] Scholars have since become fully cognizant of the value of Ray's formulation. Consequently, Bede's entire oeuvre is now seen as a site where various kinds of cross fertilization may be detected and productively examined.[13] In the present volume, the essays by Ray, Thacker,

---

[11] This is the approach of *Bede: His Life, Times, and Writings* and, with the exception of Ray's essay, of *Famulus Christi. Bede and Anglo-Saxon England* and *Beda Venerabilis* meanwhile provide no coverage of Bede's exegetical writings. By contrast, a number of the essays in *Bède le Vénérable* reflect the move towards more integrative approaches, on which see the next two notes.

[12] Roger Ray, "What Do We Know about Bede's Commentaries," *Recherches de théologie ancienne et médiévale* 49 (1982): 8. See also his "Bede, the Exegete, as Historian," in *Famulus Christi*, pp. 125–40, as well as Judith McClure, "Bede's Old Testament Kings," in *Ideal and Reality in Frankish and Anglo-Saxon Society: Studies Presented to J. M. Wallace-Hadrill*, ed. Patrick Wormald (Oxford, 1983), pp. 76–98.

Wallis, DeGregorio, and Holder all model such approaches to a greater and a lesser extent. Wallis's essay, for example, successfully integrates Bede's historical, hagiographical and exegetical writings with his computistical works to offer a new and revealing interpretation of Bede's "science," thus proving the interconnectedness of what have usually been treated as different if not wholly unrelated genres.

The third development in Bedan Studies that may be detected in this volume concerns a shift in understanding Bede's own self-conception of himself as a writer and scholar. The tendency of much earlier scholarship was to emphasize Bede's conservatism—his commitment to tradition, his impeccable orthodoxy, his humility and deference to authority, his calculated unoriginality, his quiet idealism, his saintly piety.[14] As a commentator, he was to be seen as little more than a compiler, concerned only with channeling the writings of others; as a historian, he was a master of technique, sagacious, tranquil, an idealist. Collectively, his output was admired for its erudition and polish, while the man himself could be hailed as "one of the outstanding figures of the whole medieval period,"[15] to quote Max Laistner. But it

[13] Some recent examples include Georges Tugene, "L'histoire 'ecclesiastique' du peuple anglais: Réflexions sur le particularisme et l'universalisme chez Béde," *Recherches Augustiniennes* 17 (1982): 129–72, along with his larger study of the theme in his book *L'idée de nation chez Bède le Vénérable*, Collection des Études Augustiniennes, Série Moyen Âge et Temps Modernes 37 (Paris, 2001); Scott DeGregorio, "The Venerable Bede on Prayer and Contemplation," *Traditio* 54 (1999): 1–39, and "Bede's *In Ezram et Neemiam* and the Reform of the Northumbrian Church," *Speculum* 79 (2004): 1–25; Stephen Harris, "Bede and Gregory's Allusive Angels," *Criticism* 44.3 (2002): 271–89; Erik Knibbs, "Exegetical Hagiography: Bede's Prose *Vita Sancti Cuthberti*," *Revue Bénédictine* 114.2 (2004): 233–52; and Jennifer O'Reilly, "Islands and Idols at the End of the Earth: Exegesis and Conversion in Bede's *Historia ecclesiastica*," in *Bède le Vénérable*, pp. 119–45.

[14] See below, n. 16.

could never be that this eighth-century monk laboring quietly on the fringes of the civilized world would ever consider himself anything more than a follower of tradition: *patrum uestigia sequens* ("following the footsteps of the Fathers"), as his favorite phrase was taken to mean. And so it is that Laistner, in the very same article, could say the following on the subject of Bede and his library: " . . .he made the best use of it, even though it did not very greatly stimulate his own originality; for to be a scholar meant in his day, and for many years to come, being a traditionalist. Bede's importance lies not in his original ideas, but in the selfless devotion with which he digested much of the learning and doctrine of the Fathers and passed it on in a simpler and more intelligible form to his own people and to later generations."[16]

In the estimation of much recent Bede scholarship, the present essays included, there is a good deal to question about the foregoing characterization. The preference today is for a rather different Bede, this one a more imposing figure.[17] To sample some of the conceptions to emerge from the essays collected

---

[15] Laistner, "Bede as Classical and Patristic Scholar," p. 70.

[16] Laistner, "Bede as Classical and Patristic Scholar," pp. 92–93; see also p. 71. For comparable sentiments, see Jenkins, "Bede as Exegete and Theologian," pp. 167–8; Joseph de Ghellinck, *Littérature latine au Moyen Âge* (Paris, 1939), p. 34; David Knowles, *Saints and Scholars: Twenty-Five Medieval Portraits* (Cambridge, 1962), p. 17; and Gerald Bonner, "Bede and His Legacy," *Durham University Journal* 78.2 (1986), pp. 221–2. On Bede's orthodoxy and piety, see Charles Plummer, introduction to *Venerabilis Baedae opera historica*, 2 vols. (1896; reprinted as one volume, Oxford, 1946), pp. lxii–lxix.

[17] Two ground-breaking discussions that helped to initiate this shift are Roger Ray, "Bede and Cicero," *Anglo-Saxon England* 16 (1987): 1–15, which draws attention to Bede's bold critique of Jerome's views on pagan literature; and Walter Goffart, "Bede and the Ghost of Bishop Wilfrid," in *The Narrators of Barbarian History (A.D. 550-800): Jordanes, Gregory of Tours, Bede, and Paul the Deacon* (Princeton, 1988; reprinted, Notre

here, this Bede is "a creator of Christian Latin culture" (Ray), has "grand aspirations in his chosen field of religious learning" (Thacker), is "original even while following traditional paths" (Brown), has "the status of an *auctor*" (DeGregorio), is "*engagé* and an interventionist" (Goffart), and is even "a patristic figure" (Hill). None of this is to suggest that Bede did not revere authority and tradition; on the contrary, Hill's essay details how in later times Bede would come to been seen as a model for orthodoxy itself. What is different is an assumption that deference to authority and tradition on Bede's part did not always have to amount to a total drain of innovation or social engagement.[18]

According to this view, then, Bede's favorite tag means something else altogether. It implies that he is moving in the same direction as the Fathers as one of their equals (*patrum uestigia sequens*), not that he is putting his feet in the exact same tracks by undertaking a program of slavish quotation and repetition (*patrum in uestigiis sequens*). Such a shift in perspective enables us to see in his writings a process more complex than that of merely "digesting and passing on" tradition, as Laistner's view has it. For in a very real sense, the role Bede played in this regard was anything but passive: as a scholar, a writer, and a teacher, it fell to him to determine what should be brought forth from the past and what should be relegated to oblivion—in a word, to determine *what* tradition is. And alongside that task, there

Dame, 2005), which unveils the local circumstances that influenced the composition of the *Historia ecclesiastica*. These authors return to these topics in their essays below. Also significant are Alan Thacker, "Bede's Ideal of Reform," in *Ideal and Reality in Frankish and Anglo-Saxon Society: Studies Presented to J. M. Wallace-Hadrill*, ed. Patrick Wormald (Oxford, 1983), pp. 103–22; and DeGregorio, "Bede on Prayer."

[18] As DeGregorio for one has recently emphasized: see "*Nostrorum socordiam temporum*: The Reforming Impulse of Bede's Later Exegesis," *Early Medieval Europe* 11 (2002): 107–22, and "Bede's *In Ezram et Neemiam* and the Reform of the Northumbrian Church," *Speculum* 79 (2004): 1–25.

was yet another still: to remold and in this way to "make new" what he had selected so that it might best suit the needs of his eighth-century Anglo-Saxon world—and so innovation merges with tradition. The essays that follow explore some of the possibilities this dynamic interchange between tradition and innovation can be seen to take in Bede's oeuvre. They emphasize that he imaginatively redeploys received rhetorical, exegetical, and historical methods, critiques the present rather than merely synthesizing the past, and corrects the views of past *auctores* where such intervention and innovation could aid his contemporaries. Whatever the scenario, the Bede who emerges from the pages of the present volume is better seen as a creator, an innovator, and a critic of tradition and of his own age than as a follower, a popularizer, or a traditionalist plain and simple.

In reflecting these developments, the studies that comprise *Innovation and Tradition in the Writings of the Venerable Bede* offer a cross-section of the fundamentally changed world of Bedan scholarship. Accordingly, the book is best viewed in the context of its predecessor volumes as a measure of how much scholarship on Bede has progressed during the past century. The new issues that have come to the fore are reflected in the kinds of questions we ask here: How did Bede understand his own activity as a scholar and writer? What continuities and developments mark the course of his career? How do his various writings illuminate one another? To what extent can we discern in his oeuvre "footsteps" of his own, separate from those of the Fathers? And why did his writings so quickly gain him the status of a *doctor ecclesiae*? The attempt to answer such questions has resulted in a high degree of consensus among the contributors, and the results are especially productive in those instances where focused readings of individual Bedan works in one essay intersect with treatments of larger issues in another. Of course, in conversations of this kind some disagreement among contributors is to be expected, and in the end this book attempts nothing like a definitive synthesis of all of Bede's work. Its more modest aim in bringing together the work of these ten scholars will be well served if it encourages a more complex view of Bede as a sophisticated writer and activist in the culture of his day, and a figure worthy of continued study in ours.

Who Did Bede Think He Was?

Roger Ray

IN THIS ESSAY I SHALL PROPOSE that Bede saw himself as a creator of Christian Latin culture, specifically as the latest in a
line of fellow creators, like Augustine and Jerome.[1] He would
never have claimed to be one of the *patres*; it would have been
an immense rhetorical blunder that would have driven his (or
Augustine's or Jerome's) readers away. By apparent contrast,
he claims occasionally to be "following the footsteps of the Fathers," *patrum uestigia sequens*, and this phrase, which is discussed
in more than one contribution to the present volume, has been
for many Bedan scholars what *fides quaerens intellectum* has been
for the students of Anselm of Bec, a caption for a large body of
thought and literature.[2] In his autobiographical sketch at the
end of the *Historia ecclesiastica*, Bede tells us that he all but made
a career of excerpting patristic works.[3] Over against these well

---

[1] In a footnote I raised this possibility in *Bede, Rhetoric, and the Creation of
Christian Latin Culture* (Jarrow Lecture, 1997), p. 18, n. 10. See Joseph
Kelly, "Bede on the Brink," *Journal of Early Christian Studies* 5 (1997):
85–103, who views Bede not as a father but as a conduit between the
patristic and medieval worlds; and Richard W. Pfaff, "Bede among the
Fathers: The Evidence of Liturgical Commemoration," *Studia Patristica*
28 (1993): 225–9, who treats not Bede's own self-estimate but English
liturgical evidence of his subsequent reputation.

[2] E.g., *In Sam.* 1 (p. 10, lines 52–54). Other cases of Bede's use of this
phrase include *In Regum* Prol. (p. 293, lines 22–30); *In Cant.* Prol. (p. 180,
lines 501–04); *Exp. Act. Apost.*, Praef (p. 3, lines 9–10); *Hom.* 2.11 (p. 258,
lines 191–92); and *DTR* 5 (p. 287, line 86).

[3] Bede, *HE* 5.24 (p. 566).

known words of apparent subordination I would place three observations.

Many Fathers, Few and Faint Footprints,
and Rhetorical Deference

First of all, we might bear in mind that the notion of only four Doctors of the Latin church (Jerome, Ambrose, Augustine, and Gregory I) was not promulgated until 1298, during the pontificate of Boniface VIII. This is helpful to remember since in Bede's writings he never counts the number of Fathers. In a single sentence of his commentary on Luke, acknowledging his major sources, he is the first writer to name the four future canonical Fathers together, but he quickly adds that he relied also on *ceteri patres*, other Fathers.[4] Throughout his career he revered and used the works of many previous Christian writers besides those of the canonical four, as even Laistner's incomplete catalogue of Bede's library shows.[5] The ubiquitous view that the age of the western Fathers ended with Isidore of Seville is arbitrary and would have irked and even shocked Bede, given his sharp reservations about Isidore.[6] At any rate, "patristics" meant nothing to Bede. *Auctoritates* meant everything, and for him there

---

[4] Bede, *In Lucam* Prol. (p. 7, lines 95–105). The topic is treated in a recent essay by Bernice M. Kaczynski, "Bede's Commentaries on Luke and Mark and the Formation of a Patristic Canon," in *Anglo-Latin Literature and Its Heritage: Essays in Honour of A. G. Rigg on His 64th Birthday*, ed. Siân Echard and Gernot R. Wieland, Publications of the Journal of Medieval Latin 4 (Turnhout, 2001), pp. 17–26.

[5] M. L. W. Laistner, "The Library of the Venerable Bede," in *Bede, His Life, Times, and Writings: Essays in Commemoration of the Twelfth Centenary of his Death*, ed. A. Hamilton Thompson (Oxford, 1935), pp. 237–66.

[6] See e.g., Frank Cross and Elizabeth A. Livingstone, *The Oxford Dictionary of the Church*, 2nd edn. (Oxford, 1974), p. 504. On Bede and Isidore, see n. 18 below.

were many. In all, his works give us no reason to think that *patres* and *doctores* were a thing of the past and that no new ones would ever rise up to shape the Christian Latin tradition. His abbot Hwaetberht obviously saw that Bede was, as Malcolm Parkes has observed, at least a best-selling star, for after 716 he charged the Wearmouth-Jarrow scriptorium to undertake a furious production of his works, which were in increasing demand elsewhere.[7] Soon after Bede's death his writings were called to the continent by the Anglo-Saxon missionaries, the chief of whom, Boniface, thought Bede was *candela ecclesiae*, the lamp of the church, presumably of all the church.[8] Apparently Bede was to Boniface what Gregory the Great was to Bede, a catholic apostle. Many know that in the ninth century Bede was often put among the *patres*.[9] Alcuin, for example, thought there were five Fathers: Jerome, Augustine, Ambrose, Gregory the Great, and Bede.[10] Notker Balbulus was especially enthusiastic, claiming that "God . . .who on the fourth day of the creation of the world brought forth the sun in the east, ordained in the sixth age of mankind Bede as a new sun in the west, to illuminate the whole globe."[11] In the twelfth-

[7] See Malcolm B. Parkes, *The Scriptorium of Wearmouth-Jarrow* (Jarrow Lecture, 1982), p. 22; Joyce Hill, *Bede and the Benedictine Reform* (Jarrow Lecture, 1998), pp. 3–6; and David Rollason, *Bede and Germany* (Jarrow Lecture, 2001), pp. 9–14.

[8] Boniface, *Epistola*, no. 76 (MGH, Epistolae selectae, I, p. 159). Also Parkes, *Scriptorium*, p. 569.

[9] See Hill's essay in this volume.

[10] Alcuin, *Epistola*, no. 216 (MGH, Epistolae 4, p. 2).

[11] Quoted and translated from Notker's *De interpretationibus divinarum scripturarum* by Dorothy Whitelock, *After Bede* (Jarrow Lecture, 1960), p. 10. This magisterial essay is a fine discussion of Bede's legacy. See also George Hardin Brown, *Bede the Venerable* (Boston, 1987), pp. 97–103; and J. E. Cross, "Bede's Influence at Home and Abroad," in *Beda Venerabilis: Historian, Monk and Northumbrian*, ed. L. A. J. R. Houwen and A. A. MacDonald (Groningen, 1996), pp. 17–29.

century revival of thought and letters, scribes voluminously copied Bedan manuscripts as if his works were, as Peter Abelard remarked, "accepted in the entire Latin church."[12] According to Benedicta Ward, Thomas Aquinas thought the same thing.[13] Arthur Holder reckons that Bede would have "blushed" to think that posterity would put him among the *patres*.[14] I have come to doubt that in his heart Bede would have turned from all this praise. It is interesting and perhaps telling that in his later works, as Alan Thacker has found, Bede was fascinated with *spirituales magistri, sancti praedicatores, rectores,* and *doctores ecclesiae*.[15] Since in the latter half of his scholarly career his works became an industry, it must surely have occurred to Bede that others would use such language to speak of him and that there would surely be those who would follow in *his* footsteps, as indeed so many did.

Obviously he felt authorized to walk where the four Latin Fathers never trod. He was indeed a pioneer in a number of his works—the school treatises, several biblical commentaries (on the Apocalypse, on the Acts of the Apostles, on the Temple and the Tabernacle, on Ezra- Nehemiah), the historical martyrology, the *Historia abbatum,* and the *Historia ecclesiastica.* In the preface to *De templo,* Bede speaks of his work as *res noua,* and indeed, as Holder has found, here and in the companion work on the Tab-

---

[12] Abelard, *Historia calamitatum,* trans. Betty Radice and M. T. Clanchy, *The Letters of Abelard and Heloise* (New York, 2003), p. 26.

[13] Benedicta Ward, *The Venerable Bede* (London, 1990), p. 142.

[14] Arthur G. Holder, "Bede and the Tradition of Patristic Exegesis," *Anglican Theological Review* 72 (1990): 401.

[15] Alan Thacker, "Bede's Ideal of Reform," in *Ideal and Reality in Frankish and Anglo-Saxon Society: Studies Presented to John Michael Wallace-Hadrill,* ed. Patrick Wormald, Donald Bullough, and Roger Collins (Oxford, 1983), pp. 122–3, as well as his essay in this volume, pp. 43-46. See also Scott DeGregorio, "Bede on Prayer and Contemplation," *Traditio* 54 (1999): 5–8, and "Bede's *In Ezram et Neemiam* and the Reform of the Northumbrian Church," *Speculum* 79 (2004): 13–16.

ernacle the Fathers gave him very little to go on.[16] For him the patristic map of Christian Latin culture was apparently not fully drawn. There was need for new leadership, and from the success of his books over several centuries it appears that he provided it. In Laistner's incomplete list of Bede's manuscripts the extant texts of his biblical commentaries fill almost sixty pages, a number worthy of any *pater*, and we can only guess how many the Vikings destroyed or were otherwise lost.[17]

It is we who are fascinated with the canonical view of the four Latin Church Fathers, the definition of which came much after Bede. And it is irrelevant here that in 1298 Boniface VIII did not follow a strong tradition and count Bede as the fifth doctor of the Latin Church. It was not a good year for papal honor to England, since the English crown was in bad odor at the papal court. What is relevant is that, when it came to the makers of Christian Latin culture, Bede himself did not think four was a sacred number. For him the world of the *patres* was both vouchsafed and unfolding, both old and new.

In the second place, the tearing hurry in which Bede seems to have written major work after major work in the last decade of his life, one of the most remarkable authorial runs in the history of Latin literature, suggests that to his mind the footsteps of the Fathers were too few and sometimes too faint. In his gray whiskers he may have produced more than a dozen major titles, including perhaps as many as ten exegetical works, not to mention the *Historia ecclesiastica*. It may well be true that, as the *Epistola Cuthberti de obitu Bedae* relates, Bede rose up on

---

[16] See Arthur G. Holder, "New Treasures for Old in Bede's *De tabernaculo* and *De templo*," *Revue Bénédictine* 99 (1989): 237–40. The same is true for the third installment of the trilogy, *In Ezram et Neemiam*: see DeGregorio, "Reform of the Northumbrian Church," p. 3, and also his essay below.

[17] M. L. W. Laistner with H. H. King, *A Hand-List of Bede's Manuscripts* (Ithaca, N.Y., 1943), pp. 20–82.

his deathbed and wrote copy, and even used his last energies to attack a reputed church father, Isidore of Seville.[18] If it is not true, it is striking that those shortly after him were prepared to believe it. Among his final writings was certainly the triumphant and all but complete bibliography of his works given at the end of the *Historia ecclesiastica*. The list comes just after Bede remarks that he had given most of his career to excerpting the Fathers, and he revealingly adds that he had to do some work on them: " . . . ex opusculis uenerabilium patrum breuiter adnotare, siue etiam ad formam sensus et interpretationis eorum superadicere curaui."[19] Apparently unable to believe that Bede would have been so bold as to improve the Fathers, Plummer mistranslated him: " . . . I have endeavored . . . to make brief notes on the holy Scripture, either out of the works of the venerable Fathers or in conformity with their meaning and interpretation."[20] Bede's words are in fact a rather aggressive and immodest thing to say: " . . . I have made it my business . . . to make brief extracts from the works of the venerable Fathers . . . or to add notes of my own to clarify their sense and meaning."[21] Was he, tired and perhaps ill, vaguely but honestly complaining that the footsteps of the

[18] *Epistola Cuthberti de obitu Bedae*, in *Historia ecclesiastica gentis Anglorum*, ed. Bertram Colgrave and R. A. B. Mynors, Oxford Medieval Texts (1969; reprinted with corrections, 1991), pp. 580–7. See esp. 582–3 on the *exceptiones* Bede took to the "lie" in Isidore's *Liber rotarum*. For a different view of Bede's attitude toward Isidore, see the two articles by William D. McCready, "Bede, Isidore, and the *Epistola Cuthberti*," *Traditio* 50 (1995): 75–94, and "Bede and the Isidorian Legacy," *Mediaeval Studies* 57 (1995): 43–73.

[19] Bede, *HE* 5:24 (p. 566).

[20] Charles Plummer, *Venerabilis Baedae opera historica*, 2 vols. (1896; reprinted, 2 vols. in 1, Oxford, 1946), p. x.

[21] This is Bertram Colgrave's translation, taken from *Historia ecclesiastica gentis Anglorum*, ed. and trans. Bertram Colgrave and R. A. B. Mynors (1969; reprinted with corrections, Oxford, 1991), p. 567. All subsequent translations from Bede's *Historia ecclesiastica* are from this edition.

Fathers had not always been clear and suggesting that others will need his guidance too if they are to understand the Bible? Next he straightaway lists almost all of his books, and I cannot believe that as he looked over his finished bibliography he felt nothing but gratitude to the Fathers. "It is human to rejoice in one's judgments on things, if they have been prudently set forth," wrote Bede in his comment on Proverbs 15:23.[22] As Bede reviewed the list of his books I would think he rejoiced. They are an architecture of knowledge, rising up to an entire edifice of Christian Latin learning, founded on educational treatises, elevated by biblical commentaries and homilies, pierced and illumined by saints' lives, and covered majestically by a great book of Latin historiography written for the king. No Christian Latin writer before him had ever built anything so complete. We cannot account for this accomplishment if we do not recognize that, in the world of prime Latin Christian authorities, Bede wanted to take his place among the others, as of course he did.

My third observation is that his rhetorical skill may have led us astray to think that his vocational aspirations are expressed well in language like *patrum uestigia sequens*. He was the master of appeals to what the Greco-Roman rhetors called *ethos*, the character of the author or speaker. In particular, he was an expert at *captatio benevolentiae*, capturing the good will of the reader, including us. In a classic history of medieval literature, W. P. Ker observes that Bede's perennial reputation as "a great man" suffered nothing even from Enlightenment rationalists; he apparently worked his magic even though his books contain things that Voltaire and others usually wanted to throw on the rubbish heap.[23] The preface to the *Historia ecclesiastica*

---

[22] Bede, *In prou. Sal.* 2 (p. 88, lines 76–77): "Humanum quidem est de sua sententia quasi prudenter prolata quemque laetari . . ." Quoted and translated by Paul Meyvaert, "Bede the Scholar," in *Famulus Christi: Essays in Commemoration of the Thirteenth Centenary of the Birth of the Venerable Bede*, ed. Gerald Bonner (London, 1976), p. 66.

[23] W. P. Ker, *The Dark Ages* (London, 1958), p. 95.

illustrates this captivating modesty exceptionally well. It is built from the Greco-Roman rhetorical topos of narrative truth, and it is mainly about *ethos*, his own character as a Latin author. At the end he tells his reader that, although he had gone to great lengths to find authoritative documents and eyewitness testimony, he had no choice but to write mainly from *fama vulgans,* and he asks that no one blame him if in these oral traditions there are events that never occurred. The genre of history, *uera lex historiae*, permits him, he asserts, to write from common report if he does not personally claim that it is true. All this is stated with grace and strength that bespeak an earnest and well-meaning person. Occasionally in his writings there is the picture of a deferential, self-restrained monastic servant, *famulus Christi.* I am not suggesting that there is no truth to all of this, but I am sure that exordial rhetoric, like all rhetorical discourse, need only be credible, not true. Bede well knew the conditions of rhetorical verisimilitude.[24] Nor does the rhetorical writer ever put all of his cards on the table. One must take him mainly for what he does and from this practice extrapolate the undisplayed cards, which are usually the aces. I believe that the preface of the *Historia ecclesiastica,* for all its foregrounded humility, skillfully masks an anti-Isidorean agenda.[25] In the *Etymologiae* (1.41–44), Isidore wrote the absurd view that in antiquity no one wrote history except those who had eyewitness experience of the events in question. If that were really the rule of history, the *Historia ecclesiastica* (and, for that matter, the Gospels or Isidore's own historical works) would travesty the

---

[24] See my "Bede the Exegete, as Historian," in *Famulus Christi*, pp. 128–9, and "Bede and Cicero," *Anglo-Saxon England* 16 (1987): 12–13, on Bede's use of the *circumstantiae* (who, what, when, where, why, and so on) with which the Greco-Roman rhetors sought to establish the credibility of narrative.

[25] For the following, see my "Bede's *Vera Lex Historiae,*" *Speculum* 55 (1980): 1–21.

genre. Bede knew better, and so, in language that seems partly to ape Isidore's, he declared correctly that the historiographical tradition permits the historian to use sources for whose truth he cannot himself vouch. It was, in any event, a winning demurrer if one considers the enormous number of surviving manuscripts, most of them full copies and a burst of them having been written in the twelfth-century revival of the Latin verbal arts. In our century it even created the illusion that Bede was a proto-historicist, when in fact he wrote in the tradition of Latin rhetorical historiography.[26] For Bede it was a rhetorical disclaimer, part of his long prefatory appeal to *ethos.*

Collegial Differences

In my view *patrum uestigia sequens* is itself a phrase that is mainly rhetorical, an appeal to *ethos*, and as I shall argue later it expresses in only a limited sense a scholarly program. He certainly did not emulate the Fathers in his choice of early projects. The school treatises and the commentaries on the Apocalypse, the Acts of the Apostles, and the Catholic Epistles were all virtually unprecedented. Tackling the Book of Revelation was an especially heady thing for a young man to do. This most difficult of New Testament books is a mine field of hermeneutical problems, and none of the Fathers except the obscure Primasius had dared to cross it.[27] The Acts of the Apostles had

---

[26] See William D. McCready, *Miracles and the Venerable Bede,* Texts and Studies 118 (Toronto, 1994), pp. 195–213, who seems to think that Bede knew how to undertake factual reconstruction on the analogy of modern historical criticism. On Bede as rhetorical historian, see my "The Triumph of Pagan Rhetorical Assumptions in Pre-Carolingian Historiography" in *The Inheritance of Historiography, 300–900,* ed. Christopher J. Holdsworth and Timothy P. Wiseman (Exeter, 1986), pp. 66–84.

[27] See Gerald Bonner, *Saint Bede and the Western Apocalyptic Commentary* (Jarrow Lecture, 1966), pp. 7–8.

scarcely been touched by previous writers, except for the poet Arator.[28] In the authorial frenzy of his last decade, Bede would come back to write learned "retractions" on this book, and in so doing became the first Christian writer after Augustine to have the courage of second thoughts.[29] Studying Acts also prompted him to learn Greek, a feat that separates him from all but one of the four Latin *doctores*. Of course in all the early commentaries, as ever, Bede owed much to the Fathers, but it is none the less telling that he brought them to bear on projects they never attempted. Augustine was the only one of the four Latin Fathers to write about the liberal arts and teaching, but he expressly refused to write textbooks. The young Bede acted to fill this gap too.

One of his school treatises, the first book on chronology, was so daring and original that it brought a charge of heresy. Bede was convinced that the best authority for the Old Testament was Jerome's translation from the Hebrew, which had been worrying to Augustine.[30] Though Bede knew the nearly canonical Eusebian chronology of the Old Testament, he set out to create his own from the study of the Vulgate, since, as he says, Eusebius did not know Hebrew. The final count of years between Adam and Christ fell more than a thousand years short of the millenarian calendar, which was an illegitimate offspring of the Eusebian chronology. Hence a millenarian member of Bishop Wilfrid's household, and even during a meal with Bede's diocesan, charged that he had committed the heresy of making it seem that Jesus was born in the fourth age of the world.

---

[28] See Lawrence T. Martin, introduction to *The Venerable Bede: Commentary on the Acts of the Apostles*, Cistercian Studies Series 117 (Kalamazoo, Mich., 1989), p. xviii.

[29] The text of the *Retractatio* is printed in CCSL 121, pp. 103–63.

[30] J. N. D. Kelly, *Jerome: His Life, Writings, and Controversies* (London, 1975), p. 218, treats Augustine's doubts about Jerome's resolve to translate the Old Testament from the Hebrew.

Bede's response was anything but deferential and conciliatory. In a letter of 708 he replied in Latin vituperation that almost puts Jerome in the shade.[31] He unleashed the fire of the high style, which should put to rest the widely held view that Bede never wrote anything except in the *sermo simplex*. And the brunt of his argument rests on four authorities—Augustine, Jerome, Origen, and Josephus, an interesting quadriga. In the second, mature treatise on chronology, another product of his crowded last decade, there is no concession to the millenarians, only a confident reaffirmation of his earlier views. Indeed there seems to be a consistency of vision throughout his works. He was dedicated always to the building of Christian Latin culture.

Yet the most striking show of a sense of original authority is the defense of *saecularis eloquentiae* written against Jerome in Bede's commentary on 1 Samuel.[32] Elsewhere I have discussed at some length this extended and highly important passage, but I here return to it because it was the text above all that prompted me to ask again about Bede's self-estimate. I will give only a summary of it. Saul took an oath that he and his warriors would fast through a long day in preparation for a battle with the Philistines. Jonathan, his son, did not hear about the oath, and in a forest sweet with honey he took a bite. The honey made his eyes newly keen, all the more ready for the fight. Then he heard about the oath, and angrily complained that his father had forbidden too much by denying food to his people in a pagan land on the eve of a major battle with unbelievers. Against this backdrop Bede takes Jerome to task for having sworn, in his famous Letter 22, that he would never again read or own pagan litera-

[31] Bede, *Epist. Pleg.* (pp. 617–26). For more on this letter and its background, see Faith Wallis, introduction to *Bede: The Reckoning of Time*, trans. Faith Wallis, Translated Texts for Historians 29 (Liverpool, 1999), pp. xviii–xxxiv; on its rhetorical significance, see my "Bede and Cicero," pp. 9–12.

[32] See my "Bede and Cicero," pp. 2–7, for a full discussion of Bede's remarks on *saecularis eloquentiae* in the Samuel commentary.

ture. Without naming him Bede refers to the famous nightmare in which Jerome stood before the heavenly judge and was found to be *non christianus sed Ciceronianus*. Bede affirms that too much eagerness for pagan books can be hurtful to the soul. Yet he adds that the faithful teacher knows that sometimes only the taste of a Tullian text will do if one is to prevail in verbal combat with unbelief.[33] This focus on *saecularis eloquentia*—on argument and debate (*inventio*)—shows that Bede felt some urgency to tout the Christian use of it. A taste of honey in the land of the heathen had lit up Jonathan's eyes even though his father Saul had proscribed it. He forbade too much, Bede says, as did Jerome in Letter 22. The point is that pagan rhetoric, though it can be dangerous, can arm the church for verbal battle.

The exegesis of 1 Sam. 14 was written in the tradition of the ancient myth of civilization, given in books like Cicero's *De inventione*. Its point is that eloquence called together cities and civilizations, but it is morally neutral, equally useful in rival camps, and so good men must know it if they are to prevail over the bad. I used to think that this legacy probably came to Bede through the first paragraphs of Augustine's *De doctrina christiana*, Book 4,

---

[33] Bede, *In Sam.* 2 (p. 120, lines 2173–9; p. 121, lines 2227–36): "Et nobiles saepe magistri ecclesiae magnorumque uictores certaminum ardentiore quam decet oblectatione libros gentilium lectitantes culpam quam non praeuidere contrahebant adeo ut quidam eorum [viz., Jerome] se pro hoc ipso scribat in uisione castigatum obiectumque sibi a domino inter uerbera ferientia quod non christianus sed Ciceronianus potius esset habendus...Videtis, inquit, quia efficacior sum factus et acutior promptiorque ad peroranda quae decent eo quod gustauerim paululum de flore Tullianae lectionis; quanto magis si didicisset populus christianus sectas et dogmata gentilium, nonne multo confidentius et certius eorum derideret simul et conuinceret errores multo deuotius de sua sana fide gauderet patrique luminum pro hac gratias redderet. Neque enim aliam ob causam putandum est Moysen uel Danihelem sapientiam uoluisse discere saecularem quam ut cognitam destruere melius et deuincere possent."

which seems to pummel Jerome's Letter 22 in the course of defending the Christian study of Greco-Roman eloquence. In his exposition of the Apocalypse, Bede copied the exegetical rules of Tyconius from the very end of *De doctrina christiana*, Book 3.[34] Since Augustine's commendation of the Christian use of pagan rhetoric comes in the very first paragraphs of Book 4, I thought it likely that Bede's eyes would have continued on to read it.

Perhaps because I had gone on record with this belief, I was asked a few years ago to present a paper on Bede at a conference on *De doctrina christiana* held at the University of Notre Dame. I was to read immediately after Thomas Amos finished his paper on the *De doctrina christiana* in the massive sixth-century Augustinian compilation of Eugippius. It was, however, shattering to hear Amos conclude convincingly that Bede knew *De doctrina christiana* only from Eugippius. Sitting beside Professor Amos on the dais, I was stunned to remember that Eugippius includes not a word from *De doctrina christiana*, Book 4. An entire section of my paper wafted away. On my feet I tried to save the day by claiming that it is all the more remarkable that Bede, without knowing Book 4, nonetheless developed a critique of Jerome's Letter 22 and a defense of rhetoric similar to Augustine's.

Isn't it remarkable? Referring obviously to Jerome's Letter 22 and so all but mentioning the author by name, Bede did not hesitate to raise his voice against the translator of the Vulgate, of which he was a champion throughout his career and on which his abbey spent a fortune to produce not one but three full copies. Bede wrote the rather serene exegesis of 1 Sam. 14 as if he had authority in the circle of the Fathers, even on white hot topics like the limits of Latin literacy. And it is too much to think that in his apology for the Christian study of pagan rhetoric Bede was lucky to hit upon some old textbook ideas. I prefer a less highly charged possibility—that Augustine and Bede took similar positions because both had read the ancient myth of

[34] Bede, *Exp. Apoc.*, Praef. (p. 223, line 37–p. 231, line 113).

23

civilization in a pagan work, like Cicero's *De inventione*, and had baptized it for the creation of Christian Latin culture.

If Bede habitually subordinated himself to the Fathers, why is there no mention of Augustine in the preface to his early treatise on figures of speech?[35] Here again Bede was moving in the orbit of the Latin verbal arts, a circle in which he obviously thought he had weight even as a young scholar. Like Augustine in *De doctrina christiana*, Bede argues that the biblical writers were first with the best use of the Latin figures of speech. Yet he gives no hint that Augustine ever thought this, even though Bede could well have gleaned Augustine's view from the excerpts of *De doctrina christiana* in Eugippius.[36] *Patrum uestigia sequens?*

Reframing the Fathers

I could give further evidence that Bede wrote as if he were blazing—not following—trails, but I must come to a further question. Does Bede have his own mind even when he is following the vestiges of an *auctoritas*? For nearly a hundred years scholars have been saying yes: Henri Quentin, Charles Jones, Robert B. Palmer, Paul Meyvaert, among others.[37] The publication of almost all of Bede's commentaries and biblical treatises

[35] See Bede, *DST* Prol. (p. 142, line 1–p. 143, line 24).

[36] *Eugipii excerpta ex operibus Sancti Augustini* (CSEL 9: pp. 803–77), contains about half of the first three books of *De doctrina christiana*, quite enough to drive home the biblicization of Latin literacy.

[37] Meyvaert, "Bede the Scholar," pp. 42–44, discusses Palmer, Quentin, and Jones, with all of whom he agrees. For other examples, see Ansgar Willmes, "Bedas Bibelauslegung," *Archiv für Kulturgeschichte* 44 (1963): 281–314, where the author observes that Bede's exegesis lies between "receptivity and independence" (p. 291) in a realm of his own making; Brown, *Bede the Venerable*, pp. 42–51; Holder, "New Treasures for Old," p. 144. For still others, see DeGregorio, "Bede on Prayer," pp. 3–4 and the ample notes.

in modern if not perfect editions, together with broadening recognition that his lifework was exegesis not history, have been major developments. Yet the close study of Bede's voluminous scriptural works has only begun. It is, to my mind, the most important and promising field of Bedan research, one which will likely be transformative.[38] Early results of this work may suggest a trend. For example, in the first major study in Bede's spirituality since M. T. A. Carroll's book published more than fifty years ago, Scott DeGregorio considers the interplay of Gregory the Great and Bede on the subject of prayer. Among the Fathers Gregory was, DeGregorio believes, Bede's favorite, for the two shared a deep concern for the practice of the Christian faith, for a lived spirituality. Both fixed their gaze mainly on *praxis.* Yet Bede did it with a difference. He did not walk with the pope when it came to "exploring the interior workings and slippery paradoxes of the spiritual life that so captivated Gregory."[39] Bede took from Gregory only those things that fit well with his own practical vision. He did not reject Gregory's explorations of the inner life; he simply had no use for them. For Bede, prayer was certainly hearts and minds lifted up to God, but it was above all an unremitting life of love and justice enacted toward others. Prayer was not solitary but social. Bede took his own path too when discussing the contemplative and active lives. Bede was no mystic. Contemplation was preparatory to action, which was the greater good. DeGregorio concludes that Bede owed much to Gregory but "did not hesitate to emphasize certain themes over others, or conversely to downplay some themes entirely . . ."[40]

---

[38] For an excellent bibliography of recent studies in, and translations of, Bede's commentaries, see Scott DeGregorio, introduction to *Bede: On Ezra and Nehemiah,* trans. Scott DeGregorio, Translated Texts for Historians 47 (Liverpool, 2006), pp. xii–xv.

[39] DeGregorio, "Bede on Prayer," p. 14.

[40] DeGregorio, "Bede on Prayer," p. 39.

On the strength of this far-reaching study, I would add that Bede clearly felt authorized to interact with patristic thought in his own voice, as if he were a full participant in the great conversations. When in his previously mentioned autobiographical statement he says that he excerpted the Fathers but clarified their sense and meaning, it was an understatement. I believe that further study of Bede's relationship to the Fathers will show that he was less a follower than a colleague. At any rate, in light of recent research it seems clear that the words *patrum uestigia sequens* were rhetorical, not programmatic, for what we are learning about his use of patristic sources suggests that his program was different and broader than anything that can be summed up under these words.

Latin Literacy and Authorial Identity

If Bede saw himself as a creator of Christian Latin culture, what were his literary ambitions? In what tradition of Latin discourse did he try to write? It has long been thought that the caliber of his audience set at least the level of his Latinity. In the commentary on the Apocalypse he remarks, after all, that he would write with "inert" contemporary readers in mind.[41] Did the young Bede really think that any manner of plain talk could deliver to sluggish readers the mysteries of the Revelation? For that matter, is the exposition of the Revelation, or any other of his books, written in the *sermo simplex*? Bede wrote with a habitual lucidity and moderation, in a fluent and correct style, but his Latin is anything but simple. What then were his affinities? Late Latin or classical? If he was taking a stand among the Fathers, could he keep the literary pace?

In 1938 David Ross Druhan published a book-length study of the Latin syntax of the *Historia ecclesiastica*, and so far as I know it seldom or maybe never thereafter saw the light of day in Bedan studies. Using as his standard the great inventory of

---

[41] Bede, *Exp. Apoc.*, Praef. (p. 233, lines 140–6).

Roman syntactical authorities put together by nineteenth-century German philologists, Druhan tries to document and assess every instance in which Bede departs from classical usages. He ranges over all the parts of Latin syntax, from gender and number to the various kinds of dependent clauses, and concludes that Bede's practices are "decidedly classical," much more so than those of his early European predecessors, including Gregory the Great. Druhan reckons that Bede learned classical idioms from the quotations given in the grammarians known to him, but adds that the classicism of his style suggests that he must have had "a more direct acquaintance with Virgil and Cicero."[42] More recent studies, none of them nearly as extensive, have lent weight to this view.[43] At the same time the number of grammarians known to Bede has shrunk away from the total Druhan and, after him, Charles Jones added up, while there is now more reason than ever to think that Bede had a firsthand knowledge of Virgil and Cicero.[44] How Bede learned to write in a "decidedly classical" way is more interesting than Druhan thought.

[42] David Ross Druhan, *The Syntax of Bede's Historia ecclesiastica*, Catholic University of America Studies in Medieval and Renaissance Latin 8 (Washington, D.C., 1938), pp. 212–13.

[43] See Calvin B. Kendall, "Bede's *Historia ecclesiastica*: Rhetoric of Faith," in *Medieval Eloquence*, ed. James J. Murphy (Berkeley, 1987), pp. 145–72, and also his "Imitation and Bede's *Historia ecclesiastica*," in *Saints, Scholars, and Heroes: Studies in Medieval Culture Presented to Charles W. Jones*, ed. Margot H. King and W. M. Stevens, 2 vols. (Collegeville, Minn., 1979), 1:161–90; and in the same volume, see Donald K. Fry, "The Art of Bede: Edwin's Council," pp. 191–207. See also Martin Irvine, *The Making of Textual Culture: Grammatica and Literary Theory*, Cambridge Studies in Medieval Literature 19 (Cambridge, 1994), pp. 277–9.

[44] On grammarians see Anna Carlotta Dionisotti, "Bede, Grammars, and Greek," *Revue Bénédictine* 92 (1982): 11–41; on Cicero, see my "Bede and Cicero"; and on Virgil, see Neil R. Wright, "Bede and Virgil," *Romanobarbarica* 6 (1981): 361–79. and Irvine, *Textual Culture*, pp. 277–9.

Roger Ray

Gabriele Knappe is the latest scholar to argue, however, that
Bede was virtually cut off from the world of Cicero and classical rhetoric and knew nothing of it except the rehash contained in the late antique grammarians and Isidore of Seville.[45]
This position begs several questions. Are surviving manuscripts,
quotations, and book-lists the final test of Bede's knowledge of
classical rhetoric? If the exegesis of 1 Sam. 14 discussed earlier
does not endorse the Christian study of *saecularis eloquentia* and
approve the reading of Cicero, what does it do? If the exegesis
means what it says, who are we to deny to Bede the rhetorical re-
sources which he defends against Jerome? And if Bede is really
talking about grammar, why does he speak of rhetoric, i.e. *saecularis eloquentia*? Clearly Bede here and elsewhere defends the
Christian use of rhetorical argumentation, not just style.[46] How
much can one learn of rhetorical *inventio* from the *grammatici*?
Can we account for the making of his books if we think he knew
nothing of rhetoric beyond the cut-flowers of the grammarians
and Isidore? When did anyone else, having only secondhand
knowledge of Greco-Roman rhetoric, ever write Latin books at
the literary level of Bede's? Druhan seems not to have known
the exegesis of 1 Sam. 14, which would have been grist for his

[45] Gabriele Knappe, "Classical Rhetoric in Anglo-Saxon England," *Anglo-Saxon England* 27 (1999): 5–29, which sums up the results of her *Traditionen der klassichen Rhetorik in angelsächsischen England*, Anglistische Forschungen 236 (Heidelberg, 1996). Both titles are curious, since she concludes that there was no tradition of classical rhetoric in Anglo-Saxon England.

[46] See Bede, *In Sam.* 4 (p. 262, line 2127–p. 263, line 2175), where Bede argues that faithful people can be swept away in a flood of words if they are not ready to defeat shrewd arguments with better ones, as Athanasius did at Nicaea when faced with clever Arians. In *In prou. Sal.* 2 (p. 93, lines 133–7), Bede observes that "per eloquentiam" one can teach good things even though one does not love them. The lure of language overcomes even a lack of heart by the speaker, which seems to be an endorsement of verbal illusions.

mill; but he nonetheless concluded that Bede's Latinity is inconceivable unless we assume that he had firsthand knowledge of standard-setters like Cicero. Bede wrote deliberately in the same tradition as had the Latin Fathers in whose company he mainly wanted to run. I believe that he did so with direct knowledge of the Ciceronian eloquence which he calmly defends in the exegesis of 1 Sam. 14.

The ancient rhetors allowed that some people have *ingenium*, the knack for speaking and writing well, without going to school. Bede, by contrast, prized, fostered, and in the school treatises even pioneered formal education. Hence when he argues that *magistri ueritatis*, Christian teachers, need pagan eloquence and its authorities, he leaves nothing to luck; he is talking about learning. Bede's literary practice often seems cut to the pattern of classical rhetorical theory. Was this hit-and-miss? Take, for example, the locus classicus of Hellenistic historiographical theory in Cicero's *De oratore* 2.62. I am not suggesting that Bede somehow saw this work, but I nevertheless see nothing in Bede's practice of history that departs from Cicero's precepts. He wrote as if he thought, with Cicero, that history has no separate rules; it borrows them from the Latin verbal arts, especially the art of persuasion and instruction. Clearly he saw history as a form of high moral instruction, "the teacher of life," as Cicero says. He certainly agreed that the identity of history lies in its subject matter, the truth, that is, real or at least credible events reported didactically in the vast imaginative space that lies between malice and flattery. He surely concurred with Cicero that the historian ought to reveal what he approves, or disapproves of, in human conduct and that he should recount events in chronological order, giving a narrative of them from the onset of the story to its outcome. Undoubtedly he took the view that the language of history should be, as Cicero says, "flowing, full, smooth, and placid." And he could not have written the *Historia ecclesiastica* without knowing the difference between, to use Cicero's words, *tantummodo narratores* and *exornatores rerum*, mere chroniclers and expansive historians. Bede wrote chronicles, he wrote expansive history, and he knew that the difference lay in the rhetorical quality of the latter, or, as Cicero put it, "the voice of the orator."

Bede also agreed with Cicero that the real historian should give attention to ethnography and geography. Book 1, chapter 1, of the *Historia ecclesiastica* may be the most ignored part of the entire work, but to my mind it reflects much about Bede as a practitioner of Latin letters. I do not accept Calvin Kendall's suggestion that this geographical passage is Bede's paradise, to be followed by a pentateuch of books.[47] It is basically a secular piece, with only one sentence of religious reference. Bede quotes one *pater*, Basil of Caesarea, but the subject is not faith but how water becomes hot. Book 1 was written partly to set the scene and locate the story, but partly too to be the first glimmerings of literary pleasure to come. It brings to mind not Orosius or Gregory of Tours, whose ethno-geographical surveys fall with a thud, but pagan historians and poets who wrote ethnographical and geographical bits mainly to excite the minds and imaginations of readers.[48] Britain is, Bede says,

> an island rich in crops and trees, and has good pasturage for cattle and beasts of burden. It produces vines in certain districts . . .and is remarkable too for its rivers, which abound in fish, especially salmon and eels, and for copious springs. Seals as well as dolphins are frequently captured and even whales; besides these there are various shellfish, among which are mussels, and enclosed in these are often found excellent pearls of

[47] Kendall, "Imitation and Bede's *Historia ecclesiastica*," passim.

[48] On ethnography and geography in Latin historical works, see Timothy P. Wiseman, "Practice and Theory in Roman Historiography," *History* 28 (1981): 392. Colgrave, in *HE* 1.1 (p. 14, n. 1), suggests that Bede may have taken the idea of an ethno-geographical beginning from Orosius or Gregory of Tours. If so, he did not emulate what and how they wrote.

every color, red and purple, violet and green, but mostly white. There is also a great abundance of whelks, from which a scarlet-colored dye is made, a most beautiful red which neither fades through the heat of the sun nor exposure to the rain, indeed the older it is the more beautiful it becomes. The land possesses salt springs and warm springs and from them flow rivers which supply hot baths, suitable for all ages and both sexes, in separate places and adapted to the needs of each.[49]

The most recent commentary on the *Historia ecclesiastica* says that these lines spring from no known source and probably owe much to Bede's imagination.[50] Aren't they a purple patch, vivid and evocative scenery painted into the text for sheer artistic effect, written in the classical tradition of the rhetorical set piece? Henry Mayr-Harting makes me think that this first chapter of Book 1 may even contain Bede's only joke. He believes that the famous and ludicrous passage about the lack of snakes in Ireland

---

[49] Bede, *HE* 1.1 (p. 14): "Opima frugibus atque arboribus insula, et alendis apta pecoribus ac iumentis, uineas etiam quibusdam in locis germinans . . .fluuiis quoque multum piscosis ac fontibus praeclara copiosis; et quidem praecipue issicio abundat et anguilla. Capiuntur autem saepissime et uituli marini et delfines nec non et ballenae, exceptis uariorum generibus concyliorum, in quibus sunt et musculae, quibus inclusam saepe margaritam omnis quidem coloris optimam inueniunt, id est et rubicundi et purpurei et hyacinthini et prasini sed maxime candidi. Sunt et cocleae satis superque abundantes, quibus tinctura coccinei coloris conficitur, cuius rubor pulcherrimus nullo umquam solis ardore, nulla ualet pluuiarum iniuria pallescere, sed quo uetustior eo solet esse uenustior. Habet fontes salinarum, habet et fontes calidos, et ex eis fluuios balnearum calidarum omni aetati et sexui per distincta loca iuxta suum cuique modum accommodos." Trans. Colgrave, p. 15.

[50] J. M. Wallace-Hadrill, *Bede's Ecclesiastical History of the English People: A Commentary* (Oxford, 1988), p. 6.

and the use of scrapings from Irish manuscripts to cure snakebite in England may parody the views of Isidore of Seville who in his *Etymologiae* first propounded what Mayr-Harting calls "this nonsense."[51] A little later Bede enlivens the legends and lore of early Britain by imputing direct discourse to the whole Irish nation speaking apparently in unison, which is a rather funny image, maybe joke number two.

Bedae Vestigia Sequens

In all, Bede wrote as if he thought he was working at the top of the field, among the other builders of Christian Latin culture, both in contents and style. This view fits the shape of his total corpus, suits his inclination to take initiatives and exercise discretionary judgment among previous *patres*, and respects the level and caliber of his Latin literacy. I have one further consideration. In the bio-bibliography at the end of the *Historia ecclesiastica*, Bede gives pride of place to two of his teachers, Benedict Biscop, the founder and first abbot of Wearmouth, and Ceolfrid, the first abbot of its twin house at Jarrow. These two, for all their practice of monastic *stabilitas loci*, were, as Patrick Wormald has argued, internationalists when it came to their sense of the relevant Christian world.[52] Before he founded Wearmouth, Biscop, a former Northumbrian nobleman, had made three trips to the continent, had visited Rome on four occasions, had received the tonsure at Lerins and lived there as a monk for two years, and had woven a web of relationships that reached from the Midi to northern and eastern Gaul. He spent two years at Canterbury with the Mediterranean savants Theodore and Hadrian before he went north in 674 to found Wearmouth. Between this date

[51] Henry Mayr-Harting, *The Coming of Christianity to Anglo-Saxon England* (London, 1972), p. 50.
[52] For what follows here on Biscop and Ceolfrid, see Bede, *HA* (pp. 364–82). On Biscop's internationalism, see Patrick Wormald, "Bede and Benedict Biscop," in *Famulus Christi*, pp. 141–69.

and his death in 689, Biscop made three further trips to the continent, with two more stops in Rome. To support this travel and the purchase and transport of the books from which Bede wrote his works, he amassed and spent enormous wealth, which underscores the centrality of these continental connections to Biscop's outlook. He personally escorted to Wearmouth stone masons from Gaul to rebuild the abbey church in the Gallican style, and in the course of his abbatial travels he brought home many works of art to adorn the new stone building. He even recruited from the continent a Roman cantor to teach his brothers how to sing *more Romanorum*. Obviously he wanted his foundation to have large horizons. Ceolfrid was with Biscop from 674 onward and after his death succeeded him as sole abbot of Wearmouth-Jarrow. He had accompanied Biscop on a visit to Rome and in 716 died at Langres attempting to take to the pope what now is known as the Codex Amiatinus. This oldest of all the surviving full copies of the Vulgate Bible was one of three pandects produced in the abbey scriptorium at Ceolfrid's behest.[53] This spectacular accomplishment reflects the international scale of his own vision.

When Biscop died, Bede was apparently sixteen and had been under his eye for almost nine years, enough time for the founder to recognize a youngster of potential genius. Ceolfrid doubled the size of the abbey library, and this occurred while Bede was realizing his potential. Bede clearly internalized the internationalism of his two main teachers. After Ceolfrid died, he soon broke into a blazing authorial sprint, writing one major work after another, especially biblical commentaries, as if the stakes had risen higher. In these same years the demand for his books elsewhere in England gave the scriptorium a new major project, which even caused the scribes to change to a more

[53] Richard Marsden, *The Text of the Old Testament in Anglo-Saxon England*, Cambridge Studies in Anglo-Saxon England 15 (Cambridge, 1995), pp. 76–201, provides exhaustive discussion of Amiatinus and its sister pandects.

economical bookhand.[54] With a growing readership at home
and Anglo-Saxon missionaries forging a new world of Christians
readers abroad, it may have crossed Bede's mind that his books
would sail the seas, as they did not long after he died. Surviving
manuscripts, book-lists, and quotations and references to Bede
show that by the mid ninth century his textbooks and biblical
writings were *libri catholici,* books necessary for the reading of
the Bible anywhere, like those of other *patres.* The *Historia ecclesiastica,* despite its insular themes, also found a vogue beyond
the Channel, no doubt because, as part of the patristic legacy,
it was a unique work that recounted something of great interest
to the missionary field—namely, how a barbarian people had
grown up to Catholic Christianity and then had taken the message abroad.[55] Did Bede write all these works, especially those
finished with a rush in his last ten years, without an inkling that
at some point they would likely repay with interest the international world which, through the tireless travels of his chief
mentors, had given patristic riches to him? And if, as many now
think, thanks to Robert Hanning, Bede saw the English as a new
people of God foreordained to preach the true faith across the
seas, did he write his later books unmindful of this transmarine
destiny, as if his works would have no part in it?[56] The answer
is, I believe, emphatically no. The authorial frenzy of his mature years surely took place because he saw a growing audience,
both in England and elsewhere. Bede the builder of Christian

[54] See Parkes, *Scriptorium.*

[55] Whitelock, *After Bede,* pp. 45–47, discusses the extraordinary continental
travels of the *HE* in the eighth and ninth centuries.

[56] Robert Hanning, *The Vision of History in Early Britain* (New York, 1966),
pp. 63–90.

I am very grateful to Janet Nelson for her penetrating comments on an
earlier draft of this paper, to Richard Sharpe for illuminating discussion
of Bede's Latin, and above all to Scott DeGregorio for generously making
available his translation of Bede's *In Ezram and Neemiam* and work arising
from it in advance of publication.

Latin culture went to work with new urgency, with an eye on the international world of his beloved abbots and the Anglo-Saxon missionaries, where indeed his works would have a great future. Bede did not write them to hold a second place among the *patres*.

Bede and the Ordering of Understanding

ALAN THACKER

B EDE WAS FOR LONG REGARDED as the very model of a saintly
and humble teacher.[1] His primary aims—essentially practical—were thought to be the establishment of "sound foundations of knowledge" for "the unlearned reader," and hence it
was held that for him "the quest for originality was of secondary importance."[2] Such views, at once affectionate and patron-
izing, imply a modest and unassuming personality concerned
primarily with the transmission of knowledge derived from writers more sophisticated and creative than himself. Of course, it
was always recognized that his *Historia ecclesiastica* was a master-
piece; indeed, in a seminal essay written over forty years ago,
James Campbell noted the complexity and sophistication of
that great work and memorably concluded that "Bede defies patronage."[3] But most of the remainder of Bede's writings, above
all the biblical commentaries, styled—dire word—"textbooks,"
were regarded as conventional compilations, little more than
catenae of quotations culled from the far more original Christian writers of Late Antiquity. As the introduction to this volume
notes, and as Roger Ray's essay eloquently demonstrates, such

---

[1] Charles Plummer, *Venerabilis Baedae opera historica,* 2 vols. (1896; reprint,
2 vols. in 1, Oxford, 1946), pp. xxi–xxiv, lxxviii–lxxix; Benedicta Ward,
Venerable Bede (London, 1990), p. 19.

[2] Claude Jenkins, "Bede as Exegete and Theologian," in *Bede, His Life,
Times, and Writings: Essays in Commemoration of the Twelfth Centenary of his
Death,* ed. A. Hamilton Thompson (Oxford, 1935), pp. 167, 171.

[3] James Campbell, "Bede I," in *Essays in Anglo-Saxon History* (London,
1986), p. 27.

views have recently been subject to increasing revision.[4] Bede's achievements in computus and natural science were recognized long ago by Charles Jones and were the focus of a distinguished Jarrow Lecture in 1985.[5] His knowledge of classical rhetoric has been discussed by Roger Ray.[6] The sophisticated and complex program of the *Historia ecclesiastica* has been much analyzed over the last thirty years and is the subject of continuing debate. Above all, Bede's exegesis has been increasingly scrutinized and its qualities reassessed, especially in a succession of annotated translations that do much to remedy the lack of a decent scholarly edition.[7] It is the aim of this paper to look at some of the implications of this work for Bede's overall educative agenda—to discuss, in a word, Bede's ordering of knowledge.

Bede was blessed with a clear and orderly mind. He was, very evidently, extremely learned—and his learning touched on many themes and subjects: on classical grammar, rhetoric and poetics, on natural science and computus, on history and hagiography, and most centrally of all, of course, on Scripture.[8] Bede, however, was not simply concerned to transmit as much of this encyclopedic knowledge as he could. He had a program—a program which became increasingly idiosyncratic, or perhaps we should say increasingly tailored to the needs of his own society, as time progressed. Bede's role as an educator was

---

[4] See above, pp. 5–9, 11–19.

[5] Charles W. Jones, *Baedae Opera de Temporibus*, Medieval Academy of America 41 (Cambridge, Mass, 1943); Wesley Stevens, *Bede's Scientific Achievement* (Jarrow Lecture, 1985).

[6] Roger Ray, "Bede and Cicero," *Anglo-Saxon England* 16 (1987): 1–15; *Bede, Rhetoric, and Christian Latin Culture* (Jarrow Lecture, 1997); and his remarks in his essay above, pp. 21–24, 28–32.

[7] See above, Introduction, p. 4, n. 9.

[8] In the personal note appended to *HE* 5.24 (p. 566), Bede says he was given to Benedict Biscop and then to Ceolfrid to be educated; and in *HE* 4.3 (p. 342) he refers to Trumberht, a monk educated at Lastingham, as "one of those who taught me the Scriptures."

excellently discussed by George Brown in his Jarrow Lecture of 1996 and his "edifice of Christian learning" formed the theme of Roger Ray's lecture the following year.[9] I would like to build on their work by looking in more detail at the aims, structure and development of that educative edifice.

Bede's Status and Environment

Bede's origins are famously obscure. He was almost certainly a child oblate at Jarrow, where he was the pupil and protégé of Benedict Biscop's coadjutor, Abbot Ceolfrid. Now Ceolfrid was a very grand figure. He was the principal founder of the richly-endowed monastery at Jarrow, with which King Ecgfrith was especially closely associated and where, it has been suggested, he intended to be buried.[10] Ceolfrid's anonymous biographer says that he was nobly born and he may even have been royal. Members of his family were rulers of the important royal monastery of Gilling, and he and his brother bore names which alliterated with those of that branch of the house of Ida, which achieved the kingship in 716.[11]

It is perhaps significant that Ceolfrid's name heads the list of priest-abbots commemorated in the Durham *Liber Vitae*,[12] a work which may have begun as a Wearmouth-Jarrow manuscript.[13]

[9] George Hardin Brown, *Bede the Educator* (Jarrow Lecture, 1996); and Ray, Rhetoric, and *Christian Latin Culture.*

[10] Ian Wood, *Abbot Ceolfrid* (Jarrow Lecture, 1995), p. 3.

[11] See *Vita Ceolfridi* 2, ed. Charles Plummer, in *Opera historica*, p. 388, and David Kirby, Earliest English Kings (London, 1990), p. 147.

[12] *Liber Vitae Ecclesiae Dunelmensis*, ed. J. Stevenson, Publications of the Surtees Society, vol. 13 (London, 1841), p. 6; and "*Liber Vitae Ecclesiae Dunelmensis*, BL MS Cotton Domitian A vii," ed. D. Dumville and P. Stokes, Trial version, Dept. Anglo-Saxon, Norse and Celtic (Cambridge, 2001). I am grateful to Andrew Wareham for supplying me with a text of the latter.

[13] Wood, *Abbot Ceolfrid*, p. 17. For recent discussion, see Jan Gerchow, "The Origins of Durham *Liber Vitae*," in *The Durham Liber Vitae and its Context*,

That Bede was very closely connected with Ceolfrid and that Ceolfrid was a leading figure in the Northumbria of his day is of course well-established. Less certain, but potentially even more significant, is the fact that Bede may have been a relative of Benedict Biscop himself. Biscop, who heads the list of non-priested abbots in the Durham *Liber Vitae*, was clearly very rich and well-connected.[14] That he may have been related to Bede and that both may have been of royal descent is suggested, as James Campbell has recently pointed out, by the fact that a Bede occurs in succession to a Biscop in a list of the kings of Lindsey, dating from about 800.[15]

Such high status would help to explain Bede's famously incensed outburst when accused of heresy, and his dismissal of his detractors as drunken boors.[16] It would also go a long way towards explaining the confident and abrasive tone of the letter which he wrote late in his life to the prince-archbishop Ecgberht.[17] Bede was not a humble or a modest figure. He was probably socially very grand and, as we shall see, he certainly had equally grand aspirations in his chosen field of religious learning.

Bede was based at one of the richest and best equipped scholarly institutions in the England of his day.[18] Yet, as William of Malmesbury noted, he does not appear to have had many able

---

ed. David Rollason, A. J. Piper, Margaret Harvey, and Linda Rollason (Woodbridge, 2004), pp. 47–57; and, in the same collection, E. Briggs, "Nothing but Names: the Original Core of the Durham *Liber Vitae*," pp. 63–5.

[14] *Liber Vitae Ecclesiae Dunelmensis*, p. 8.

[15] James Campbell, "Bede," in *The Oxford Dictionary of National Biography*, ed. H. C. G. Matthew and Brian Harrison, vol. 4 (Oxford, 2004), pp. 758–65.

[16] See Bede, *Epist. Pleg.* 17 (p. 626).

[17] See Bede, *Epist. Ecg.* 4, 12 (pp. 407, 415).

[18] See J. D. A. Ogilvy, *The Place of Wearmouth-Jarrow in Western Cultural History* (Jarrow Lecture, 1968); also M. L. W. Laistner, "The Library of the Venerable Bede," in *Bede, His Life, Times, and Writings*, pp. 237–66.

disciples to continue his work.[19] We can in fact name only two: Cuthbert, the author of the celebrated and pellucidly written letter on the death of his master, and Cuthbert's addressee and fellow pupil Cuthwine.[20] Indeed, Wearmouth-Jarrow in general does not seem to have been especially well-endowed with students. We can identify at most three or four authors: Bede himself, Cuthbert, Eusebius, author of a collection of Latin *enigmata* (if he is to be identified with Ceolfrid's successor, Abbot Hwætberht),[21] and the anonymous author the *Life of Ceolfrid* (if he is to be distinguished from Bede).[22] We know of at least one other scholarly associate: Witmaer.[23] That, however, is a meager haul for an establishment as rich and influential as Wearmouth-Jarrow. The contrast with Canterbury is marked. Bede himself spoke in the highest terms of the achievements of the school there and of the crowds of students who resorted to it. Among their number we can identify Aldhelm, three bishops, a senior abbot, and the legist Eoda.[24] And we may perhaps suspect that figures later

[19] William of Malmesbury, *Gesta Regum Anglorum*, 1.62–63, ed. R. A. B. Mynors, R. M. Thompson, and M. Winterbottom (Oxford, 1998), p. 95.

[20] The letter is printed in Colgrave and Mynors' edition of *HE*, pp. 580–7.

[21] Bede tells us that he gave Hwætberht the cognomen Eusebius "because of his love and zeal for holiness": see *In Sam.* 4 (p. 212, lines 12–20); also s.v. "Hwætberht," in *The Blackwell Encyclopaedia of Anglo-Saxon England*, ed. Michael Lapidge, pp. 245–6. Hwætberht's scholarly standing, asserted in *HA* 18 (p. 383) and *Vita Ceolfridi* 29 (pp. 398–9), is confirmed by the fact that Bede dedicated to him *De temporum ratione* and the commentaries on Acts and the Apocalypse.

[22] Like Wood, *Abbot Ceolfrid*, I assume that the anonymous author of the *Vita Ceolfridi* was not Bede.

[23] Bede, *HA* 15, 20 (pp. 380, 385); *Vita Ceolfridi* 29 (pp. 398–9).

[24] Bede, *HE* 4.2 (pp. 332–6), 5.8 (p. 474), 5.20 (p. 530), 5.23 (p. 556); Bernhard Bischoff and Michael Lapidge, *The Biblical Commentaries of Theodore and Hadrian*, Cambridge Studies in Anglo-Saxon England 10 (Cambridge,1994), pp. 150–1, 267–8.

prominent in Canterbury, such as the scholarly archbishops Ta-twine and Nothelm, also had their links with its school.[25]

We should of course think of the schools at both Canterbury and Jarrow as elite institutions. Michael Lapidge has suggested that we might regard Canterbury as a sort of Institute of Advanced Study.[26] To my mind, however, Theodore's Canterbury was, so to speak, Oxford with its undergraduates, offering practical training to those destined for the highest elements of the church hierarchy, while Bede's Jarrow was the Princeton Institute (or, perhaps, All Souls).

Bede was, as it were, a research professor. For while he had few students, he undoubtedly had many and well-connected helpers. His sources for the *Historia ecclesiastica* have often been analyzed and I do not propose to go into them here. Suffice it simply to note their status, that they were mostly senior figures such as Nothelm, soon (735) to be archbishop of Canterbury, Daniel, bishop of Winchester, Trumwine, former bishop of Abercorn, the abbots of Lindisfarne, Melrose, and Partney, as well as his own diocesan, Acca.[27]

Bede moreover had research assistants for other projects. Wesley Stevens in his Jarrow Lecture noted how much help in the form of practical first-hand observation he would have needed to gather together the information upon which his improved theories about the operation of the tides were based. We know indeed that competent investigators at Lindisfarne, Whithorn, and the Isle of Wight reported back to him in his research base at Jarrow.[28] Clearly Bede had distinguished correspondents and capable assistants. Whether, however, especially

---

[25] Bede, *HE* Praef. (p. 4) and 5.23 (p. 558); *In Regum* Prol. (p. 293).

[26] Bischoff and Lapidge, *Biblical Commentaries*, p. 268.

[27] See David Kirby, "Bede's Native Sources for the *Historia ecclesiastica*," *Bulletin of the John Rylands Library* 48 (1965–66): 341–71.

[28] Stevens, *Bede's Scientific Achievement*, pp. 13–15.

in his later years, he spent much time in personally instructing scholars in his monastic school, is much more questionable.

Bede's favorite word for teacher was *doctor*, a word that crops up with ever increasing frequency in his later works. It is a term with distinctly elitist implications, and I will pause for just a moment to consider its resonance for Bede and the way in which he applied it to himself. I discussed this at length a long while ago and my arguments were thereafter themselves the subject of considerable debate, so I propose only to summarize here.[29]

For Bede, the *doctor* was essentially the initiate who had penetrated beyond the veil of the literal sense of Scripture to the *arcana* beneath. He (or indeed she) had to combine the active pursuit of learning with contemplative prayer and exemplary living in order to infuse the active pastorate not just with basic understanding but with right doctrine and true ideals. The *doctores* formed, so to speak, the intellectual powerhouse which inspired and instructed the practical preachers (*praedicatores*) who were to carry out the evangelizing work on the ground.

Bede habitually spoke of the *doctores* as constituting a distinct order within the Church.[30] In doing so, he was not setting them up as separate from the established ordained hierarchy, with which they clearly overlapped. Nevertheless, not all bishops (let alone priests) were *doctores* and not all *doctores* were ordained— that is especially clear in Bede's allowing doctoral status for women. But, ordained or not, the *doctores* were fundamental to the well-being of the Church and indeed, as Bede's own actions make clear, could reprove and seek to instruct even the highest

---

[29] See Alan Thacker, "Bede's Ideal of Reform," in *Ideal and Reality in Frankish and Anglo-Saxon Society: Studies Presented to John Michael Wallace-Hadrill*, ed. Patrick Wormald, Donald Bullough, and Roger Collins (Oxford, 1983), esp. pp. 130–5.

[30] For some representative examples, see the passages listed in Thacker, "Ideal of Reform," esp. pp. 130–1, nn. 2–8.

ordained authorities, even bishops and archbishops. This was a notably ambitious role to take on, and it could be said that in a number of late commentaries Bede dwelt upon the duties of this high order almost obsessively.[31]

I would argue that this conception of himself as *doctor* was absolutely fundamental to Bede's oeuvre. Although he was by nature a practical moralist, he had an almost mystical sense of his educative role. In later years, these preoccupations determined his entire scholarly output. In the famous autobiographical note which concludes the *Historia ecclesiastica*,[32] Bede offered a definition of his life's work: it was ever his delight, he asserted, to learn or to teach or to write. For his own sake and for that of his brethren, he had made brief notes from or added to (the verb used is *superdicere*) the sense and interpretation of the Fathers in their commentaries on the Scriptures. This has been regarded as a modestly understated claim. But it seems to me to be nothing of the kind.[33] Bede is putting himself alongside the greatest of Christian teachers, as capable of adding to their work. Like them he was a *doctor*. His vision of his own role is apparent in a passage in his commentary on 1 Samuel, as we shall see a key work:

> For, with my aid in the present (*meo praesente auxilio*), the church has restrained itself (*continuit . . .se*) from idolatries and other disgraceful acts from that time when, having emerged

[31] In addition to Thacker, "Ideal of Reform," see now Scott DeGregorio, "*Nostrorum socordiam temporum*: The Reforming Impulse of Bede's Later Exegesis," *Early Medieval Europe* 11 (2002): 107–22, and "Bede's *In Ezram et Neemiam* and the Reform of the Northumbrian Church," *Speculum* 79 (2004): 1–25.

[32] Bede, *HE* 5.24 (pp. 566–70).

[33] On this point, see also the comments in this volume by Ray, pp. 11–19 and passim, and DeGregorio, pp. 7–9.

by confession from the darkness of ancient blindness, it came near to the light of knowing the holy Trinity which is God.[34]

This unusually personal reference occurs in the context of God sending forth apostles to teach the gentiles. It is clear, therefore, that Bede regarded himself as standing in an exalted succession of aid-givers. His attitude appears equally clear in his publication of a volume of retractations relating to his early commentary on Acts.[35] By so doing he explicitly put himself on a level with the author of another and more famous Retractatio: Augustine of Hippo.[36] And in the work itself he unabashedly corrects a second *doctor ecclesiae,* Jerome, who had, he claimed, misled him over the identity of the apostle Thaddeus.[37]

---

[34] Bede, *In Sam.* 3 (p. 195, lines 2493–7): "Continuit enim se ecclesia meo praesente auxilio ab idolatria ceterisque flagitiis ex eo tempore quo egressa per confessionem a priscae latebra caecitatis usque ad lucem cognoscendae sanctae quae Deus est trinitatis accessit . . ." The text may also be interpreted as part of an extended comment in which Bede takes on the voice of Christ (lines 2491–2502), but in my view the more directly personalized reading offered above is more plausible.

[35] For Bede as for Augustine, *retractatio* (from the verb *retractare*) implies revision, reconsideration and correction, rather than retraction in the modern sense.

[36] Bede opens the preface of his *Retractatio* by observing that Augustine, that *eximius doctor ac pontifex,* in his maturity had issued a book of retractations on certain works that he had composed in his youth. He adds that it was not that he was confounded by early unskilfulness but rather that he was rejoiced by his increase of wisdom over the years to leave appropriate literary memorials to posterity. He, Bede, was pleased to imitate such *industria:* see *Retract. Act.* Praef. (p. 103, lines 1–9). For a fuller discussion of the degree to which Bede identified with Augustine, see Alan Thacker, *Bede and Augustine: History and Figure in Sacred Text* (Jarrow Lecture, 2005), forthcoming.

[37] Bede, *Retract. Act.* 1 (p. 107, lines 75–85).

In his latter years, Bede was clearly in no danger of underestimating his standing.

Bede's Educative Program

I want now to look a little more closely at Bede's educative program, how it evolved and took its final form. Although Bede's early works were distilled from his authorities with exceptional skill and clarity, they were (except perhaps for his celebrated recalculation of the age of the world) on the whole cautious and derivative. He ended, however, writing treatises on biblical books which nobody else had commented upon, and, as we shall see, using those commentaries as vehicles for his own concern as a *doctor* for the well-being of the Church Universal and of his own *ecclesia gentis Anglorum* in particular.

He was, moreover, aware of his own originality. No longer simply following the footsteps of the Fathers, he was contributing new perspectives. In the moving conclusion to his late commentary on Ezra–Nehemiah, for example, he states this eloquently and unambiguously. Invoking the "most high Father of Lights," he asserts that He had manifested to him, the "unworthy" Bede, "grace not only of comprehending ancient offerings in the treasury of this prophetic book, but of finding new ones beneath the veil of the old."[38]

It is difficult for us to elucidate fully the stages by which he attained this confidence and originality, since so few of Bede's works can be securely dated. Nevertheless, we can at least discern the lineaments of the process. In the autobiographical

---

[38] Bede, *In Ezram* 3 (p. 392, lines 2108–15); trans. Scott DeGregorio, *Bede: On Ezra and Nehemiah*, Translated Texts for Hisorians 47 (Liverpool, 2006), p. 226. See below DeGregorio, p. 166, where the passage is quoted in the original and more fully discussed. For the late date of the commentary, see DeGregorio, "Reform of the Northumbrian Church," pp. 21–22, and introduction to *Bede: On Ezra and Nehemiah*, pp. xxxvii–xlii.

note at the end of the *Historia ecclesiastica,* to which I have already referred,[39] Bede surveyed his output. Interestingly, he arranged his work in a highly structured manner. He began with the scriptural commentaries, catalogued not in the order in which they were written but in the canonical order of the biblical books to which they relate. It is quite a comprehensive list. From the Old Testament Bede had covered the crucial origin myths in Genesis, Israel's first focus of worship, the Tabernacle, the history of Israel under its kings, with especial reference to the Temple, and then had sampled the prophets, wisdom literature, and the apocrypha. From the New Testament he covered the main categories of text—the fundamental Gospels and the Epistles, the historical Acts and the mystical Apocalypse. All this represents the most ambitious and carefully planned program of biblical commentary since Late Antiquity.

From the Scriptures, Bede moves on to hagiography, history and martyrology, hymns and epigrams, and natural science and computus, concluding with orthography, meter and grammar. Now there is nothing random or accidental in all this. For Bede, knowledge was highly interconnected. Its primary focus was the Christian Scriptures and the body of authoritative learned commentary on those Scriptures. It was natural therefore to begin with biblical exegesis. Hagiography and history follow since they demonstrated the teaching elucidated in abstract terms in the commentaries in action, in the theater of human affairs. The close connections in Bede's mind between exegesis and history are particularly evident in the links between the late commentaries, such as *De tabernaculo, De templo,* and *In Ezram et Neemiam,* and the *Historia ecclesiastica,* issues to which I shall return in a moment.

After history and historiography, the next significant section in Bede's list of his writings focuses on his scientific treatises on chronology and the natural world. Computistical calculation of

---

[39] See n. above 32.

course had considerable practical implications for monks and liturgists, and Bede was, as we all know, an outstanding computist. At a deeper level, however, he was interested in chronology as revealing the structure of time, that structure which, as Faith Wallis has recently pointed out, represented the "continuity and pattern" of divine providence.[40] Both his chronological treatises therefore culminate in discussion of the ages of the world, of the progress of time from creation to the sixth and present age, the last of historical time that will usher in "the eternal stability and stable eternity" of the seventh and final age.[41] That doctrine of the seven ages of the world, predicated on the seven days of creation, brings us of course back full circle to the creation myth of Genesis and biblical exegesis.

Such concerns are intimately connected with Bede's analysis of the natural world. That world could only be understood through the lens of Genesis, and *De natura rerum* begins with a discussion derived from Augustine of the biblical creation story. What follows (in which the principal sources—Augustine, Pliny and Isidore—are carefully indicated) is designed to bring the ancients' understanding of the world into a scriptural perspective.[42]

Computus also naturally intersected with history.[43] Both Bede's treatises on time ended in world chronicles, dating events by *annus mundi*, the age of the world. In them, as Faith Wallis has pointed out,[44] Bede was writing universal history with

---

[40] Faith Wallis, introduction to *Bede: The Reckoning of Time*, trans. Faith Wallis, Translated Texts for Historians 29 (Liverpool, 1999), p. lxx.

[41] Bede, *DTR* 71 (p. 544, lines 92–93); trans. Wallis, *Reckoning of Time*, p. 249.

[42] The work was intended to supersede Isidore's *De natura rerum* and the Irish Pseudo-Isidore's *De ordine creaturarum*, both of which Bede seems to have found unsatisfactory: see Charles Jones, introduction to CCSL 123A, p. xii; and Wallis, introduction to *Reckoning of Time*, pp. lxxx–lxxxi.

[43] Wallis, introduction to *Reckoning of Time*, pp. lxvii–lxviii.

[44] Wallis, introduction to *Reckoning of Time*, pp. lxvii–lxxi.

a universal dating system. In the *Historia ecclesiastica*, he is specific, focused upon the salvation history of a single nation—and here, in work solely devoted to the last age, he uses a different dating system, centered on the incarnation, thereby Christianizing the structure of time.

The contribution of grammar and metrics, as discussed in *De arte metrica* and *De schematibus et tropis*, is equally clear. As Charles Jones pointed out, Bede was the first to adapt the teaching of grammar, within which he included metrics and figures, for Christian and more specifically monastic, purposes.[45] Metrics had an obvious application to hymnody and the *opus Dei* and to a number of poetic books in the scriptural canon. Indeed, Bede is the first to distinguish the rhythmic verse used in early hymns from the quantitative verse of the ancients.[46] Again, as in *De natura rerum*, Bede integrated the basic elements of classical learning into his new program of Christian knowledge. This emerges with particular clarity in the concluding chapter of *De arte metrica*, in which Bede lists the three poetic genres of classical composition, the dramatic or active, the narrative or expository and the common or mixed, explaining that such genres were employed not only by the great classical poets but also by the Scriptures.[47]

In the second book of his grammatical work, Bede enumerates the figures of speech derived from rhetoric. He opens by saying that he is discussing these "schemes" or "tropes" solely in relation to the Scriptures. In other words, the work is to constitute a summary of Christian hermeneutics. It offers with a particularly clear and unambiguous statement of Bede's aims in his educative program:

[45] Jones, introduction to CCSL 123A, p. x.

[46] See Bede, *DAM* 24 (p. 138, line 1–p. 139, line 31), along with Calvin Kendall's comments, *Bede: The Art of Poetry and Rhetoric*, ed. and trans. Calvin Kendall, Bibliotheca Germanica Series Nova, vol. 2 (Saarbrücken, 1991), p. 23.

[47] Bede, *DAM* 25 (p. 140, line 12–p. 141, line 25).

> In order that you, my beloved son (he means the deacon Cuthbert) . . . , may know that holy Scripture takes precedence over all other forms of writing not only by virtue of its authority, in that it is divine, and its utility, in that it leads to eternal life, but also because of its antiquity and its very use of rhetoric, I have decided to demonstrate by means of examples gathered from its pages that there is not one of these schemes and tropes which teachers of classical rhetoric (*saecularis eloquentiae magistri*) boast of which did not appear in it first.[48]

Bede goes on to list seventeen schemes, which, true to his word, he illustrates with scriptural exempla. He then discusses tropes, concluding with an extended discussion of allegory. In this section he defines the celebrated fourfold levels of meaning in Scripture: the literal, typological, tropological or moral, and anagogical or mystical. Interestingly, he illustrates these meanings with reference to the Temple, which embodies all these levels of meaning at once. In the literal sense it is the house which Solomon built; allegorically (i.e. typologically) it represents Christ's body or the Church; tropologically, each of the faithful; anagogically, the joys of the heavenly mansion.

The grammatical treatises have been regarded as textbooks for use in the schoolroom by Bede's pupils. And because he refers to himself as *conlevita*, "co-deacon" when addressing Cuthbert, the designated recipient of the work, they have been thought to be early, written before Bede had attained priestly orders at the age

---

[48] Bede, *DST* 1 (p. 142, line 12–p. 143, line 19): "Sed ut cognoscas, dilectissime fili, cognoscant omnes qui haec legere uoluerint quia sancta Scriptura ceteris omnibus scripturis non solum auctoritate, quia diuina est, uel utilitate, quia ad uitam ducit aeternam, sed et antiquitate et ipsa praeeminet positione dicendi, placuit mihi collectis de ipsa exemplis ostendere quia nihil huiusmodi schematum siue troporum ualent praetendere saecularis eloquentiae magistri, quod non in illa praecesserit."

of thirty (i.e. before 702).[49] To my mind, however, they represent Bede's mature reflections on his educative program; they are the foundations on which he reared his edifice of Christian knowledge. While taking the form of schoolbook, they are in fact a highly original manifesto for an education wholly focused upon the Christian and more especially the monastic life. They are linked, moreover, with Bede's concerns in the 720s and early 730s when he was writing his greatest chronological, exegetical and historical works. In particular, the reference to the fourfold nature of the allegorical interpretation of Scripture is very close to similar expositions in Bede's commentaries on the Tabernacle and the Song of Songs, both works of his maturity.[50] It is particularly significant that in *De schematibus* Bede chose the Temple as a subject which could be interpreted in all four senses, since he was to write a commentary expounding the spiritual significance of the Temple in the 720s. Thus I would follow the latest editor of *De schematibus*, Calvin Kendall, in ascribing to it a much later date than is commonly allowed.[51] The Cuthbert, who is Bede's disciple, is almost certainly that Cuthbert who was present at his deathbed and was later abbot of Wearmouth-Jarrow. Bede's use of *conlevita* is best regarded as a courtesy to his pupil, rather than a literal description of his own clerical status.[52]

---

[49] This is the view put forth by Plummer, *Opera historica*, pp. cxlv, and M. L. W. Laistner with H. H. King, *A Handlist of Bede Manuscripts* (Ithaca, N.Y., 1943), pp. 131–2.

[50] Bede, *In Cant.* 3 (p. 260, lines 617–25); and *De tab.* 1 (p. 25, lines 781–811).

[51] Kendall, *Art of Rhetoric and Poetry*, pp. 28–29. Cf. Martin Irvine, "Bede the Grammarian and the Scope of Grammatical Studies in Eighth-Century Northumbria," *Anglo-Saxon England* 15 (1986): 43, and Arthur Holder, "(Un)Dating Bede's *De Arte Metrica*, in *Northumbria's Golden Age*, ed. Jane Hawkes and Susan Mills (Stroud, 1999), pp. 390–95.

[52] Cf. Holder, "(Un)Dating Bede's *De Arte Metrica*," p. 395.

I am arguing then that by the 720s Bede viewed his oeuvre as an interconnected program for a monastic education. His so-called school treatises or textbooks constituted a fundamental element in this program. Although clearly suited to practical use, they are not primarily straightforward books of instruction intended by Bede to be employed in his own schoolroom.

Bede's Exegetical Technique: the Earlier Years

To assess Bede's mature educative program, it is necessary to look a little more closely at the development of his technique as a biblical exegete. Bede was never primarily a speculative theologian. His originality lay rather in his ordering of knowledge and connecting it with God's purposed salvation of mankind. Concern to follow established authority is especially apparent in his early exegesis, almost all of which was devoted to the New Testament. In works such as the commentary on the Apocalypse, written around 703 and addressed to Hwaetberht, later abbot of Wearmouth-Jarrow, and that on Acts, written around 709 and one of the first works addressed to Bishop Acca, Bede was brief, highly allegorical and highly dependent of the work of earlier commentators, such as Tyconius, Primasius and Arator.[53] The Seven Catholic Epistles, where Bede had few predecessors, was equally brief, but here by contrast he was strongly literal and moral.[54] After these early works Bede turned to the Gospels. In his

---

[53] On the Apocalypse, see Gerald Bonner, *Saint Bede in the Tradition of Western Apocalyptic Commentary* (Jarrow Lecture, 1966), and Roger Gryson's new edition of the commentary: *Explanatio Apocalypseos*, ed. Roger Gyrson, CCSL 121A (Turnhout, 2001). On Acts, see Lawrence Martin, introduction to *The Venerable Bede: Commentary on the Acts of the Apostles*, trans. Lawrence Martin, Cistercian Studies Series 117 (Kalamazoo, Mich., 1989).

[54] George Hardin Brown, *Bede the Venerable* (Boston, 1987), p. 59; Ward, *Venerable Bede*, pp. 56–8.

massive commentary on Luke, his most ambitious work to date, the stress remained literal and moral, and the technique highly derivative: Bede relied heavily on Ambrose, Augustine, Jerome and Gregory the Great—indeed, he seems to have been the first to recognize these four as the Latin Fathers.[55] In the preface, addressed to Acca, he defended himself vigorously against any charge of innovation, in particular concerning the ascription of symbols to the evangelists (he followed Augustine, who was unusual in awarding the lion to Matthew and the man to Mark).[56]

Bede is in general cautious in his treatment of the New Testament. He is especially careful here to declare his grounding in previous authorities: his well-known citation of the sources for his commentaries on Luke and Mark is a particularly striking instance of that concern.

In his work on the Pauline Epistles indeed he offered nothing at all in his own words. In that case, he merely put together excerpts from the works of St. Augustine, mostly culled from a previous Augustinian *collectaneum* compiled in the early sixth century by Eugippius, abbot of the Neapolitan monastery of Castellum Lucullanum. His input there comprised the considerable skill with which he selected and arranged the excerpts. In his *collectaneum*, unlike that of Eugippius, Scripture was para-

---

[55] See Bede, *In Lucam* Prol. (p. 7, lines 93–105); Ward, *Venerable Bede*, p. 44. For detailed discussion of this point, see J. N. Hart-Hasler, "*Vestigia patrum sequens*: The Venerable Bede's Use of Patristic Sources in his Commentary on the Gospel of Luke" (Ph.D. diss., Cambridge University, 1999); and more recently, Bernice M. Kaczynski, "Bede's Commentaries on Luke and Mark and the Formation of a Patristic Canon," in *Anglo-Latin Literature and Its Heritage: Essays in Honour of A. G. Rigg on His 64th Birthday*, ed. Siân Echard and Gernot R. Wieland, Publications of the Journal of Medieval Latin 4 (Turnhout, 2001), pp. 17–26.

[56] Bede, *In Lucam* Prol. (p. 7, line 123–p. 10, line 220); cf. *Exp. Apoc.* 5 (pp. 281–3, lines 63–79), and Augustine, *De consensu Euangelistarum*, esp. 1.6 (CCSL 43: p. 9, line 1–p. 10, line 14).

mount: Bede arranged his *excerpta* according to Pauline composition not Augustinian theme.[57]

Bede's Mature Works: the Commentaries

Bede's first substantial Old Testament commentary, the four
books on 1 Samuel, dedicated to Acca and written around 716,
marks a turning point in his exegesis. In this work, one of the
most elaborately allegorical[58] and in fact the longest of his Old
Testament commentaries, he first expresses in a concentrated
form his preoccupation with *doctores* and *praedicatores,* with the
teaching and preaching mission of the church.[59] 1 Samuel inaugurated a major group of mature commentaries, all focused
on the Old Testament, and all to a greater or lesser extent concerned with the same themes.[60] The group includes works on

[57] On this Bedan compilation, see the two articles by P.–I. Fransen,
"Description de la collection de Bède le Vénérable sur l'Apôtre," *Revue
Bénédictine* 71 (1961): 22–70, and "D'Eugippius à Bède le Vénérable,"
Revue Bénédictine 97 (1987): 187–94; also Thacker, *Bede and Augustine.*
Curiously, the work has been translated into English by David Hurst, *Bede
the Venerable: Excerpts from the Works of St. Augustine on the Letters of the Blessed
Apostle Paul,* Cistercian Studies Series 183 (Kalamazoo, Mich., 1999), even
though a critical edition of the text has yet to be published.

[58] Note Bede's own reference to it as *allegoricae expositionis libellum*: see *In
Sam.* 4. Prol. (p. 212, line 23). For additional comment, see Brown's essay
in this volume, pp. 122–23.

[59] See, for example, the following statistics relating to *doctores*—*In Lucam*:
63 references in 420 pages of CCSL text; *In Marcum*: 29 in 217 pages;
In Sam.: 112 in 265 pages; *De tab.*: 61 in 136 pages; *De templ.*: 38 in 91;
In Ezram: 43 in 155 pages; *In prou. Sal.*: 41 in 140 pages; and *In Cant.*: 65
in 208 pages. See also DeGregorio, "Reforming Impulse," pp. 112–13,
which also views this commentary as crucial to the development of Bede's
views on pastoral care.

[60] The themes particularly developed include the Church's universal
mission to spread the Gospel (e.g. *In Sam.* 1, p. 28, line 711–p. 29, line

the Song of Songs, Proverbs, and the interrelated compositions devoted to the Tabernacle, the Temple, and Ezra and Nehemiah. In a general sense these works are all concerned with salvation history and with *aedificatio ecclesiae*, the building up of the church—both through the refutation of error and the spreading of the word. Behind them lies an eschatological concern for the process by which ultimately the world would arrive at that day when all its peoples had received the message of salvation and the Last Judgment could be inaugurated.

More specifically, Bede particularly develops in these works the theme of the role of Christian teachers and preachers in promoting the Church's universal mission and in combating obdurate resistance to that mission. He shows particular anxiety that contemporary spiritual leaders, including members of both the ordained hierarchy and of the order of teachers and preachers, are not up to the task, because they are corrupt or ignorant and unskillful. All these works are much concerned with the Jews. Those of the old dispensation have a key role,

737); the need for *boni rectores, doctores* and *praedicatores* to accomplish that work (e.g. *In Sam.* 2, p. 122, line 2281–p. 123, line 2300); the destiny of the Jews and the penance required of them (e.g. *In Sam.* 4, p. 252, lines 1699–1723); and the correction of error and heresy (e.g. *In Sam.* 2, p. 96, lines 1163–79). Linked with this is a concern about the corrupt priests (e.g. *In Sam.* 1, p. 30, lines 778–803) and unskillful spiritual leaders and teachers of his own day and the contemporary persistence in disregarding the saving message of Christ (e.g. *In Sam.* 2, p. 90, lines 945–50; p. 112, lines 1851–9). All this, of course, relates to his own key role, "his present aid," expressly mentioned in the same commentary (see above p. 44, n. 34). These concerns were presumably exacerbated by the sudden departure of Ceolfrid at a period of turbulence in Wearmouth-Jarrow's history, perhaps connected with the political upheaval that saw the killing of Osred and his replacement by a distant kinsman, Cenred (*HE* 5.22, p. 553). Bede refers to the *conturbatio* arising from this departure in unwontedly personal terms in his introduction to the fourth book of his commentary (*In Sam.* 4 Prol. p. 212, lines 1–28).

since they may prefigure well-disposed pagans or offer a type of the exemplary pastors of the past who built up the Church and implemented its saving mission. Those of the new dispensation, by contrast, are viewed as obdurately rejecting Christ and their conversion is a matter of especial concern. Linked with this is an equally obtrusive preoccupation with heresy, also seen as obdurate and willful separation from the church.

All this, of course, links closely to Bede's contemporary concerns about the Church in England, first expressed in the Samuel commentary, developed in its successors and fully articulated in the letter to Bishop Ecgberht. The resonance for Bede's native cultural world is intense. The children of Israel in the Old Testament provide a comfortable analogy for Bede's own pre-Christian ancestors; they could be presented as having virtue and a role in salvation even though in their position as forerunners, they could not in the nature of things participate in the full Christian revelation. It was no casual search for simile that prompted Bede to refer to that paragon of pagan *uirilitas*, the Northumbrian king Æthelfrith (592/3-616), in biblical terms. To him, as to a second Saul, could be applied the words of Israel himself, the patriarch Jacob, when he blessed his youngest son: "Benjamin shall ravin as a wolf; in the morning he shall devour the prey and at night divide the spoils."[61] These admiring words, it should be remembered, were being bestowed on Æthelfrith in the context of his defeat of the Christian Irish and in the knowledge that he would shortly be depicted as the instrument of the death of some 1200 Christian British priests and monks.[62]

The unregenerate Jews, keeping their message of salvation to themselves and ultimately rejecting the new dispensation, provided a further image of contemporary resonance. They were a figure so to speak of the hated British, that *gens perfida* which

[61] Gen. 49:27, quoted by Bede, *HE* 1.34 (p. 117).
[62] *HE* 2.2 (p. 140).

had failed in its missionary duty to convert the pagan English.[63] Here the theme of universal mission blended with the theme of the English as a chosen people, a new Israel.[64] Unlike the British, the English were destined for a missionary role—to bring the faith to their own continental kindred. In so doing, they were demonstrating their chosen status and distinguishing themselves from the British. The preoccupation with heretics, often linked with Jews in the commentary on Samuel,[65] may well have sprung from a similar root. The British were firmly associated with heresy in Bede's mind, since he knew the arch-heretic Pelagius to be British and linked him personally with Julian of Eclanum whose works he condemned in his commentary on the Song of Songs.[66] The obstinacy so frequently ascribed to heretics (as to the Jews) is also clearly a characteristic of the British as they appear in the *Historia ecclesiastica*.

Let us look now at Bede's technique as an exegete in these later commentaries. Unquestionably, they display a sophisticated use of allegory, along the lines of Alexandrine scriptural analysis pioneered in the Latin West by Tyconius and Augustine, and driven to its extreme by Gregory the Great. In an age when the Scriptures were believed to be of divine inspiration, such a methodology freed its practitioners from the tyranny of literal fundamentalism. The problem is of course that such techniques, if pushed too far, are inimical to structured discourse. When inner meaning may be discerned (as in Gregory) without apparent relation to, indeed at times in clear contradiction of, the literal sense, it is all too easy for a certain randomness of

[63] Jennifer O'Reilly, introduction to *Bede: On the Temple*, trans. Seán Connolly, Translated Texts for Historians 21 (Liverpool, 1995), pp. xxxix–xxxv.

[64] As such, the English, prefigured by the "good" Jews of the Old Testament, superseded the British, representative of the unregenerate Jews of the New Testament.

[65] See, for example, *In Sam.* 4 (p. 252, lines 1712–21).

[66] Bede, *HE* 1.10 (p. 38); and *In Cant.* Prol. (p. 167, line 1 – p. 180, line 513).

thought to pervade the writing. At its best, however, Gregory's most elaborate work of exegesis, the *Moralia* on the Book of Job, is a moving text, a series of meditations on interrelated themes. All Bede's later commentaries also have something of this meditative, thematic quality.

In England around 700 Alexandrine allegory was not the only exegetical option, a fact of which Bede was most certainly aware. At Canterbury, Theodore had taught an exegetical technique that followed the principles of the school of Antioch and privileged the literal sense of Scripture, making use of historical and above all philological analysis.[67] Bede too had always been interested in literal interpretation, and in his *De octo quaestionibus,* when he discussed what Paul meant in his statement that "For a day and a night I was in the depth of the sea" (2 Cor. 11.26), he cited Theodore's reading of the passage.[68] Unlike Theodore, however, Bede followed this with a discussion of the mystical meaning of the text. In his late work he went further and sought greater integration of the literal and allegorical senses. By then he usually chose his texts with great skill so that their surface meaning had some relationship to the spiritual and moral themes he wished principally to discuss. That is particularly obvious in the three late interrelated works on the Tabernacle, the Temple, and Ezra and Nehemiah. For one who wished to discuss *aedificatio ecclesiae*, the building up of the Church through mission and reform, there is an obvious appropriateness in commenting on texts centered upon the main foci of Old Testament worship. Ezra and Nehemiah, as Scott DeGregorio has recently pointed out, are especially apposite texts, in that their theme is the rebuilding of the Temple, the refortification of the Holy City and the prophet's and the

---

[67] For Theodore and the Antiochenes, see Bischoff and Lapidge, *Biblical Commentaries,* esp. pp. 18–24, 205–9, 243–9.

[68] *De oct. quaest.* 3 (PL 93, cols. 456–7); for an English translation, see *Bede: A Biblical Miscellany,* trans. W. Trent Foley and Arthur G. Holder, Translated Texts for Historians 28 (Liverpool, 1999), pp. 152–3.

governor's role therein. The biblical Ezra and Nehemiah were themselves spiritual and moral reformers.[69] Significantly, none of the Fathers had attempted a scheme like this; indeed no commentary on Ezra and Nehemiah existed at all. Bede thus had a blank page on which to inscribe his exegetical concerns.

One result of this approach was an increasing unease with allegorical discourse that radically contravened the literal sense. This was already apparent in the commentary on Samuel where Bede offered an elaborate justification of his use of the evil Philistines to typify Gentile catholic believers and the chosen people, Israel, to typify contemporary unbelieving Jews and heretics.[70] The text that posed the most crucial problems in this respect, however, was the commentary on the Song of Songs, a work of uncertain date but undoubtedly composed in Bede's maturity. Although on the surface his subject was a poem about erotic love, Bede's commentary was, as Arthur Holder argues in his essay in this volume, a meditation on salvation history focused on the Incarnation.[71] Bede equated the bride in the poem primarily with the Church as a whole, not like later commentators, such as St. Bernard, with the individual soul.[72] He thus tied it in with his overriding concerns of the period. The sense of the work as a whole is, however, completely divorced from this interpretation and Bede was therefore forced to dismiss it. Basing himself on an earlier commentator, Apponius, and attacking the Pelagian Julian of Eclanum, he categorically asserted that the work had no carnal meaning.[73] Even so,

---

[69] See DeGregorio, "Reform of the Northumbrian Church," esp. pp. 3–20, together with his earlier article, "Reforming Impulse," pp. 115–16.

[70] See *In Sam.* 4, p. 252, line 1712 – p. 253, line 1739, where he justifies using the evil Philistines to typify gentile believers and Israel to typify the perfidy of contemporary Jews and heretics.

[71] Holder, "Christ as Incarnate Wisdom," p. 169 and passim

[72] Holder, "Christ as Incarnate Wisdom," pp. 171–2.

[73] Bede, *In Cant.* 3 (p. 337, lines 1–4); for comment, see Holder, "Christ as Incarnate Wisdom," pp. 172–3.

he clearly preferred its interpretation to accord as far as possible with the literal sense. Holder highlights the opening passage in the Vulgate, "Let me kiss you with the kisses of my mouth for your breasts are better than wine," which Bede wishes to be read as the Old Testament Synagogue addressing her bridegroom, Christ.[74] Bede, ever alert to surface meaning, has an elaborate explanation of why feminine body parts are attributed to Christ, an issue that had not troubled his sources.[75]

Thus, in their themes and techniques, and indeed in their originality in launching out on subjects not hitherto attempted by the Fathers, Bede's final exegetical works represent a coherent, ordered, interconnected program. He had a consistent and distinctive intellectual approach that integrated the literal and mystical meanings. He was, moreover, especially interested in the historical books of Scripture and his interpretation of these works bore upon his own approach to history as expressed in the *Historia ecclesiastica*.[76]

Bede's Mature Works: History and Computus

I want to conclude by looking briefly at Bede's other works in the 720s and early 730s and to argue that they too are contributions to this ordered program. This is especially obvious in the case of the *Historia ecclesiastica*. That work is clearly dominated by the twin themes of the providentially ordained conversion of the English, a new Israel with a divine mission, and the ur-

---

[74] See Bede, *In Cant.* 1 (p. 191, line 31 – p. 191, line 43), along with Holder, "Christ as Incarnate Wisdom," pp. 173.

[75] Holder, "Christ as Incarnate Wisdom," pp. 174–5. Cf. Bede, *In Sam.* 4 (p. 252, line 1712 – p. 253, line 1739).

[76] Compare the historical and chronological prologue to *In Sam.* 2 (p. 68, line 1 – p. 70, line 95), in which Bede discusses the period of Israel's history from the end of the *ducatus* of Samuel, to the beginning of the reign of Saul.

gent need for exemplary *doctores*, preachers and pastors to guide the *gens* along that path in the present. The great teachers and preachers of the golden age of the English church clearly provide concrete illustration of the qualities, duties, and functions of the *doctores* and *praedicatores* discussed in a more abstract way in the commentaries.[77]

What is less obvious is how computus links into this. For Bede's third major enterprise of his latter years (together with the Old Testament commentaries and the Histories) is his great work on Time, *De temporum ratione*. This, as Faith Wallis's contribution to this volume makes abundantly clear, was no textbook. It is, as she puts it, "an exceptionally wide-ranging, coherent and successful analysis of calendar construction, which for the first time set this problem within the context of ancient cosmology and a Christian understanding of nature and history."[78] Bede's meditations on Time are closely linked with his other preoccupations. As Wallis further emphasizes, they are concerned with the Christian—and more specifically monastic—qualities of order and *stabilitas*.

But Bede's computistical preoccupations also intersect with his historical and exegetical interests, and more specifically with his particular concern for the elect status of the English, in a quite precise way. That point of connection is the perceived eschatological role of *Britannia* and *Ultima Thule*. As Diarmuid Scully has pointed out, the conversion of the English was crucial to the whole millenarian scenario.

For Bede, as for the Ancients, the islands of Britannic archipelago were the isles of the Ultimate West, the edge of the world, whose conversion represented the completion of the conversion of the Gentiles. That conversion preceded the con-

---

[77] On these points, see especially Campbell, "Bede I," pp. 24–25, and Thacker, "Ideal of Reform," pp. 142–50.

[78] Wallis, "New Approach to Bede's 'Science'," pp. 69–70.

version of the obdurate Jews of the new dispensation.[79] And the conversion of the Jews ushered in the reign of Antichrist, the prelude to the Last Judgment and the onset of the unending final age of everlasting rest. All that was spelt out by Bede in the eloquent and moving final chapters of *De temporum ratione*. It is the essential backdrop to his preoccupation with Jews and heretics in his later commentaries. Here then computus and chronology fused with exegesis and history and Bede's sense of the special and chosen nature of the *gens Anglorum* linked into his interest in universal salvation history.

Conclusion

I would argue then that Bede's later years saw the forging of a remarkably ordered and interconnected program of writing. Focused upon salvation as attained through understanding, and observance, of the teachings of Scripture and more specifically upon the salvific role of Bede's own English and indeed Northumbrian *gens*, it linked his three main interests, scriptural exegesis, history and computus. And it was underpinned by his studies of grammar and meter which were probably also published during this period. Although Bede was not a speculative thinker, he had conceived a program of great originality and cohesiveness. For him education, moral teaching and spiritual understanding were inextricably linked. Taking what was available, he selected and integrated Christian and classical learning, to shape a new educative framework. He also produced an oeuvre

---

[79] Diarmuid Scully, introduction to *Bede: On Tobit and Habakkuk*, trans. Seán Connolly (Dublin, 1997), esp. pp. 33–36; idem, "The Atlantic Archipelago from Antiquity to Bede: The Transformation of an Image" (Ph.D. diss., University College, Cork, 2000), esp. 30–41, 146–50, and 154–68; and Jan Davidse, "The Sense of History in the Works of the Venerable Bede," Studi medievali 23 (1982): 647–95, pp. 664–70.

designed to meet its needs. That oeuvre was intended to be at once of universal application and carefully attuned to the needs of his present-day and of his people. Those in Bede's eyes were the duties of a Doctor of the Church. It is undoubtedly time to abandon all talk of the humble teacher of Jarrow. Bede, I suspect, was aware of his eminence. He thought of himself as the Augustine of his age. And who is to say that he was not right?

Si Naturam Quæras: Reframing Bede's "Science"

Faith Wallis

Reframing Bede's "Science"

IN 1970, BEDE WAS ADMITTED into a distinctively modern "hall of fame," the *Dictionary of Scientific Biography*.[1] This accolade was the climax of a movement initiated largely in the mid-1930s to identify what were seen as Bede's "contributions" to science.[2] Many historians are now quite accustomed to referring to Bede's "scientific writings," which usually means his survey of cosmology *De natura rerum*, his two works on time reckoning *De temporibus* and *De temporum ratione*, and sometimes his account of cosmogenesis in the first part of his commentary on Genesis. What seems less certain is exactly what claim the term "science" makes about Bede. For some, Bede was a "scientist" as we moderns understand the term—someone who conducted investigations which resulted in new positive knowledge about the natural world. He held "advanced" views on questions pertaining to nature, launched a rationalist critique of earlier writ-

---

[1] Charles W. Jones, "Bede," *Dictionary of Scientific Biography*, ed. Charles C. Gillispie, vol. 1 (New York, 1970), pp. 564–6.

[2] The pioneering studies were by Franz Strunz, "Beda Venerabilis in der Geschichte der Naturbetrachtung und Naturforschung," *Zeitschrift für deutsche Geschichte* 1 (1935): 311–32; and Beda Thum, "Beda Venerabilis in der Geschichte der Naturwissenschaften," *Studia Anselmiana* 6 (1936): 57–71. Bede's "science" did receive some passing mention in earlier works, e.g. Charles Homer Haskins, *Studies in the History of Mediaeval Science*, 2nd edn. (Cambridge, Mass., 1927), but the articles of Strunz and Thum were the earliest specialized studies.

ers, conducted a program of observation and experimentation, and even achieved "breakthroughs."[3] Not everyone, however, has felt comfortable with this approach. Charles Jones preferred to emphasize the close connection between Bede's scientific writings and his work as an exegete, especially his commentary on Genesis. Jones also argued that these scientific writings were didactic works intended for a clerical audience; therefore they must be evaluated in the light of clerical-monastic modes of teaching and ideas about the nature of learning, as embodied in Augustinian *doctrina christiana*.[4] Jones also situated Bede's interest in the natural world in his computistical project: indeed, his *Dictionary of Scientific Biography* article discusses only computus. Attention to computus also informs the work of Wesley Stevens, though even here, a broadly positivist model of science continues to dominate the analysis. Most of Stevens' Jarrow Lecture on Bede's science concerns Bede's store of scientific facts, his position on questions

[3] This is particularly characteristic of the work of Thomas R. Eckenrode, "The Growth of a Scientific Mind: Bede's Early and Late Scientific Writings," *Downside Review* 94 (1976): 197–212; see also his "Venerable Bede as a Scientist," *American Benedictine Review* 22 (1971): 486–507, "Venerable Bede's Theory of Ocean Tides," *American Benedictine Review* 25 (1974): 56–74, and his 1970 Ph.D. dissertation from St. Louis University, "Original Aspects in Venerable Bede's Tidal Theories with Relation to Prior Tidal Observations." Bede's discussion of tides is found in *DTR* 29; see commentary in Faith Wallis, *Bede: The Reckoning of Time*, trans. Faith Wallis, Translated Texts for Historians 29 (Liverpool, 1999), pp. 307–12.

[4] See particularly his *Saints' Lives and Chronicles in Early England* (Ithaca, N.Y., 1947), and "Bede's Place in Medieval Schools," in *Famulus Christi: Essays in Commemoration of the Thirteenth Centenary of the Birth of the Venerable Bede*, ed. Gerald Bonner (London, 1976), pp. 261–85. Jones's lead has been followed by Benedicta Ward, *The Venerable Bede* (London, 1990), who discusses the scientific works in chapter 2 "Bede the Teacher," and George Hardin Brown, *Bede the Venerable* (Boston, 1987), who groups them with "The Educational Treatises" (ch. 2).

like the sphericity of the earth, and the reconstruction of observations or experiments which Bede might have conducted.[5]

Accepting computus as "Bede's science" has, however, generated its own debates. For Brigitte Englisch, computus is science only when Bede severs its links with *doctrina christiana*. Englisch argues that Bede's scientific achievement was to combine elements of the classical liberal arts and natural history with the technical, problem-oriented literature of the Christian calendar, and that this helped to emancipate science from its exclusive identification with philosophical speculation. Bede's particular contribution was to demonstrate the calendar's rationality as a consistent and replicable cycle governed by mathematical and astronomical principles. But in Englisch's view, Bede achieved this by subverting religious authority. His allegiance to the alleged decisions of the Council of Nicaea about the date of the spring equinox, for instance, is merely a "theologizing of the functional cosmological-computistical directives." Having made this purely formal submission, Bede is then "liberated" to select other authorities, including writers on the liberal arts, to promote a computistical system whose proofs are strictly internal.[6]

For Peter Hunter Blair, on the other hand, *doctrina christiana* effectively disqualifies "science" as a category applicable to Bede; hence he grouped the "scientific works" under the theme of "Number and Time."[7] Blair preferred the term "number" to "mathematical sciences," not only because it is the term Bede

[5] See Wesley Stevens, *Bede's Scientific Achievement* (Jarrow Lecture, 1985).

[6] Brigitte Englisch, "Realitätsorientierte Wissenschaft oder praxisferne Traditionswissen? Inhalte und Probleme mittelalterliche Wissenschaftsvorstellungen am Beispiel von *De temporum ratione* des Beda Venerabilis," in *Dilettanten und Wissenschaft. Zur Geschichte und Aktualität eines wechselvollen Verhältnisses*, ed. Elisabeth Strauss (Amsterdam, 1996), pp. 19–21; and her *Die Artes liberales im frühen Mittelalter (5.–9. Jh.): Das Quadrivium und der Komputus als Inidkatoren für der exacten Wissenschaften zwischen Antike und Mittelalter*, Sudhoffs Archiv, Beiheft 33 (Stuttgart, 1994), section 2.1.

[7] Peter Hunter Blair, *The World of Bede* (London 1970), ch. 24.

himself used, but because it embraces the religious symbolism of number. However, this reduces the "scientific works" to *De temporibus* and *De temporum ratione*, moreover, half of Blair's treatment of these works is devoted to the world-chronicles and the issue of *annus domini* chronology. What little is left of Bede's "science" is swallowed up in history.

It would seem, then, that Bede's "science" is both uncertain in its boundaries and unclear in its definition. The presentism of the term "science" is also an embarrassment, not least because Bede himself, in his autobiographical note at the close of the *Historia ecclesiastica*, claims that his exclusive intellectual concern was the study of Scripture.[8] To continue to isolate Bede's "science" also seems out of step with new approaches that stress the interpenetration of the genres within which Bede worked, especially history, exegesis, and hagiography.[9]

The challenge, then, is to understand Bede's interest in the natural world in a manner which acknowledges its prominence in Bede's world-view, without dissolving its context.[10] So in this essay, I shall use the term "science" to designate Bede's ideas about the material creation and his response to its intellectual

[8] Bede, *HE* 5.24 (pp. 566–71). Cf. William D. McCready, *Miracles and the Venerable Bede*, Texts and Studies 118 (Toronto, 1994), p. 88; Roger Ray, "What Do We Know about Bede's Commentaries?" *Recherches de théologie ancienne et médiévale* 49 (1982): 5.

[9] Important examples of this approach are Jan Davidse, "The Sense of History in the Works of the Venerable Bede," *Studi medievali* 23 (1982): 664–70, and "On Bede as Christian Historian," in *Beda Venerabilis: Historian, Monk and Northumbrian*, ed. L. A. J. R. Houwen and A. A. MacDonald (Groningen, 1996), pp. 1-15; Roger Ray, "Bede, the Exegete, as Historian," in *Famulus Christi*, pp. 125–40, and "Bede's *vera lex historiae*," *Speculum* 55 (1980): 1–21; Robert A. Markus, *Bede and the Tradition of Ecclesiastical Historiography* (Jarrow Lecture, 1975); Glenn Olsen, "Bede as Historian: the Evidence from his Observations on the Life of the First Christian Community at Jerusalem," *Journal of Ecclesiastical History* 33 (1982): 519–30; and Claudio Leonardi, "Il venerabile Beda e la cultura del secolo VIII," *Settimana di*

challenges. Even this minimalist definition comes with further qualifications. First, Bede wrote books specifically devoted to cosmology, cosmogenesis, and chronology, though this does not exhaust the range of scientific topics that he was curious about.[11] Secondly, there were some kinds of science that Bede did not involve himself in: he is very much less concerned than the Irish "Augustine" who composed *De mirabilibus sacrae scripturae* in rationalizing scientific allusions and problems in Scripture, and he did not attempt to compile an encyclopaedia, as did Isidore or Pliny. Some topics were inaccessible or of little interest to him, such as Boethian number theory. Finally, neither the form nor the content of his scientific writings is exceptionally original. He was not the first Christian scholar to write a hexaemeron, or a treatise on "the nature of things," or a manual of time-reckoning. On the other hand, in *De temporum ratione*, Bede composed an exceptionally wide-ranging, coherent and successful analysis of calendar construction, which for the

studi 20 (1973): 603–58. Bede was nonetheless aware of the demands of different genres: see esp. Judith McClure, "Bede's Old Testament Kings," in *Ideal and Reality in Frankish and Anglo-Saxon England: Studies Presented to J.M. Wallace-Hadrill*, ed. Patrick Wormald (Oxford, 1983), pp. 76–98, and Arthur G. Holder, "Allegory and History in Bede's Interpretation of Sacred Architecture," *American Benedictine Review* 40 (1989): 115–131.

[10] There are many excellent models for such an approach to medieval science, notably: Jacques Fontaine, *Isidore de Séville et la culture classique dans l'Espagne visigothique*, 2nd edn. (Paris, 1983), pt. 5, ch. 3, and *Isidore de Séville: genèse et originalité de la culture hispanique au temps des Wisigoths* (Turnhout, 2000), pt. 4, ch. 14; R. W. Southern, *Robert Grosseteste: The Growth of an English Mind in Medieval Europe* (Oxford, 1986), pt. 2; Roger French and Andrew Cunningham, *Before Science: the Invention of the Friars' Natural Philosophy* (Aldershot, 1996).

[11] Geography, biology, and medicine, for example, find their way into the niches of computus, which serves as a sort of "filing system" for the fragmented heritage of ancient scientific erudition: see Wallis, *Reckoning of Time*, pp. xviii-xxxiv.

first time set this problem within the context of ancient cosmology and a Christian understanding of nature and history. The range of *De temporum ratione* defines the specific quality and level of Bede's interest in the material creation, and his ability to synthesize several scientific genres in a manner not paralleled in his sources, or the works of his contemporaries. *De temporum ratione* is also remarkable for its pedagogical "experiments" to demonstrate natural phenomena,[12] and for its inclusion of hitherto unrecorded knowledge about tides, some of which Bede may have gathered through personal inquiry of some kind. However, it is well to remember that Bede never claims to have made any independent investigation into the pattern of tides; on the contrary, he states that the principle of port is a matter of common local knowledge.[13] Similarly, his repeated invitation to confirm the date of the spring equinox by consulting a sun-dial cannot be construed as evidence of anything more than casual inspection; it is certainly not the trace of a research program.[14] Most importantly, Bede never regards his own insights or innovations as in any way distinct from, let alone superior to, the account of the world found in his authorities. As far as Bede was concerned, his job was to explain tradition, and this principle applied as much to his scientific writings as to his exegesis.

[12] E.g. the "experiment" of the hanging lamps in the church, used to demonstrate that the Sun can appear to be closer to the Earth than the Moon, although it is higher in the heavens: *DTR* 26 (p. 359, line 3–p. 362, line 55); see also the commentary in Wallis, *Reckoning of Time*, pp. 304–6.

[13] Bede, *DTR* 29 (p. 370, lines 74–77): "Scimus enim nos, qui diuersum Britannici Maris litus incolimus, quod ubi hoc aequor aestuare coeperit ipsa hora aliud incipiat ab aestu deferuere."

[14] *DTR* 31; confirmation of the equinox by sundial is also mentioned in Ceolfrid's letter to King Nechtan of the Picts: see *HE* 5.21 (p. 542). An elaborate experiment involving the *dioptrae* or "sights" described by Pliny has been reconstructed by Harrison, "Easter Cycles"; cf. Stevens, *Scientific Achievement*, p. 16 and nn. 48–49. For discussion and reservations, see Wallis, *Reckoning of Time*, pp. 315–17.

A new approach to Bede's science should therefore define what Bede understood the material creation to be, and integrate that understanding into *doctrina christiana* as a Christian intellectual praxis and pedagogy. Since Bede's scientific interests were selective, a simple inventory of what he knew about the world will not advance us very far; rather, we should look for clues to Bede's ideas about the fundamental structures of the universe. My argument is that these structures are encapsulated by Bede in the word *natura*. This word appears frequently, and in consistent semantic patterns, throughout his scientific corpus. Its centrality to his concept of the universe is signalled by the fact that his survey of cosmology is entitled *De natura rerum*, and that his major sources, Isidore's book of the same name and Pliny's *Historia naturalis*, both contain the word *natura* in their titles.[15] However, Bede never defines *natura*. Instead, he regularly associates it with a restricted circle of related penumbral terms, notably *ratio* and *ordo*, which occasionally almost serve as synonyms. As a first step, we should look at how Bede uses the term *natura* when he is consciously thinking about the material creation, paying close attention as we do so to other terms that will help us to situate the larger meaning of his science. To test these extended meanings, we will look briefly at how Bede uses *natura* and its related terms when he is *not* directly discussing the phenomena or problems of creation.

The corpus of Bede's scientific writings outlined above may be divided into two broad categories. *De natura rerum* and *In Genesim* are descriptions of the cosmos, while *De temporibus* and *De temporum ratione* are manuals of time-reckoning and calendar construction. Both types of writings contain references to *natura*, but the

[15] Bede explicitly refers to *DNR*'s title in the preface of *DTR* (p. 263, lines 1–2) and in his enumeration of his own writings in *HE* 5.24 (p. 570). He refers to Pliny's work by title frequently, for example in *DTR* 33 (p. 382, line 8), but never refers to Isidore's *De natura rerum* by title. Thus we cannot be certain whether he knew it as *De natura rerum*, or by its alternate title of *Liber rotarum*.

word carries a different connotation depending on the genre of the work. When he is writing cosmology, Bede uses the word *natura* almost exclusively to mean the "property" or "attribute" of some specific thing. However, when he is writing about time, he uses *natura* in a very original manner to connote the way a particular kind of time is measured—God's "real time," established at Creation and embodied in the motions of the Sun and Moon. The distinction between the two "natures" is particularly striking in *De temporum ratione*, where cosmology and computus are fused. It is in *De temporum ratione* as well that the penumbral terms make their most distinctive appearance.

Natura in Cosmological Context:
De natura rerum *and* In Genesim 1

Bede's understanding of *natura* in his cosmological writings is fairly restricted, even by the standards of patristic and early medieval thinking.[16] To a certain degree, this reflects the circumstances of their composition. His youthful *De natura rerum* corrects and supplements Isidore of Seville's treatise of the same

[16] The literature on early medieval concepts of nature is not abundant, and the period between Augustine and Eriugena is especially barren. Useful, if partial, analyses include Giselle de Nie's study of Gregory of Tours, *Views from a Many-Windowed Tower* (Amsterdam, 1987); Marina Smyth, *Understanding the Universe in Seventh-Century Ireland*, Studies in Celtic History 15 (Woodbridge, 1996); Arno Borst, *Das Buch der Naturgeschichte: Plinius und seine Leser im Zeitalter des Pergaments*, 2nd ed. (Heidelberg, 1995), chs. 1–3, and Jennifer Neville, *Representations of the Natural World in Old English Poetry*, Cambridge Studies in Anglo-Saxon England 27 (Cambridge, 1999). For the patristic period, see Jean Pépin, *Théologie cosmique et théologies chrétiennes* (Paris, 1964); D.S. Wallace-Hadrill, *The Greek Patristic View of Nature* (Manchester, 1968), George Economou, *The Goddess Natura in Medieval Literature* (Cambridge, Mass., 1972), and Jaroslav Pelikan, *What Has Athens to Do with Jerusalem? Timaeus and Genesis in Counterpoint*, Jerome Lectures 21 (Ann Arbor, 1997).

title,[17] while excising Isidore's material on the units of time, and thereby throwing the cosmology into stronger relief.[18]

This cosmology is essentially an account of the four elements—fire, air, water and earth—understood as both a circle of paired characteristics combining hot/cold, and wet/dry, and as a vertical hierarchy based on relative weight and lightness. Fire, the lightest element, and earth, the heaviest, occupy the highest and lowest places respectively, with water and air as the intermediaries.[19]

Following Isidore, Bede structures *De natura rerum* according to the second schema, as a descent from the fiery region of the heavens, through the atmosphere with its meteorological phenomena, to the watery zone of rivers, oceans and tides, and finally to the geography of earth. This vertical schema is a convention of ancient natural history, as found for example in the first two books of Pliny's *Historia naturalis*.

Parallel to cosmography was another model available for describing the natural world, namely cosmogenesis, which for Bede meant the account of the six days of creation found in Genesis. Bede was aware of the connections between the two: for example, he inserts an abbreviated account of the Creation in chapters 1–2 of *De natura rerum*, a feature not found in Isidore. In fact, God's separation of heavens from earth, and His subsequent division of the heavens into the regions above and below the firmament, and of earth into water and dry land, replicate in narrative form the vertical structure of the cosmos. Moreover, *In Genesim* uses many of the same classical and patristic sources as *De natura rerum*, and echoes with a slightly different accent

[17] Edited with French translation by Jacques Fontaine, *Traité de la nature* (Bordeaux, 1960). To avoid confusion with Bede's work of the same title, I will hereafter cite this work by Isidore as *De natura rerum* (ed. Fontaine, *Traité*).

[18] For a fuller discussion, see Wallis, *Reckoning of Time*, pp. lxiii–lxvii.

[19] Isidore, *De natura rerum* 11 (ed. Fontaine, *Traité*, pp. 212–17); Bede, *DNR* 4 (pp. 195–96); cf. *DTR* 35.

exactly the same issues addressed by *De natura rerum.*[20] So it is perhaps not surprising to find that *De natura rerum* and *In Genesim* use the word *natura* in much the same way. In these works Bede generally uses the word as a substantive which almost always carries a dependent genitive. *Natura* is therefore the *natura* of something—in the epigraph of the book, Bede states that its purpose is to discuss "the various natures *of things* (*naturas rerum uarias*)." (189.3). *Natura* in this context connotes "attribute," "property," or "characteristic behavior." For example, in *De natura rerum* 38 (p. 223, line 3 – p. 224, line 8)—*De natura aquarum duplici*—the double "nature of waters" is their property of being either fresh or salt. But if both fresh water and salt water are "water", which is *naturalis?* The answer is: both. Fresh water can be rendered salt by being filtered through the ashes of burnt seaweed, and salt water made fresh by being filtered through earth. In short, it is the *natura* of water to be either fresh or salt, and to be able to change from one into the other.[21] However, each of these states of water has its own *natura.* Salt water is of a heavier *natura* than fresh (*DNR* 40, p. 226, line 8, quoting Pliny), and fresh water when it flows into salt is *naturaliter* consumed by it (p. 225, lines 2–3, quoting Isidore). *Natura* is therefore an "attribute," but one which is in some sense constitutive or definitive of a particular entity. Drawing on Isidore again in *De natura rerum* 42 (p. 226, lines 2–5), Bede observes that the Red Sea does not have its ruddy hue *naturaliter* but because it is tinted by the red color of the earth that lines its shores. This red color could be said to be the *natura* of the earth of this region, since it produces red gems, and the red lead (*minium*) used for artist's pigments. But it is not the *natura* of the Red Sea.

---

[20] See Charles W. Jones, introduction to *In Gen.*, p. vii; see also his fuller discussion of these themes in "Some Introductory Remarks on Bede's *Commentary on Genesis,*" *Sacris Erudiri* 19 (1970): 115–98.

[21] Bede's source here is the Irish *De ordine creaturarum*: on the Irish tradition of speculation on this problem, see Smyth, *Understanding the Universe*, pp. 227–36.

For Bede *natura* most typically means the inherent properties of the four elements. Chapter 4 of *De natura rerum*, "De elementis," contains more appearances of the word *natura* than any other chapter in the treatise. *Natura* designates both types of properties associated with the elements, namely the qualities of hot, cold, wet and dry, and the qualities of relative weight and lightness. *Natura* connotes the first when Bede states that the shared properties of hot/cold and wet/dry allow the elements to mingle with one another "by a certain propinquity of nature" (*quadam naturae propinquitate*. p. 195, lines 9–10). Position, which is determined by weight, is also referred to as *natura*: fire, for example, "continually seeks its natural seat" (*naturalem sui sedem*) above the air (p. 195, lines 6–7). "Furthermore, the elements themselves are called *naturae* insofar as they manifest one or other of these types of property. "Earth," says Bede, "is the heaviest [element] and the one which cannot be borne up by any other *natura*" (p. 195, line 34; a modified quotation from the Irish *De ordine creaturarum*). This association of *natura* with the elements and their properties extends to the regions dominated by each of the elements, as well as their contents. The heavenly zone for instance is "of a subtle and fiery nature" (*Caelum, subtilis igneaeque naturae*. . . p. 196, line 2), and the Sun is "by nature" fiery (p. 211, lines 6–7). What is notably absent throughout is any notion of *natura* as a general category (meaning e.g. the ensemble of the universe), or as an abstraction.[22]

---

[22] The one apparent exception is in *DNR* 45 (p. 228, lines 4–6), where Bede quotes from Pliny, *Historia Naturalis* 2.55.162: "Sic terrae arcentibus cunctis nisi in se locus non est, natura cohibente et quo cadat negante." Pliny may have, indeed probably did, mean *natura* here to denote the law or principle governing natural entities, but I would venture that Bede understood it to mean "[its] nature," i.e. the property of heaviness inherent in earth itself which prevents it from falling any lower. It is noteworthy that Bede's unique use of *natura* to denote the ensemble of the universe is again a quotation from Pliny in *DTR* 27 (p. 362, lines 12–13): the theory of eclipses reveals "the magnitude of the dimensions

When he is working in the cosmogenic genre, Bede uses *natura* in very similar ways, though very sparingly: the word appears only eight times in Book 1 of *In Genesim* in the section devoted to the creation story, covering 39 pages in Jones' edition. Here too, *natura* almost always means "property." For example, it is the *natura* of water always to flow, and to seek the lowest place (p. 10, lines 259–60). Once again, it is particularly associated with the elements: the *natura* of water, for instance "is very close to the quality of air" (p. 20, lines 589–93) as we can see in the condensation of atmospheric moisture into clouds.[23] "Everything that we are accustomed to see on land or in the water," says Bede, "takes the beginning of its nature either from these [elements] or from nothing" (p. 6, lines 10–12). In using "nature" in this sense, Bede is following a well-documented tradition. Boethius' last definition of nature in *Against Eutyches*, for example, is "the specific difference that gives form to anything."[24] Bede's immediate model, however, is Isidore of Seville, who uses *natura* almost exclusively in the sense of "property" in his own *De natura rerum*.[25] However, in the 11th book of his *Etymologies*, on the human body, Isidore provides a formal definition of *natura* which is quite different: "Nature takes its name from that which causes something to be born (*nasci*). For it has the capacity to generate and to make. Some say

of the three largest things in nature" (*trium maximarum rerum naturae partium magnitudinem detegit*: *Historia Naturalis* 2.10.49, p. 198).

[23] On the other hand, there are a few interesting variations. In the plural, "natures" is almost a synonym for "creatures": e.g. Bede says that God is the *naturarum optimus conditor* (*In Gen.* 1, p. 31, line 960, quoting Augustine), and *dispositor naturarum* (*In Gen.* 1, p. 10, lines 257–8).

[24] Boethius, *Contra Eutychen* 1 (LCL: p. 80, lines 57–58): "Natura est unam quamque rem informans specifica differentia." There is little evidence that Bede knew the work of Boethius: see below, n. 54.

[25] Isidore uses *naturae* to mean "entities in the physical world" collectively, but like Bede, never uses *natura* to signify an abstraction, such as "the laws governing the physical world": indeed, when Isidore wants to allude to the latter, he prefers *ratio mundi*: see *De natura rerum* 25.2 (ed. Fontaine,

that [nature] is God, by whom all things were created and exist."[26] In short, Isidore acknowledges a meaning of *natura* that links it to ancient religious or mythological concepts of nature as a divine force of fecundity and generation in the sublunary world, but does not introduce this meaning into his *De natura rerum* because *De natura rerum* is not about living things. So it is not surprising, perhaps, that it does not appear in Bede either. What is more surprising is that Bede never uses *natura* in this sense in his commentary on the creation story in Genesis, even when his patristic authorities do.[27] Ambrose in particular uses the term *natura* quite frequently. For him *natura* means a number of things, including the power which perpetuates creation through reproduction, embodied in God's command to "increase and multiply." Ambrose even personifies Nature: discussing the creation of the Sun on the fourth day of the world, he makes Nature say that the Sun is good "as one that assists my fecundity, but not as one that creates; good as nourisher of my fruits, but not as their maker."[28] Bede, however, seems consciously to avoid using *natura* in any way that would suggest an independent principle with creative powers of

Traité. p. 265, line 15). Isidore only comes close to suggesting that *natura* might connote an abstraction on one occasion, in chapter 30 (*De pestilentia*), when he claims that plagues are caused by "disruption in the balance of the natural order" (*sicque naturalis ordinis perturbata temperie.* pp. 303–8). However, the notion of "natural order" is here reduced to the properties of physical elements, which become "infected" as a result of this disequilibrium. On Bede's temporal reading of *naturalis ordo* in connection with pestilence, see below, p. 96.

[26] Isidore, *Etymologiae* 11.1.1: "Natura dicta ab eo quod nasci aliquid faciat. Gignendi enim et faciendi potens est. Hanc quidam Deum esse dixerunt, a quo omnia creata sunt et existent." Cf. *Etymologiae* 9.5.19.

[27] As we shall see below, he occasionally uses *natura* in the muted sense of "reproductive capacity of living things" in other parts of the commentary.

[28] Ambrose, *Hexaemeron* 4.1.4 (CSEL 32.1: p. 112, line 25–p. 113, line 16); cf. Economou, *Goddess Natura*, 56–57.

some kind. This is all the more remarkable in that the principle by which things replicate their kind gets considerable attention from Augustine, an author on whom Bede depends heavily, in the form of the *rationes seminales* "programmed" by God into the primal creation to ensure its stable reproduction. Bede, however, is somewhat cautious about even the *rationes seminales*. It is possible that he was reacting to texts like the Irish Augustine's *De mirabilibus sacrae scripturae*, which argue that God's blueprint for creation is a fixed and irrevocable law, which even He cannot suspend. But it is equally likely that Bede wished to distance himself from the related notion of simultaneous creation, not because he judged Augustine to have erred on this point, but because the distinction between the creation of light on the first day, and the creation of the celestial luminaries on the fourth, was of such deep significance for him.[29] I shall return to this point shortly.

Natura in Computistical Context: De temporibus *and* De temporum ratione

The materials on the units of time which Bede dropped from Isidore's *De natura rerum* when he composed his own *De natura rerum*, formed the nucleus of *De temporibus*. They were considerably expanded in *De temporum ratione* by the re-incorporation of cosmological material from *De natura rerum* and elsewhere, which Bede here redistributed under new computistical ru-

---

[29] On the Irish Augustine, see Smyth, *Understanding the Universe*, pp. 63, 73, 301. On Bede's reserve regarding *rationes seminales*, see McCready, *Miracles*, pp. 20–21. He makes only a few muted allusions to the idea: in *In Gen.* 1 he refers to the *substantiam seminalem* by which the nature of water lay hidden within the primordial chaos (p. 40, lines 1259–60); in *DNR* 1 (p. 192, lines 12–15) to the *seminibus et primordialibus causis* which ensure the continuity of creation in time; and in *DTR* 5 (p. 285, line 48) to the primal chaos as a *seminaria . . .materies* from which the entire creation devolved. He understood the concept and was not in principle hostile to it: see Wallis, *Reckoning of Time*, 270–1.

brics. While it blends cosmology and computus, *De temporum ratione* nonetheless distinguishes the two meanings of *natura*. When describing the cosmos, Bede uses *natura* in the sense of "property" or "attribute" discussed above. For example, Mars is "fiery in color and likewise in nature" because it is close to the Sun.[30] When writing about time, though, Bede understands *natura* in a very different way. Considering that *De temporibus* was written at about the same time as *De natura rerum*, the difference is striking, and obvious in the very first chapter of the work (*De momentis et horis*). Here Bede states:

> To avoid mistakes, it should be noted that computus rests partly on nature, partly on authority and partly on custom: on nature, when the common year [is said] to have twelve lunar months; on custom, when the months are counted as having 30 days; on authority, when the week [is said] to comprise seven days.[31]

This distinction of the three modes of time-reckoning is original to Bede, being found neither in Isidore nor in prior computistic literature. Furthermore, *natura* here does not signify a property, but rather is presented as an abstraction, comparable to *consuetudo* and *auctoritas*.

Further on in *De temporibus*, Bede uses *natura* in another way, apparently unrelated to the first, but in fact connected. In chapter 12, Bede observes that the beginning of the lunar month

---

[30] Bede, *DTR* 8 (p. 301, lines 44–45): "Martis stella, utpote soli proxima, colore simul et natura est feruens." Trans. Wallis, *Reckoning of Time*, p. 33. Bede also occasionally uses *natura* in Isidore's extended sense of "cause," e.g. in *DTR* 7 (p. 295, line 6–p. 296, line 8), where earth's shadow is described as the *natura* of night.

[31] Bede, *DT* 1, p. 585, lines 9–14: "Et notandum propter errorem cauendum quod computus partim natura, partim auctoritate uel consuetudine nitatur: natura, ut annum communem duodecim menses lunares habere; consuetudine, ut menses triginta diebus computari; auctoritate, ut hebdomadam septem feriis constare."

seems to occur earlier and earlier in the day with each passing month. Over 19 years, in fact, it will retreat across an entire day; hence it is necessary once every 19 years to drop one day from the lunar reckoning to compensate.

This "leap of the Moon," says Bede, occurs because people compute with a notional lunar month of 29½ days, thereby preferring "ease of calculation to the truth of nature" (*non in hoc tamen ueritatem naturae sed calculandi facilitatem*). "If, on the other hand, you investigate nature" (*si naturam quaeras*), you will discover that the true lunation is a bit shorter, which is why the beginning of the lunation falls a little earlier each month.[32] *Natura* or *ueritas naturae* is, therefore, the duration of the Moon's course. It is time as the Moon measures it, and not as humans manipulate it.

These two meanings converge in chapter 2 of *De temporum ratione*, where Bede re-visits the theme of the three kinds of time-reckoning to explain in greater depth what he means by authoritative and customary time. By custom, months are thought of as having 30 days "even though this does not match the course of either the Sun or the Moon."[33] The lunar month is actually about 29½ days, and the solar month 30 days and 10½ hours. "Thus," says Bede, "with nature as our guide" (*natura duce*) we discover that the solar year is made up of 365¼ days, but the lunar year is finished in 354 days if it is common and 384 days if it is embolismic."[34] The *natura* that is our guide is the actual periodicity of the planets themselves, rather than

[32] Bede, *DT* 12 (p. 595, lines 5–7).

[33] Bede, *DTR* 2 (p. 275, line 19–20): "...cum hoc nec solis nec lunae cursui conueniat." Trans. Wallis, *Reckoning of Time*, p. 13.

[34] Bede, *DTR* 2 (p. 275, lines 23–25): "Porro natura duce repertum est solis annum ccclxv diebus et quadrante confici; lunae uero annum, si communis sit cccliiii, si embolismus ccclxxxiiii, diebus terminari." Trans. Wallis, *Reckoning of Time*, p. 14.

our calendar's conventions. But Bede is suddenly aware that by personifying *natura* as *dux*,[35] he is implying that *natura* is an independent entity, and wields authority of some kind. So he hastens to explain that "[t]his 'nature' was created by the one true God when He commanded that the stars which He had set in the heavens should be the signs of seasons, days and years; it is not, as the folly of the pagans asserts, a creating goddess, one amongst many."[36] Where Bede learned about the pagan goddess *Natura* is not clear,[37] but his anxiety is revealing. Computistical *natura* is not a quality of anything, not even of the heavenly bodies themselves, but rather something perilously close to a law or regulatory principle, and as we have seen, the notion of na-

[35] The phrase has a strikingly literary flavor, but if Bede derived it, its source has not been traced. In Statius' *Thebaid*, the Argive women appeal to Athens to restore order in the name of *natura princeps* (12.561–2) and Theseus consents, invoking "Nature our guide" (12.642–8); cf. Economou, *Goddess*, pp. 44–45. However, there is no evidence that Bede knew the *Thebaid*: see M. L. W. Laistner, "The Library of the Venerable Bede," in *Famulus Christi*, pp. 263–6, as well as the indices of the critical editions of Bede's works in CCSL.

[36] Bede, *DTR* 2 (p. 275, lines 28–31): "Sed et errantia sidera suis quaeque spatiis zodiaco circumferri, quae natura non iuxta ethnicorum dementiam dea creatrix una de pluribus sed ab uno uero Deo creata est, quando sideribus caelo inditis praecepit ut sint in signa et tempora et dies et annos." Trans. Wallis, *Reckoning of Time*, p. 14.

[37] Jones' apparatus refers to Lucretius, but it is unlikely that Bede knew *De natura rerum* other than as citations embedded in other works. Moreover, though Lucretius describes *natura* as creating and nourishing all things in 1.21, he does not refer to her as a goddess; indeed, in 2.1117, he contrasts *natura* with the gods, whose help she does not require to run the universe. A rather distant analogue is Prudentius' *Contra orationem Symmachi*: Theodosius 1.9–13, but there is no indication that Bede knew this work.

ture as legislator made Bede nervous. He rarely uses the phrase "natural law";[38] as we shall see, he preferred to associate *natura* with *regula*, stressing nature's obedience over its legislative prerogatives. Hence his care to assure the reader that this *natura* is nonetheless something created and not creating. Nature was created together with the Sun, Moon and stars, and its office is bound up with their mission to be signs of seasons, days and years. The *natura* that is our guide is the actual periodicity of the planets themselves, as distinct from calendar conventions.

This periodicity is grounded in the specific situation of the celestial time-keepers at the moment of creation, when God calibrated the cosmic chronometer, so to speak. *Natura* is therefore the *measurement* of periodicity. As he explains in *De temporum ratione* 5, there were days—three of them in fact—before there were Sun, Moon and stars to *measure* the days. God not only created light on Day One, but He also called it "day," and this primal light produced real days and nights by circling around the earth from east to west. What the creation of the Sun on the fourth day produced was something else, namely the equinox. Of course, God divided light and darkness into equal parts on the first day of creation, but they could not be *known* to be equal before there was something to *measure* their equality, namely, hours. Hours measure the Sun's passage across the sky, because the Sun casts shadows which can be read on the numbered segments of a sundial. After sunset on the fourth day, the hours could continue to be measured by the motions of the

---

[38] Bede uses "natural law" to designate the moral law prior to the promulgation of the written law under Moses: see for example *DTR* 64 (p. 456, lines 27–28): "Prima namque saeculi tempora lege naturali per patres . . ." He also says that Ishmael was born "permixtione sexus utriusque lege naturae" (*In Gen.* 4, p. 239, lines 1630–31), but this is intended to underscore the typological distinction of Ishmael (law, flesh) from Isaac (grace, spirit).

newly-created stars.[39] The *natura* created on the fourth day was, therefore, the measurement of time, not time itself.[40] The Moon was created full on Day Four, for all things came into being in their perfect state; therefore the Moon was created at sunset. In Bede's view, these details are critical, for what he calls the "rule of Easter" (*paschae regula*: p. 291, line 29) is nothing other than locating the moment every year when the Sun and Moon return to the positions and states they held at the moment of their creation. The Sun must "inaugurate the equinox" (*aequinoctium . . . inchoauit*: p. 291, lines 17–18); the Moon that follows this event must be full.

It is essential to grasp that for Bede, the status of the celestial time-keepers at creation, and the cyclical resumption of that status, is itself *natura*. For example, Bede points out that the first day of creation must have been March 18. March 18 is also when the Sun is in the first degree of Aries, the beginning of the zodiac. But Bede is not comfortable with starting the zodiac at the creation; *quantum ad naturam* (p. 295, line 105)—"as far as nature is concerned"—the zodiac should begin at the equinox itself, because all celestial cycles began there at creation.

This is not a minor technicality for Bede, but a matter to which he returns many times. For example, Bede would like the leap-year day to be inserted at the equinox, not on 24 February (the 6th kalends of March) as was customary in the Julian calendar, since the Sun began to accumulate the extra day from the moment of its creation. In his *Letter to Wicthed*, Bede is particularly emphatic that the solar year *iuxta naturam* starts on the equinox. The extra leap-year day will thus be complete on the equinox, and this is where it ought to be inserted *secundum naturam* "because according to human custom, it is [added] at

---

[39] See Bede, *DTR* 6 (p. 290, line 1–p. 292, line 44).

[40] Cf. Bede, *In Gen.* 1 (p. 15, line 431–p. 16, line 456): what was created on Day Four was the *ordo temporum*.

various times of the year, as it pleases each people to insert it. But according to natural computation (*naturalis . . . rationis*) it is to be added at the completion of the solar cycle."[41] The cycles of the Moon should likewise be calibrated to the equinox. In chapter 42, Bede argues that *ratio naturalis* dictates that the leap of the Moon should, like the leap year day, also take place at the equinox. In practice it is inserted in different locations by different computistical schools. But the equinox is the "natural" place "because, of course, of the origin of the creation of the stars" (*propter originem uidelicet . . .conditionis siderum*).[42] Finally, "in discussing natural truth" (*in naturalis assertione ueritatis*), the age of the Moon on any given day is determined by its age at sunset, since the Moon "first rose upon the world at eventide."[43] The Moon's state at sunset determines the lunar phase, "lest the order of primal creation be disturbed."[44] People insert the embolismic months—extra lunar months added every two or three years to bring the lunar and solar years back into alignment—wherever it suits them, though *ratio naturae* dictates that they should do so at the end of the lunar year, i.e. at the equinox. This, as Bede observes, causes no end of confusion over the age of the Moon: is it 14, 15 or 16 days old?[45] Since the 15th day of the lunation is the lunar marker for Easter, human arbitrariness can be held responsible for Paschal controversies.[46]

---

[41] Bede, *Epist. Wicht.* 7 (p. 638, lines 110–13): "Ideo autem addimus naturaliter quia consuetudinis est humanae uariis illum temporibus anni prout cuilibet genti complacuit inserere. Naturalis uero est rationis in completione et circuli solaris adici . . ." Trans. Wallis, *Reckoning of Time*, p. 421.

[42] Bede, *DTR* 42 (p. 412, lines 67–69). Trans. Wallis, *Reckoning of Time*, p. 115.

[43] Bede, *DTR* 43 (p. 412, line 9–p. 413, line 13); Trans. Wallis, *Reckoning of Time*, p. 116.

[44] Bede, *DTR* 43 (p. 414, lines 46–47). Trans. Wallis, *Reckoning of Time*, p. 117.

[45] See Bede, *DTR* 11 (p. 317, line 79–p. 318, line 84).

[46] Other examples of the distinction between *natura* and human custom can be cited. The siderial lunar month is 27 days and 8 hours long, but "a more painstaking inspection of nature (*diligentior inquisitio naturarum*)" shows

Naturalis ratio, ratio naturae, and *natura* are interchangeable terms because computistical *natura* is a *ratio,* a measurement or reckoning of time marked out by God when he created His cosmic indicators of time, the Sun, Moon and stars. Time itself can only be grasped as *ratio* or measurement: *tempus,* says Bede, "takes its name from 'measure' (*temperamentum*) either because every unit of time is separately measured (*temperatum*) or because all the courses of mortal life are measured (*temperentur*) in moments, hours, years, ages and epochs."[47] Months (*menses*) also "take their name from the measure (*mensura*) by which each of them is measured."[48] It is interesting to note that Bede did not derive either of these etymologies from Isidore of Seville. Their source, if they have one, has not been traced; neither has the source of his etymology for the word "year" (*annus*) "from the renewal (*innouando*) of all things which pass away according to the natural order" (*naturali ordine*).[49] This last etymology highlights the notion of *natura* as cycle, and indeed, it is found in a chapter entitled "Natural Years." A "natural year" is defined as the period required for any natural temporal cycle to return to a given point. The Great Year, for instance, is the period required for all the planets to "return at one and the same time

that the Moon's "proper course" is 29½ days, that is, from conjunction to conjunction (*DTR* 11, p. 316, lines 55–60). Humans being as they are, "custom or authority or at least convenience of calculation prevails over nature (*DTR* 11, p. 317, lines 73–75)," and so the lunar month is normalized to alternate between 29 and 30 days.

[47] Bede, *DTR* 2 (p. 274, lines 2–5): "Tempora igitur a 'temperamento' nomen accipiunt, siue quod unumquodque illorum spatium separatim temperatum sit, seu quod momentis, horis, diebus, mensibus, annis, saeculisque et aetatibus omnia mortalis uitae curricula temperentur." Trans. Wallis, *Reckoning of Time,* p. 13.

[48] Bede, *DTR* 11 (p. 312, line 2): "Menses dicti a mensura, qua quisque eorum mensuratur." Trans. Wallis, *Reckoning of Time,* p. 41.

[49] Bede, *DTR* 36 (p. 395, lines 2–3): "Annus uel ab innouando cuncta quae naturali ordine transierant . . ." Trans. Wallis, *Reckoning of Time,* p. 103.

to where they once simultaneously were."[50] What makes these years "natural" is the fact that they are measured by the planets themselves, as opposed to the mathematical divisions of the hour into "moments," "points" and "atoms," which Bede terms "unnatural";[51] what makes them "years" is their cyclical character. This identification of "nature" with "cycle" is applied in a particularly interesting way in chapter 29 of *De temporum ratione*, Bede's justly famous discussion of tides. Though the time of the tide will vary from place to place (the principle of port), its periodicity is constant, because "*naturalis ratio* convinces us that the tides flow according to the pattern of the Moon's cycle of 19 years."[52] "In any region, the Moon holds to whatever rule of fellowship (*regulam societatis*) with the sea it received in the beginning,"[53] that is, at the beginning of creation. Even something as local as the tide has a *naturalis ratio*—a cyclical pattern, and a starting post fixed by God Himself.

Bede's computistical definition of *natura* is, as I pointed out earlier, not explicitly found in any of his sources. So why did he choose this term to signify measurement of cosmic time? Did he see any connection between cosmological *natura*-as-property and computistical *natura*-as-temporal-cycle? While a direct source remains elusive, I think that a likely place to look for clues is an anonymous Irish computistical treatise known to Bede, and

---

[50] Bede, *DTR* 36 (p. 397, line 30–31): "Annus magnus est cum omnia simul errantia sidera ad sua quaeque loca quae simul habuere recurrunt." Trans. Wallis, *Reckoning of Time*, p. 104.

[51] Bede, *DTR* 3 (p. 276, lines 14–15). Trans. Wallis, *Reckoning of Time*, p. 15.

[52] *DTR* 29 (p. 371, lines 98–99): "Aestus adfluere naturalis ratio cogit, per denos autem et nouenos annos, iuxta lunaris circuli ordinem." Trans. Wallis, *Reckoning of Time*, p. 85.

[53] Bede, *DTR* 29 (p. 371, lines 91–92): "Seruante quibusque in regionibus luna semper regulam societatis ad mare quamcumque semel acceperit." Trans. Wallis, *The Reckoning of Time*, p. 85.

preserved in the 11th century copy of his personal anthology of computistical materials. The first part of the treatise is a dialogue between *magister* and *discipulus*. *Magister* defines computus as *ratio numerorum*, and illustrates his remarks with two quotations from Boethius' *De institutione arithmetica*.

> Boethius says: Everything which is fashioned from the first nature of things (*a prima rerum natura*), is perceived to be given form by the *ratio* of numbers. For this was the principal exemplar in the Creator's mind. From it is derived the multiplicity of the four elements, and from it the changes of the seasons, and from it we understand the cycle (*conversio*) of the motion of the stars and of the heavens. Boethius also says: Properly speaking, every course of the stars and every astronomical *ratio* is constituted by the nature of numbers itself (*ipsa natura numerorum*). For thus we compute (*colligimus*) risings and settings, thus we track the slowing down and acceleration of the planets, thus we come to know the eclipses and manifold variations of the Moon.[54]

Here *ratio numerorum* is at once the form of the elements, and the measurement of time and celestial motion; both are linked to God's act of creation. *Magister* further explains that computus is a part of *philosophia*; in particular, it pertains to "Natural [philosophy] which the Greeks call *physike*, that is *physica*, which discourses about the investigation of nature . . ." Each of the three parts of philosophy—*physica, ethica* and *logica*—is found in Scripture, and physica is found in Genesis. But when *Magister* finally describes the contents of *physica*, we learn that it is the mathematical sciences of arithmetic, geometry, music and astronomy. *Naturalis philosophia, ratio numerorum* and computus coincide in a manner

---

[54] "Et dixit Boethius: Omnia quaecunque a prima rerum natura constructa sunt, numerorum uidentur ratione formata. Hoc enim fuit principale exemplar in animo conditoris. Hinc enim quatuor elementorum

Faith Wallis

which is not found elsewhere in computistical literature. Bede's original experiment of fusing the cosmology he found in books with titles like *De natura rerum*, and *Historia naturalis*—not to mention Genesis—with time-reckoning, may have been inspired by this Irish tract. So also, I would argue, was his adoption of the term *natura* into the computistical lexicon.

Finally, we have seen how Bede uses *naturalis ratio*—"natural measurement" or "natural calculation"—to denote the measures of time divinely instituted at creation. But *ratio* is a word with many meanings. In mathematical contexts it denotes "reckoning" in the sense of calculation or accounting. But it can also mean reckoning in the sense of reasoning, as well as the product of this reasoning, an explanation or reason that *accounts* for something. In principle, then, *naturalis ratio* could mean "an explanation of a natural phenomenon" or "reasoning based on facts about the physical world."

This is indeed how Bede uses the phrase *naturalis ratio* in chapter 25 of *De temporum ratione*. Bede's aim in this chapter is to refute the belief that the position of the horns of a crescent Moon (pointing up or pointing down) presages the weather of

multitudo mutuata est, hinc temporum uices, hinc motus astrorum coelique conuersio intelligitur. Item Boethius dicit: Proprie ipsa natura numerorum, omnis astrorum cursus, omnisque astronomica ratio constituta est. Sic enim ortus occasusque colligimus: sic tarditates uelocitatesque errantium siderum custodimus; sic defectus et multiplices lunae uariationes agnoscimus." Oxford, Bodleian Library, MS Bodley 309, fols. [62v–64v]. This is the "Sirmond manuscript," a copy of an Irish computus anthology used by Bede: see Charles W. Jones, "The 'Lost' Sirmond Manuscript of Bede's computus," *English Historical Review* 51 (1937): 204–19. This text, composed in seventh-century Ireland, is printed in PL 90, col. 649A. Quotations from Boethius are from *De institutione arithmetica*, ed. G. Friedlein (Leipzig, 1867), 1.2 (p. 12, lines 14–19), and 1.1 (p. 12, lines 6–10). There is no evidence that Bede knew any work of Boethius at first hand, but his fusion of natural property and cyclic time bears some resemblance to the second *metrum* of book 3 of

88

the coming month. *Naturalis ratio*, he says, shows that this cannot be the case. Here, *naturalis ratio* means factual knowledge about the natural world, and rational inferences drawn from this knowledge. We know that the Moon is fixed (*lunae statum, qui fixus . . . permanet*) in the ether: how can her position be changed by the atmospheric conditions beneath her, so that she would turn her horns other than as *naturae ordo* dictates? Bede goes on to explain that the direction of the horns depends on the position of the crescent Moon *vis-à-vis* the setting Sun, and that this follows an annual pattern. He concludes: "Therefore the alteration of the Moon, which is natural and fixed (*quae naturalis est et fixa*) cannot portend the condition of the month to come."[55]

Here *natura* recovers its computistical meaning, since it is the Sun's annual course north and south of the celestial equator which produces these variable positions of the crescent Moon. Though itself without any time-measurement function, the rotation of the Moon's horns, being the product of the Sun's time-measuring movements, is *naturalis*. It is also *fixa* in that it repeats cyclically.

What is interesting, though, is the pairing of the term *naturalis* with *fixa*, since it echoes Bede's earlier statement that *naturalis ratio* proves that the Moon is "fixed" in the ether. Cosmology and computus fuse into a notion of *natura* as simultaneously the physical structure of the universe and the regularity of celestial time. *Naturalis ratio* is an explanation of the world in terms of this structure and regularity. By identifying nature with reason as well as reckoning, then, Bede invokes a *natura* which guarantees regu-

---

De consolatione philosophiae (LCL: p. 236, line 1–p. 238, line 38). Boethius' hymn to all-powerful Nature exemplifies her cosmic law in the fact that the Sun sets in the west each evening, and every morning returns in the east—the law of nature is a law of the return to origins: cf. Pelikan, *Timaeus and Genesis*, pp. 125–32.

[55] *DTR* 25 (p. 359, lines 53–55). "Non ergo lunae conuersio, quae naturalis est et fixa, potest futuri mensis portendere statum." Trans. Wallis, *Reckoning of Time*, p. 76.

larity and rationality in the universe; at the same time he avoids stirring the ashes of the defunct pagan *dea creatrix.*

Ratio as Stabilitas, Regula and Ordo

Yoking *naturalis* with *fixa* also implies that *natura* is consistent and stable, a theme of particular importance for Bede when he is thinking about the reckoning of time. Time itself is inherently unstable, "fleeting and wave-tossed" (*uolubili ac fluctiuagi*).[56] The ages of the world are "unstable" (*labentibus*),[57] being both unequal in length, and non-cyclical. They contrast with the "stable eternity and eternal stability" (*aeterna stabilitate ac stabili aeternitate*)[58] into which the world will be absorbed at the end of the age. But computus foreshadows that stability through the ordering of time into cycles. The guarantee of the correctness of the Alexandrian system of Easter reckoning is precisely that it produces a permanently repeating cycle of valid dates for the feast, thus lending time something of the permanence of eternity.[59] "We are bolstered," says Bede, "by the aid of the authority of the Fathers when we follow the decrees of the Council of Nicaea, which fixed the fourteenth Moons of the Paschal feast with such firm stability [*firma stabilitas*] that their 19-year cycle can never waver [*uacillare*] and never fail."[60] The rules of computus also

---

[56] Bede, *DTR* 71 (p. 544, line 91). Trans. Wallis, *Reckoning of Time*, p. 249.

[57] Bede, *DTR* Praef. (p. 263, lines 11–12); ch. 10 (p. 310, line 4); cf. Bede's epigraph to *DNR*: "Naturas rerum uarias labentis et aeui/ Perstinxi titulis, tempora lata citis/ Beda Dei famulus . . ." (p. 189, lines 3–5).

[58] Bede, *DTR* 71 (p. 544, lines 92–93). Trans. Wallis, *Reckoning of Time*, p. 249.

[59] The Great Paschal Cycle of 532 years gives an "eternity's-eye view" of all time: "Thus whoever reads them can, with unerring gaze, not only look forward to the past and future, but can also look back at each and every date of Easter in the past; and in order to clarify an ancient text, he can clearly identify all the years . . ." (*DTR* 65, p. 460, lines 24–29).

[60] Bede, *DTR* 43 (p. 415, lines 62–66): "Paternae etenim auctoritatis subsidio fulcimur dum Nicaenae Synodi scita sectamur, quae quartas decimas festi

have "a fixed course" and do not "waver."[61] Faulty calculation, on the other hand, engenders instability and collapse: failure to add in the leap-year day to the lunar reckoning "will mean that the fourteenth Moon of Easter will waver, and then the course of the year will reel, and that ever-inviolable state of the 19-year cycle, being more and more perturbed, will be overthrown."[62]

Regula was another element in the formula of stability associated with *natura* in the computistical sense. It can mean both divine prescription—Abbot Ceolfrid's response to the Pictish King Nechtan's request for guidance on the computus begins by setting out the "three rules (*regulae*) given in Holy Scripture" for the Paschal reckoning[63]—and the astronomical and mathematical principles of calculation—as in the *regula paschae* cited above. It is connected, therefore, with both the notion of law, and the notion of measurement. Bede, as a monk, was particularly sensitive to the word *regula*.[64] He lived under a *regula* which was both a law demanding obedience and a norm of measurement. The ideal of living *regulariter* shaped every dimension of monastic experience according to a spiritual ideal of uniformity and deliberateness: nothing, not even the quantity of wine in one's cup at dinner, was unconsidered, improvised, or subject to arbitrary variation. *Stabilitas* is a particularly significant element in the Benedictine *regula*, one with which Bede was deeply

paschalis lunas tam firma stabilitate praefixit ut decemnouenalis eorum circuitus nusquam uacillare, numquam fallere possit." Trans. Wallis, *Reckoning of Time*, p. 117.

[61] See, for example, *DTR* 20 (p. 346, line 16; and p. 347, lines 26–28); and *DTR* 9 (p. 309, lines 94–95).

[62] Bede, *DTR* 41 (p. 406, lines 12–16): " . . .fit profectu ut et quarta decima luna paschalis eiusdem anni pridie quam debuerat adueniat, ideoque paschalis ratio uacillet, et totius mox anni cursus titubet, statusque ille semper inuiolabilis circuli decemnouenalis magis magisque turbatus euertatur." Trans. Wallis, *Reckoning of Time*, p. 110.

[63] Bede, *HE* 5.21 (pp. 524–5).

[64] Blair, *World of Bede*, ch. 19.

familiar.[65] *Stabilitas* is one of the three vows taken by a postulant for admission, and at the solemn profession. It is a many-layered term, signifying physical immobility within the material enclosure of the monastery, commitment to community, and perseverance in the Rule.

It has, therefore, connotations of space, time and identity that make it at times almost synonymous with the Rule itself.[66] Bede's choice of terms like *regula* and *stabilitas* to describe computistical *ratio* can hardly be meaningless, particularly given that so much of Benedict's rule is about the ordering of time.[67] The monastic resonance of these terms also lends a special flavor to Bede's derogatory use of the term *consuetudo* to designate arbitrary human custom with respect to time-reckoning. In other contexts, we find him using *consuetudo* to refer to irregular ecclesiastical, and especially monastic practice, in contrast to *regula*. In his prose *Vita sancti Cuthberti*, Bede tells how Cuthbert, on first arriving at Lindisfarne, encountered resistance to his reforms from those who "preferred to conform

---

[65] Brown, *Bede the Venerable*, p. 15; Alan Thacker, "Bede's Ideal of Reform," in *Ideal and Reality*, p. 140.

[66] E.g. in *HE* 2.1 (pp. 124–5), Bede recounts Gregory the Great's image of the monastic rule as an anchor-cable binding the soul to the calm shores of prayer while "it is tossed about on the ceaseless tide of secular affairs" (*cum incessabili causarum saecularium inpulsu fluctuaret*). Compare to Bede's image of the "fleeting and wave-tossed course of time" cited above. For the two vows of *stabilitas*, see *Regula sancti Benedicti* 58.9 and 58.17 (ed. de Vogüé, *La Règle*, 2. 628 and 630). On the multiple meanings of *stabilitas*, see de Vogüé's commentary: 4.221–2, and 6.1327. Benedict's *bêtes noires*, the *gyrovagi*, are characterized as *semper uagi et numquam stabiles*: *Regula sancti Benedicti* 1.11 (ed. de Vogüé, *La Règle*, 1.440).

[67] Bede has Cuthbert distinguish cenobitics from hermits precisely on the grounds that monks "govern all their times (*cuncta . . . tempora*) of watching, praying and fasting by [the abbot's] command": see *VCP* 22 (pp. 230–1).

to their older usage (*consuetudini*) rather than to the monastic rule (*regulari*)."[68]

This semantic overlap between the terminology of *natura*, particularly in its computistical sense, and the terminology of monastic discipline, suggests that Bede's "science" reaches deeply into his religious world-view. This has been recognized and documented in connection with Bede's accounts of miracles. McCready observes that Bede's conception of the natural world as a realm of regularity and consistency depended on his understanding of it as God's creation.[69] Miracles may operate "against the order of nature," but Bede has no conception of "the supernatural"; miracles are "manifestations of divine power,"[70] but so is creation itself. Hence the opposite of "miraculous" is sometimes, but by no means always, "natural"; natural phenomena can be distinguished from those of demonic or divine origin by terms like *materialis* or *communis*.[71] *Communis* and *natura*, however, are all but synonyms; Cuthbert's monastic habits were "ordinary garments" (*vestimentis . . . communibus*) made from "the natural [i.e. undyed] wool of sheep" (*naturalis ovium lana*).[72] *Communis*, being a word with monastic connota-

---

[68] Bede, *VCP* 16 (pp. 210–11): "qui priscae suae consuetudini quam regulari mallent obtemperare custodiae."

[69] McCready, *Miracles*, p. 20.

[70] McCready, *Miracles*, p. 21.

[71] *Materialis*: "certi quidem sumus quia contra ignem materialem nil tale audemus, incerti autem an ignem illum inextinguibilem futurae castigationis immunes euadere queamus": *VCP* 14 (pp. 202–3); *Communis*: "quia non communi infirmitate sed demonis infestatione premeretur coniunx, pro quia supplicabat": *VCP* 15, (pp. 204–5). In his homily on the miracle at Cana, Bede contrasts Christ's arrival at the wedding as *homo communis* with his miraculous manifestation of himself as *dominus caeli et terrae*. *Hom.* 1.14 (p. 103, lines 282–5).

[72] Bede, *VCP* 16, 212–13.

tions, might be added to our lexicon on overlapping scientific and ascetic terminology.

For Bede, the natural and the providential can all but converge, so that all of nature becomes a miracle. Chad, he reports, prayed for divine mercy during *every* thunderstorm; and in his commentary on Ezra, Bede states that storms and droughts—*all* storms and droughts, apparently—are signs of God's wrath and impending judgement.[73] When describing healing miracles, particularly those associated with John of Beverley, Bede sees no difficulty in attributing a natural cause to the illness, or in relating how the saint used the remedies and services of secular medicine.[74] Cuthbert ascribes his failure to cultivate wheat on the island of Farne "either to the nature of this land or to the will of God" (*telluris huiusce natura, aut voluntas Dei*), indiscriminately.[75] Perhaps the most striking example of such overlap is the famous passage in the description of the British Isles in the opening chapter of the *Historia ecclesiastica*, where Bede recounts how scrapings from the pages of Irish manuscripts, dissolved in drink, are a remedy for snake-bite. The method of cure is one usually associated with miraculous healing, but for Bede the efficacy of the remedy lies in the natural property of anything from Ireland, a land where snakes do not and cannot live.[76] In fact, Bede

[73] Chad: *HE* 4.3 (p. 343); Ezra: *In Ezr.* 2 (p. 332, lines 1785–1804). Cf. McCready, *Miracles*, pp. 25–27.

[74] McCready, *Miracles*, pp. 41–43 and references furnished there; Cameron, *Anglo-Saxon Medicine* (Cambridge, 1993), pp. 27–28.

[75] Bede, *VCP* 19 (pp. 220–21). Cf. *HE* 4.25 (pp. 420–1): the fire which destroyed Coldingham Abbey was caused "by carelessness" (*per culpam incuriae*) but also "by the wickedness of those who dwelt there" (*a malitia inhabitantium*).

[76] McCready, *Miracles*, p. 47, n. 9. Examples of miracles effected by dust, soil etc. mingled with water: *HE* 3.2 (pp. 214–16), 3.9 (p. 242), 3.13 (p. 254), 3.17 (p. 264), 4.3 (p. 346) and 5.18 (p. 514). Cf. Plummer, *Opera historica*, 2:11.

only uses the phrase "against nature" when he wishes to counter any attempt to rationalize a miracle as merely an *unusual* event. For example, in his *Expositio Actuum Apostolorum,* Bede argues that the blood which flowed from Christ's side on the cross *had* to be a sign, because it was "contrary to the nature of our bodies" (*contra naturam nostrorum . . .corporum*);[77] his bloody sweat in the garden of Gethsemane likewise was "never encountered in the usual behaviour of human nature" (*in consuetudine naturae nequaquam inveniri probatur humanae*).[78] What is noteworthy from our perspective is what *natura* actually represents here: cosmological *natura,* or the inherent property of the body. *Natura* as a force of fecundity even makes a timid appearance in this context: Sarah's sterility is cured by grace, though "nature seemed to deny" her a child (*quod natura negare videbatur*).[79] However, Bede seems particularly to identify the miraculous with events that are out of time-sequence, evoking his second, computistical conception of *natura.* In his commentary on Luke, Bede points out that the angel's guarantee to Mary that her virginity was no impediment to conception was precisely the fact that her aged cousin Elizabeth was pregnant. Elizabeth's pregnancy was "contrary to the order of nature," even though it came about in the usual way, because it happened *when* it did, in her old age. Likewise Ishmael was born "according to the customary law of nature";

---

[77] Bede, *Exp. Act.* 2 (p. 18, line 132); trans. Martin, *Commentary on Acts,* p. 32.

[78] Bede, *Retract. Act.* 2 (p. 112, line 92). Cf. *In Regum* 25 (pp. 316–17), where Bede explains that the retreat of the Sun's shadow at King Hezekiah's prayer was a true miracle, for even the midnight sun in Thule does not actually retrograde, but rather inscribes its natural circular course above the horizon instead of partially beneath it.

[79] Bede, *In Gen.* 4 (p. 236, lines 1524–6). Cf. *In Gen.* 4 (p. 206, line 459–p. 207, line 466), quoting Augustine *De civitate Dei* 16.26: Isaac was the child of grace, even though he was born "by the natural course of procreation" (*naturalem procreationis excursum*), because "nature was impaired and had ceased to function" (*vitiata et cessante natura*).

Isaac was the child of promise not because he was conceived in a different way than was Ishmael, but because he was born out of time, in his parent's old age.[80] Christ's healing miracles were truly miracles because the cure was effected instantaneously: in his comment on the healing of Peter's mother-in-law, for instance, Bede observes that "it is natural" (*naturale est*) for people recovering from fevers to convalesce slowly, but God's power confers health "totally and instantaneously" (*tota simul*).[81] This temporal distinction of natural and miraculous is echoed in Bede's scientific writings. In *De natura rerum* 37, he explains how pestilences are caused by unseasonable meteorological conditions, when summer weather, for instance, "is turned into autumn squalls and whirlwinds; for when these come in their proper time, we say that they are storms, and when they come at other times, they are prodigies or signs."[82] In sum, Bede's conceptions of *natura* as either "inherent property" or "natural cycle of time" structured his understanding of what occurs in a miracle.

The notion of *natura* in both its cosmological and computistical sense informs Bede's thinking even when he is not immediately concerned with either the created world, or the miraculous. This is illustrated by an incident from the prose *Life* of St. Cuthbert,[83] where the word *natura* is used repeatedly in the company of the related concepts of *stabilitas, ordo* and *ratio*,

---

[80] Elizabeth's conception: "omnia Deo possibilia etiam quae naturae ordine videntur esse contraria": *In Lucam* 1.36–37 (p. 34, lines 603–4); Isaac and Ishmael: *In Gen.* 4 (p. 239, lines 1629–35). Cf. McCready, *Miracles*, p. 24.

[81] Bede, *In Marcum* 1.30–31 (p. 449, lines 465–8); on instantaneity as an indicator of miracle, see McCready, *Miracles*, pp. 22–23.

[82] Bede, *DNR* 37 (p. 223, lines 4–7):"Vnde saepius omne tempus aestatis in procellas turbines brumales verti conspicuimus. Sed haec cum suo tempore venerint, tempestates; cum vero alias, prodigia uel signa dicuntur."

[83] Bede, *VCP* 1 (pp. 156–9). I have made slight modifications to Colgrave's translation.

and in both miraculous and non-miraculous contexts. Young
Cuthbert loved to play games with his companions *iuxta quod
aetatis ordo poscebat*, which Colgrave aptly translates "as was natural at his age." Notice that *ordo* denotes what is congruent with
a particular time: it is computistical *natura*. Cuthbert is good
at these games because he is "agile by nature" (*agilis natura*).
Natura here means quality, property, attribute: *natura* in the cosmological sense. However, at some point, the play starts to get
out of hand. Some of the boys "were twisting their limbs into
various unnatural contortions" (*contra congruum naturae statum
uariis flexibus membra plerique sinuarent*). "Against nature" in this
context does not connote anything miraculous, or even demonic; the lads are just playing games, *iuxta quod aetatis ordo poscebat*.
However, one of Cuthbert's young friends urges him not to join
in, "but rather by steadfastness to control both mind and limbs"
(*sed stabilitati potius mentem simul et membra subiugaret*). *Stabilitas*
here contrasts with *uariis flexibus*: it is a moral force imposed
upon the limbs that restores their *congruum naturae statum*. It
denotes firmness (as opposed to *flexibus*) and consistency (as
opposed to *uariis*). Cuthbert at first ignores the child's admonition, and the child begins to wail. Having appealed to Cuthbert
"with the gravity of an old man," he now addresses him as "holy
bishop and priest" and asks why Cuthbert would do something
so "contrary to your nature and your rank" (*et naturae et gradui
contraria*). The temporal disjuncture here—the precocious maturity of the child and his strange salutation of the boy Cuthbert as priest and bishop—signals a miracle, a stepping out of
the *ordo* of time. The miracle announces Cuthbert's destiny as a
man of God, which will entail his rejection of the thoughtless in-
dulgences of society, and particularly its complacent disregard
of *natura*. Cuthbert will have to live according to *natura*: what
is interesting here is the merging of his own *natura* as an individual (what you might call his "character"), the *natura* of his
ecclesiastical rank and vocation, and the *natura* of the physical
body. His spiritual calling is therefore a summons to the truly
"natural life." Moved by this prophetic speech, Cuthbert hence-

97

forth becomes "steadier and more mature in mind" (*stabilior . . . nimoque adolescentior*).

Bede closes the episode by remarking that the story ought not to cause surprise, since God has been known to put "rational words" (*rationabilia uerba*) even into the mouths of animals, such as Balaam's ass. I would argue that the choice of the word *rationabilia* here is calculated. *Ratio* is the mental cognate of *natura*: the summons of the child alerts Cuthbert to the demands of *natura* upon his body, mind and soul, and is at the same time a call to obey God.[84]

Conclusions

A new approach to Bede's "science" would therefore locate it within a web of interrelated ideas and images. At the centre of the web is a distinctive epistemological object, *natura*: creatures and their specific attributes on the one hand, and the ordering of time on the other. *Ratio* denotes an intellectual method adapted to *natura*: a complex concert of logic and mathematics, grounded in the authority of the scriptural account of creation, and the scriptural understanding of God. *Naturalis ratio* in turn elides into *naturalis ordo*—temporal sequence, particularly cyclical sequence—which links time to eternity, and lends it eternity's stability. The overtones here are permanence (like a

---

[84] It should be noted that Bede's source for *VCP*, the Lindisfarne *Anonymous Life*, does use some of the terms signaled here, but in a very limited way. The postures of the boys are described as *contra naturam*, the unnamed lad enjoins Cuthbert *Esto stabilis*, and reminds him that his future episcopal state is incompatible with what is *contraria nature*, i.e. such postures: see *Vita sancti Cuthberti auctore anonymo* 3, ed. Bertram Colgrave, *Two Lives of Saint Cuthbert* (1940; reprinted, Cambridge, 1985), pp. 64–65. Missing, however, are the typically Bedan elements of computistical *natura*, of *natura* as something which is ascribed to Cuthbert himself, of Cuthbert's commitment to *stabilitas* consequent on the incident, and the terms *ordo* and *ratio*.

solid building which does not waver), predictability (as distinct from arbitrariness, *consuetudo*), consistency (*regula*) and boundedness (*mensura*). These penumbral terms link the world of created things to the world of the monastery, which is also one of stability, *regula*, measurement, sequential action—the antithesis of the arbitrariness of life dominated by individual preference or social convention, the truly "natural life." What defines *natura* and underpins *ratio*, is the trustworthiness and faithfulness of the Creator, manifested as the *stabilitas, regula,* and *ordo* "programmed" into the constitutive properties of creatures and the calculable patterns of time.

The Responsibility of *Auctoritas*: Method and Meaning in Bede's Commentary on Genesis

CALVIN B. KENDALL

IN COMPLEMENTARY CHAPTERS in this volume, Roger Ray argues that the Venerable Bede, while effectively deploying modesty *topoi* of the rhetorical tradition, in fact ranked himself as an exegete in the company of the Doctors of the Church, and Joyce Hill offers evidence that, within a hundred years of his death, he was regarded on the Continent as enjoying *auctoritas* equal to that of his great predecessors.[1] The present chapter, which examines Bede's methods and his understanding of the meaning of the text of the Old Testament in his *In Genesim*, will demonstrate how seriously Bede took his duties both as a teacher and as an exegete. If from an early age he came to a just evaluation of his own worth, it was not without a full awareness of the heavy responsibility of anyone who would presume to offer authoritative commentary on the text of the Bible.

If we were to ask what, in Bede's view of things, "sacred history" was all about, a very general answer might be, it was the story of God's plan and how it worked out, or revealed itself, in the world. Bede would have regarded the events that made up the history of the created world as, in a sense, the utterance of God. In order to understand God's plan it was necessary to read his book—that is, the Bible, which recorded the events that were centrally important to the divine message. Thus, the biblical commentator had a double task: to elucidate the events

---

[1] Ray, "Who Did Bede Think He Was?" pp. 11–18; Hill, "Carolingian Perspectives on the Authority of Bede," p.227. See also, George Hardin Brown, *Bede the Venerable* (Boston, 1987), pp. 98–100.

recorded in the Bible and to discover the message that they conveyed. The former would have to do with what we usually call the literal sense of the text, and the latter with its spiritual interpretation. The commentator's task was complicated in one way, but facilitated in another, by the assumption that the core element of the divine message was hidden in the Old Testament only to be revealed in the New.

At the very beginning of *In Genesim*, Bede cautions would-be interpreters of the Bible against losing sight of the literal sense of the text in an overactive pursuit of allegorical meanings: "But it must be carefully observed," he says, "as each one devotes his attention to the allegorical senses, how far he may have forsaken the manifest truth of history by allegorical interpretation."[2] Later in the commentary, however, he puts more stress on the importance of allegory. After some extended remarks on the altar that Abram built between Bethel and Hai (cf. Gen. 12:7; 13:3–4), he observes: "I have taken considerable pains to explain these things about the altar of Abram in order that no one should think that the blessed Moses wished to describe so skillfully with reiterated narrative the location of Abram's . . . altar . . . out of fondness for a simple record of the facts (*historia*) and not rather for the sake of spiritual understanding."[3] And at the end of *In Genesim*, he accuses literalists who would insist on the obligation of Christians to carry out the letter of the old covenant, especially in regard to circumcision, of retreating

[2] Bede, *In Gen.* 1 (p. 3, lines 29–31): "Sed diligenter intuendum ut ita quisque sensibus allegoricis studium impendat, quatenus apertam historiae fidem allegorizando derelinquat." Translations of *In Genesim* are mine throughout.

[3] Bede, *In Gen.* 3 (p. 177, line 1266–p. 178, line 1270): "Haec de loco altaris Abrae idcirco diligentius explanare curauimus, ne quis putaret beatum Moysen historiae gratia diligentiae et non potius intuitu spiritalis intellegentiae tam solerter locum . . . altaris . . . eius iterata narratione uoluisse describere."

"into the shadows of figures" (*in umbras figurarum*). Such literal readers of the text are "carnal in understanding" (*carnales sensu*).[4] Reading his metaphor backwards, the "shadows of figures" are the plain, uninterpreted words of the text—the "manifest truth of history," as he styled it earlier.

These three observations from the beginning, middle, and end of *In Genesim*, respectively, taken out of context and set side by side, may sound contradictory. It would be easy to argue that Bede's thinking must have developed or changed in the intervals of his interrupted composition of the commentary over an extended period of time. But the contradictions are more apparent than real, and I prefer to take these observations as the cautions of a man who was filling a dual role in this commentary as a teacher as well as an exegete. As a master teacher, Bede surely knew the importance of giving his pupils instruction in the fundamentals before allowing them to move on to the greener pastures of mature scholarship. As an exegete, he plainly felt a heavy responsibility to speak in the true voice of the Church.

The first responsibility of the commentator, Bede implies, is the comprehensive elucidation of the biblical narrative, including all its raw edges and unresolved contradictions. What does the text literally mean *in every detail?* How does one detail relate to another? What can be inferred from silences in the text? How can its contradictions be resolved? Behind these questions lie assumptions about the text of the Bible that were shared by the exegetical tradition of which Bede was an heir. These include the assumption that the Bible was divinely inspired and that it was, therefore, "perfect and perfectly harmonious."[5] As St. Augustine put it: "It is to be noted that our authors [of the books of the Bible] do not disagree with one another in any way. . . . This agreement justifies the belief that when they wrote

[4] Bede, *In Gen.* 4 (p. 241, lines 1730 and 1725).
[5] James Kugel, *Bible as It Was* (Cambridge, 1997), p. 20.

these books God was speaking to them, or perhaps we should say through them."[6] But although the underlying message of the Bible was perfect and free of self-contradiction, the human agents of God's plan, their actions, and the words used to describe them, were not. They were nevertheless the vehicle by which the truth of history was communicated. Therefore, however messy and unedifying the literal narrative might appear to be, it would upon reflection reveal the coherent order of God's truth, and was therefore to be respected.

One source of "messiness" in the text arose from the incommensurability of God's perfect order with the defects of the human understanding. So, for example, we read in Genesis: "And God seeing that the wickedness of men was great on the earth, and that all the thought of their heart was bent upon evil, it repented him (*penituit eum*) that he had made man on the earth" (Gen. 6:5–6).[7] The sophisticated reader will object that repentance is a temporally dependent human quality that cannot be attributed to God. But, Bede says, "although to those observing with a pure heart divine providence proves to administer all things in an absolutely fixed order, nevertheless Scripture is suited to, and adapts itself to the lowly intelligence of duller persons, the multitude of whom is far greater . . . ."[8] The language

[6] Augustine, *De civitate Dei* 18.41 (CCSL 48: p. 636, lines 15–20): "Denique auctores nostri . . . absit ut inter se aliqua ratione dissentiant. Vnde non immerito, cum illa scriberent, eis Deum uel per eos locutum . . ." Trans. Henry Bettenson, *City of God*, Revised edition, (Harmondsworth, 2004), p. 816. See also *De civitate Dei* 20.1.

[7] Bede's commentary is based on the Latin Vulgate text of the Bible, except when he notes otherwise. My translations of the Vulgate are drawn from the Douay-Rheims Version revised by Richard Challoner, modified where appropriate to accord with Bede's readings and comments.

[8] Bede, *In Gen.* 2 (p. 101, lines 1015–19): "Quamquam ergo diuina prouidentia sereno corde intuentibus appareat cuncta certissimo ordine administrare; congruit tamen scriptura, et se coaptat humili intelligentiae tardiorum, quorum longe maior est multitudo. . . ."

of Scripture was at this point drawn from its author's understanding of human rather than of divine nature.

Another source of messiness stemmed from variations between translations of the biblical texts. Broadly speaking, two translations were current in Bede's day. One was the "Old Latin" version of the Greek Septuagint; the other was Jerome's Vulgate translation, a revision of the Old Latin text in the making of which Jerome consulted the Hebrew text of the Old Testament. Bede preferred Jerome's Vulgate, based as it was on "the Hebrew truth," but he conscientiously compared the two translations, and addressed discrepancies between them.[9] For example, he notes that whereas the Vulgate states that God "had planted a paradise of pleasure *from the beginning*" (Gen. 2:8), the old translation put it that God "had planted a paradise of pleasure *to the east.*"[10] In this case, he first explains how we are to understand the phrase "from the beginning" and then how we might understand the alternative, "to the east," clearly privileging Jerome's translation from the original Hebrew, but respecting the interpretation of the Latin translator of the Greek Septuagint.

But some discrepancies were more vexing. Bede explains how the Septuagint translators mistook a Hebrew common noun for a proper noun, and thereby created a phantom place, "Naid." For as they rendered it, "Cain went out from the face of the Lord God, and dwelt in the land of Naid opposite Eden" (Gen. 4:16). "But," Bede says, "'Naid,' which several commentators . . . assert is the place where Cain dwelt, means 'fugitive,' or . . . 'unsteady motion and fluctuation.' Furthermore, [Jerome] understood that this is not the name of a place, but an indication of the reality itself, that Cain would always be unsteady and in turmoil and of uncertain habitations."[11] Therefore, the Vulgate

[9] On Bede's preference for the Vulgate, see his remarks in the letter he wrote to Plegwin: see *Epist. Pleg.* 7–10 (p. 620, line 111–p. 622, line 180).
[10] Bede, *In Gen.* 1 (p. 45, line 1430–p. 46, line 1450).
[11] Bede, *In Gen.* 2 (p. 85, lines 441–7): "Naid autem in profugum, siue . . . in instabilem motum et fluctuationem uertitur, quod nonnulli . . .

version properly translates the passage as: "Cain went out from the face of the Lord, and dwelt as a fugitive on the earth, at the east side of Eden."

Still more serious was the contradiction between the ages of the patriarchs as given in the two translations, because this ultimately affected the calculation of the age of the world. Here, Bede accepts Augustine's suggestion that the discrepancy might have arisen from a copyist's error in the first transcription of the Septuagint in Ptolemy's library, which then was multiplied throughout the world. Since only one set of dates can be right, Augustine argued and Bede agrees, we should prefer the reading that appears in the original language, Hebrew.[12]

The second responsibility of the commentator, after the establishment of a clear understanding of the text, was to discover the divine meaning or message that it contained. In *In Genesim*, Bede employs four terms for the divine meaning, which is the interpreter's goal—*mysterium, allegoria, arcanum,* and *sacramentum.*[13] All these terms have to do with mysteries. God's meaning could be mysterious in at least three different ways: (1) Much of the divine meaning contained in Genesis and the other books of the Old Testament was concealed or mysterious, awaiting the revelation of the New Testament, to which, of course, the commentator had access. (2) In general, there were elements

---

locum esse in quo habitauerit Cain, autumant. Porro noster interpres non hoc nomen loci, sed rei ipsius esse significantiam intellexit; quia Cain instabilis semper *et fluctuans* atque *incertarum sedium* esset futurus."

[12] Bede, *In Gen.* 2 (p. 93, line 741–p. 95, line 800); cf. Augustine, *De civitate Dei* 15.13. Bede repeats this argument in his *Epist. Pleg.* 10 (p. 621, line 161–p. 622, line 181).

[13] Charles Jones analyzes Bede's critical vocabulary in "Some Introductory Remarks on Bede's Commentary on Genesis," *Sacris Erudiri* 19 (1970): 151–66. His summary conclusion is that "Terms normally considered technical have no definite or consistent meaning in Bede's exegesis" (p. 151).

of God's plan, mysterious to outsiders, which were revealed to the faithful. (3) Because human understanding is finite, some aspects of the divine message would always remain beyond human comprehension and therefore mysterious.

Mysterium, the most general of the four terms, could be substituted for any of the others in most contexts. Bede often uses *mysterium* in the first way, in reference to what we would call "allegory," that is, in reference to any of the spiritual meanings that were thought to be hidden in the Old Testament and revealed in the New.[14] In his discussion of Noah's ark, Bede writes, "A multiform allegory (*multiforme . . . mysterium*) is contained in the building of the ark and the sudden coming of the flood."[15] Three pages (in Jones's edition) of various allegorical interpretations of the ark and the flood follow this statement. But *mysterium* is not limited to this sense. Bede comments on the words of the voice that said to Peter: "Arise, Peter; kill and eat" (Acts 10:13). What that means, he says, is: "destroy the wicked habits of the gentiles by preaching the truth, and bring them into the body of the Church by initiating them into the sacred mysteries (*sacris mysteriis*)."[16] The sacred mysteries apparently refer to the truths of salvation and the sacraments of the Church. These were among the elements of God's plan, mysterious to outsiders, which were revealed to the faithful—the second kind of mystery.

Bede uses *allegoria* and its derivatives in the first way, that is, in reference to the meanings concealed in the Old Testament that were revealed in the New. It is surprising how rarely the noun *allegoria* itself occurs in *In Genesim.* In fact, apart from his

---

[14] The adverbial form *mystice* is always used in the sense "allegorically."

[15] Bede, *In Gen.* 2 (p. 102, lines 1060–1): "Multiforme in fabrica arcae ac superuentu diluuii continetur mysterium."

[16] Bede, *In Gen.* 2 (p. 132, lines 2123–5): " . . . extingue gentiles ab hoc quod male uixerant ueritatem praedicando, et infer in ecclesiae membra sacris mysteriis initiando."

quotation of St. Paul's influential discussion of allegory in Gal. 4:22–26,[17] Bede uses the noun only twice, both times within the space of a single paragraph in which he describes what is sometimes called "threefold allegory."[18] This refers to the assumption of biblical exegetes that the text of the Bible contains multiple layers of meaning: specifically, that it can be interpreted not only on the literal, historical level (*iuxta historiam*), but also typologically (*iuxta allegoriam*) in reference to Christ and the Church, and anagogically (*iuxta anagogen*) in reference to the Heavenly Kingdom. And Bede frequently adds another level of interpretation—the moral. When the moral level is included the system can be called "fourfold allegory,"[19] which Bede describes in his textbook *De schematibus et tropis*.

Modern usage applies the word "allegory" broadly to the whole of the threefold or fourfold system of interpretation or to any level of interpretation that goes beyond the literal or historical. The levels themselves are often referred to specifically as the "literal," the "typological," the "moral," and the "anagogi-

---

[17] Bede, *In Gen.* 4 (p. 239, line 1621).

[18] Bede, *In Gen.* 4 (p. 212, line 675–p. 214, line 744, at lines 701 and 712). On Bede's employment of "threefold" and "fourfold allegory," see Jones, "Bede's Commentary on Genesis," pp. 131–51. On his sparing use of the term *allegoria*, see Jones, "Bede's Commentary on Genesis," p. 160, and n. 137.

[19] Standard treatments are Émile Mâle, *Religious Art in France, The Thirteenth Century: A Study of Medieval Iconography and Its Sources*, ed. Harry Bober, trans. Marthiel Mathews, Bollingen Series 90.2 (Princeton, 1984), pp. 138–45; Harry Caplan, "The Four Senses of scriptural Interpretation and the Medieval Theory of Preaching," *Speculum* 4 (1929): 282–90; Beryl Smalley, *The Study of the Bible in the Middle Ages* (1959; reprinted, Notre Dame, 1964), pp. 1–36; Henri de Lubac, *Exégèse médiévale: les quatre sens de l'Écriture*, 2 vols. (Paris, 1959); Jean Daniélou, *From Shadows to Reality: Studies in the Biblical Typology of the Fathers*, trans. Wulstan Hibberd (Westminster, Md., 1960).

cal." In medieval Latin usage, "allegory" often applies narrowly to the second level of interpretation—the typological foreshadowing of the events of the New Testament in the text of the Old.[20] In the paragraph referred to above, Bede puts it this way: " . . . in holy Scripture there are three levels of meaning: namely, the historical, the allegorical (*allegoricus*), and the anagogical."[21] On the other hand, when he speaks of the "allegorical senses" (*sensibus allegoricis*) of the Bible or when he employs the verb form *allegorizando* to refer to the practice of allegorical interpretation,[22] he is using the terms in the broad sense.

Arcanum is perhaps the least problematic of the four terms. Bede uses it primarily in the second way, in reference to those of God's mysteries that are to be revealed to the faithful but concealed from all others. The *arcana* are the "secrets" of the faith. He observes, for example, that the window of Noah's ark that was opened after the flood "signifies the *arcana* of the divine mysteries with which the baptized are particularly initiated."[23] And in a similar sense, he writes that because of his faith, Abraham heard the word of God, but "the Jews were cast out from the stock of Abraham and counted among 'the offspring of vipers' (Luke 3:7), because they were unable to comprehend the *arcana* of Divinity that they heard."[24]

---

[20] For an account of various usages of *allegoria* in the patristic period, see Erich Auerbach, "'Figura'," trans. Ralph Manheim, in *Scenes from the Drama of European Literature: Six Essays* (1959; reprinted, Gloucester, Mass., 1973), pp. 47–48.

[21] Bede, *In Gen.* 4 (p. 213, lines 696–7): " . . . in scriptura sacra triplex est sensus intellegentiae: historicus uidelicet, allegoricus, et anagogicus."

[22] E.g., Bede, *In Gen.* 1 (p. 3, line 29–p. 4, line 31); both terms.

[23] Bede, *In Gen.* 2 (p. 122, lines 1762–3): " . . . designet arcana mysteriorum celestium quibus baptizati specialiter initiantur."

[24] Bede, *In Gen.* 4 (p. 203, lines 322–4): "Porro Iudei, quia audita diuinitatis arcana capere non poterant, eiecti de stirpe Abrahae et inter *genimina* sunt *uiperarum* computati."

Finally, there is the term *sacramentum*.[25] Like *mysterium* it has broad application, but it places greater emphasis on the truths of God's plan for human salvation and the rituals that embody them than on the veils that obscure the plan and the things about it we cannot know. Although it is often used in connection with allegory, it typically refers to the meaning that the allegory conveys. So, when Bede remarks in his preface that he plans to interrupt his work on Genesis to comment on the Book of Ezra, he says that in Ezra there can be found "the *sacramenta*, the sacred truths, of Christ and the Church under the allegorical figure of the release from the long captivity, of the restoration of the temple," etc.[26] Similarly, the four letters that make up the name "Adam" allegorically contain a reference to the four corners of the world, because they are the first letters of the Greek words for east, west, north, and south. This allegorical meaning is a *sacramentum*, a "sacred truth," because through his offspring Adam was destined to populate the whole world.[27] Bede speaks of the *sacramenta* of the Passover[28] and the *sacramenta* of life (the reference is presumably to baptism),[29] and the *sacramentum* of refraining from eating meat with blood,[30] the *sacramentum* of the Sabbath,[31] and the *sacramentum* of circumcision.[32] In each of these cases, an appropriate translation would be "ritual" or "rite" or "religious observance." The *sacramenta* of the Lord's

---

[25] For a survey of the original senses and acquired meanings of *sacramentum*, see Brian Stock, *The Implications of Literacy: Written Language and Models of Interpretation in the Eleventh and Twelfth Centuries* (Princeton, 1983), pp. 254–9.

[26] Bede, *In Gen.* praef. (p. 2, lines 38–39): "... Christi et ecclesiae sacramenta sub figura, solutae longae captiuitatis, restaurati templi. . . ."

[27] Bede, *In Gen.* 2 (p. 93, lines 727–35).

[28] Bede, *In Gen.* 1 (p. 20, lines 570–3).

[29] Bede, *In Gen.* 2 (p. 140, line 2415).

[30] Bede, *In Gen.* 2 (p. 134, line 2197).

[31] Bede, *In Gen.* 4 (p. 208, lines 526–7).

[32] Bede, *In Gen.* 4 (p. 209, lines 560–1).

Incarnation,[33] on the other hand, might better be translated "the mysteries," both in the second sense, of those secrets that are revealed to the faithful, and in the third sense, of those elements of God's plan that remain beyond human comprehension.

Now, I return to Bede's comment, quoted above, that Moses provided so many details about Abram's altar, not "out of fondness for a simple record of the facts," but "rather for the sake of spiritual understanding." This is another important clue to Bede's interpretative assumptions and therefore to his methods. Facts (*historiae*) are important, but a dense cluster of details or a repeated insistence upon certain facts justifies the assumption that they point to a spiritual level of interpretation. Or to put it another way, the richer the historical texture, the greater the interpretative demand.

Interpretation has to do with meaning, and meaning with signification. What can be interpreted, and how or from where do the things that are interpreted acquire their meaning? Not all things signify, but to those that do Bede applies variously the terms *signum*, "sign," *figura*, "figure," and *typus*, "type."[34]

According to Genesis: "Enoch walked with God, and lived after he begot Mathusala three hundred years, and begot sons and daughters. And all the days of Enoch were three hundred and sixty-five years" (Gen. 5:22–23). Bede comments on these verses as follows:

> And not without reason are the three hundred years taken separately, in which Enoch is specifically said to have walked with God. For indeed this number is usually represented among the Greeks by the letter T, and the letter T contains the *figura*, the figure, of the cross; and if it had only received the up-stroke

---

[33] Bede, *In Gen.* 2 (p. 107, lines 1216–17); and *In Gen.* 4 (p. 216, line 784).

[34] The indispensable discussion of *figura* is Auerbach, "'Figura'," passim. See also his comments, in the same paper, on *signum*, p. 19, and *typus*, pp. 47–48.

which is lacking in the center, it would not in that case have depicted the figure of the cross, but the *signum*, the sign, of the cross itself in plain view.[35]

It may be a measure of the importance that Bede attached to this observation that he repeated it, or part of it, twice more in the *In Genesim*.[36] It has the clarity of an illustrative formula polished by repeated use in the classroom. In any event, the point of his remark is that the letter *T*, written like our capital *T*, in this context recalls to our mind, or "symbolizes," the cross, whereas the sign of the cross itself, resembling the letter *T* but with an ascender rising above the crossbar, has a meaning which is divinely fixed and independent of context.

What Bede was searching for, I think, was a distinction between what we might call "sign" and "symbol"—a distinction that he could use to distinguish the work of commentators like himself from the express word of God.[37] Unfortunately, the word "symbol," *symbolum*, was not part of his vocabulary.[38] But

[35] Bede, *In Gen.* 2 (p. 97, lines 865–70): "Nec frustra trecenti anni seorsum excipiuntur, quibus specialiter ambulasse cum Deo Enoch perhibetur. Hic etenim numerus apud Grecos per *T* litteram solet notari. *T* uero littera crucis figuram tenet; et si apicem solum qui deest in medio suscepisset, non iam figura crucis sed ipsum crucis esset signum manifesta specie depictum."

[36] Bede, *In Gen.* 2 (p. 140, lines 2416–19), 3 (p. 187, lines 1590–7).

[37] Cf. Augustine's distinction between "natural" and "conventional" signs (*De doctrina christiana* 2.1.1–4.5), and, more importantly, between "literal" and "figurative" signs (*De doctrina christiana* 2.10.15).

[38] Even though the word, borrowed from the Greek, had been in sporadic use since at least the first half of the third century A.D. (e.g., by Cyprian [Souter, *A Glossary of Later Latin to 600 A. D.* (Oxford, 1949), p. 409]), and was glossed, for example, by Isidore (*Etymologiae* 6.19.57), it did not enter the mainstream of intellectual discourse until the twelfth century, when it was carefully distinguished from "allegory": see Marie-Madeleine Davy, *Initiation à la symbolique romane (xiie siècle)*, 2nd edn. (Paris, 1973), p. 95.

the terms "figure" and "type" act as functional equivalents and allow him to set up an implied contrast with "sign."[39]

The question then arises whether Bede made consistent use of this contrast between *signum* and *figura* or *typus*. The answer is a cautiously qualified yes. In the *In Genesim* there are just six things in addition to the cross that Bede explicitly identifies as "signs." These are: (1) the Tree of the Knowledge of Good and Evil, (2) the serpent, (3) the poison of the serpent, (4) the sign on Cain, (5) the rainbow, and (6) circumcision. (1) The Tree of the Knowledge of Good and Evil in paradise (Gen. 2:9) is "a sign to man of the obedience which he owe[s] to God."[40] (2) The irrational serpent, which is condemned to eat earth (Gen. 3:14), is a sign of the spiritual ruin of man, who is condemned to return to dust (Gen. 3:19).[41] (3) The poison of the same serpent is a sign of the enmity God placed between it and Eve and her seed (Gen. 3:15).[42] God sets a sign on Cain (4), so that whoever finds him shall not kill him (Gen. 4:15). Here the term *signum* appears in the text of the Vulgate itself, and Bede's discussion of it is borrowed from Augustine.[43] God declares that the rainbow (5) is "the sign of a covenant between me, and between the earth" that he will never again destroy all living things with the waters of a flood (Gen. 9:13–15). However, this does not exhaust

[39] For a valuable account of Bede's attempt at "a general theory of symbol" in *DST*, see Brown, *Bede the Venerable*, pp. 34–35. The distinction I am making between sign and symbol goes one step further. Brown, p. 95, points out that *signa* is Bede's preferred term for miracles in the *Historia ecclesiastica*.

[40] Bede, *In Gen.* 1 (p. 46, lines 1460–1): ". . . homini signum obedientiae quam Deo debebat. . . ." The Tree of Life, which Bede refers to in the same sentence, is almost certainly another, although he uses the term *sacramentum* instead of *signum*.

[41] Bede, *In Gen.* 1 (p. 66, lines 2100–3).

[42] Bede, *In Gen.* 1 (p. 66, lines 2115–18).

[43] Bede, *In Gen.* 2 (p. 84, lines 423–31); Augustine, *Contra Faustum Manichaeum* 12.13: (CSEL 25.1: p. 341, lines 7–14).

the meanings of this sign. Bede asserts that the rainbow

> also sets before our eyes a sign of the future judgment which
> will be upon the world by fire. For not without reason does it
> gleam blue and red at the same time, since by the color blue
> it bears witness to us of the waters that have gone past, and by
> the red, of the flames that are to come. Moreover, the heavenly
> rainbow . . . is fittingly placed as a sign of divine mercy.[44]

These supplementary meanings depend more than the original on the ingenuity of the commentator, and approach the domain of allegorical symbolism. The same tendency toward allegorical symbolism is found in Bede's discussion of circumcision, the last sign (6) that he takes up in his *In Genesim*.[45] Circumcision is a major topic of the fourth book. As with the rainbow, it is God who specifically calls it a "sign" in the Vulgate text: "And you shall circumcise the flesh of your foreskin, that it may be for a sign of the covenant between me and you" (Gen. 17:9–11). Bede explains that

[44] Bede, *In Gen.* 2 (p. 135, lines 2238–44): " . . . et futuri iudicii quod per ignem est mundo futurum . . . signum nobis ante oculos praetendit. Neque enim frustra ceruleo simul et rubicundo colore resplendent, nisi quia ceruleo colore aquarum quae praeterierunt, rubicundo flammarum quae uenturae sunt nobis testimonium perhibet. Apte autem arcus celestis . . . in signum diuinae propitiationis ponitur."

[45] I should mention, if only to rule it out, one other "sign" that Bede mentions. This is the fact that Isaac was born at the beginning of the fifteenth year of his half-brother Ishmael's life, "*as if* as a sign of the resurrection" [*quasi in signum resurrectionis*] (*In Gen.* 4, p. 208, line 528). The numerological allegory involved here is too complex to be explained briefly; the point is that Bede calls attention to the close analogy between signs and allegory. I must add that Bede uses the word "sign" to refer to things that are not of sacred significance, like the signs of the Zodiac. The sign that God set on Cain may fall into this category.

the flesh of the foreskin is ordered to be circumcised for a sign of the covenant between God and men, so that by this sign the faithful of that time were to be admonished that they should cleanse themselves "from all defilement of the flesh and of the spirit," in order that they might perfect "sanctification in the fear of God" (2 Cor. 7:1).[46]

But as he continues to elaborate on the "deeper allegory" (*altiore mysterio*) of this sign, he begins to speak in terms of "pre-figuration":

> Therefore none of the faithful doubts that, as a sign of this covenant, Abraham and his seed were circumcised in the flesh of their foreskin, in order that it might be prefigured typologi-cally that he would be born from that seed, who would cleanse his chosen ones from all stain of sins, and endow them with eternal blessing.[47]

Later, in his lengthy discussion of the significance of Isaac's circumcision on the eighth day (Gen. 21:4–5), that circumci-sion is described more cautiously as "a rite of the old covenant" (*ueteris . . . testamenti sacramentum*) which "was sent as a figure of the grace of the new covenant" (*in figuram gratiae noui testamenti*

---

[46] Bede, *In Gen.* 4 (p. 204, lines 381–5): "Circumcidi ergo praecipitur caro praeputii, in signum foederis inter Deum et homines, ut hoc signo admonerentur fideles illius temporis, *munda*ndos se *ab omni inquinamento carnis et spiritus, perfici*endam *sanctificationem in timore Dei.*"

[47] Bede, *In Gen.* 4 (p. 204, line 389–p. 205, line 394): "Quod ad gratiam noui testamenti pertinere nemo fidelium dubitat, in huius ergo foederis signum nemo fidelium dubitat, quod circumcisus est Abraham et semen eius in carne praeputii sui, ut praefiguraretur typice nasciturus de illius semine, qui electos suos ab omni macula peccatorum expurgaret, ac perpetua benedictione donaret."

praemissum).[48] The figural interpretations are Bede's. Nowhere in this passage does he use the term *signum*.

Although Bede does not develop the distinction between sign and what I am calling "symbol" into a full-fledged system, he seems implicitly to suggest that the meanings of sacred signs are authorized by God and independent of the observer, but that symbols may be interpreted differently in different contexts or by different observers. The sign of the cross always signifies the same thing. The letter T, on the other hand, may symbolize the cross in one context, but something quite different in another.

A *signum*, a sacred sign, like the cross, that has spiritual meanings in addition to its literal meaning would be in Bede's terms an "allegory," but in some sense an "open" or "unveiled" allegory. *Figurae*, "figures," and *typi*, "types," symbols whose meanings are not declared but are uncovered by the effort of human commentators, would also be allegorical. This, however, is allegory that is "veiled" or "hidden," in the usual way we understand allegory.

Precisely because veiled allegory is conveyed by symbols whose meanings are indeterminate, a heavy responsibility falls upon the commentator. Bede's sense of this responsibility emerges clearly in his warning at the beginning of *In Genesim* against over-zealous spiritual interpretation at the expense of "the manifest truth of history." No interpretation that was based on a false understanding of the literal meaning of the text could be relied upon to bear good fruit. But even after the commentator has ascertained to the best of his ability the manifest truth of history, pitfalls remain. How is one to guard against falling into error in the course of interpreting symbols whose meanings are not fixed? What if different authorities have interpreted these symbols differently? Their interpretations are the product of human ingenuity, unlike the meanings of signs, which are given by God.

Bede's solution to the problem of fallibility appears in his commentary on the episode in Genesis in which three men appear to Abraham before his tent and Abraham commands Sarah

[48] Bede, *In Gen.* 4 (p. 237, lines 1541–3).

to take three measures of flour and bake them into bread (Gen. 18). Bede compares the process of spiritual interpretation to the leavening of the bread:

> [Sara] hides the leaven of the Gospel in three measures of meal so that the whole may be leavened, whenever holy Church, which Sara signifies in this passage, either proclaims history in the Scriptures, or unveils allegory, or lifts up its interpretive eye to the contemplation of heavenly things, as it always inculcates by its words the virtue of love either of the Lord or one's brother. Let no one suppose that he has understood the Scripture rightly, in which he was unable to find the teaching of charity.[49]

The solution, therefore, was to adopt Augustine's standard for judging the validity of human interpretations, which was to ask if they fulfilled the law of Christian charity. Augustine had put it this way in *De doctrina christiana*:

> Whoever . . . thinks that he understands the divine Scriptures or any part of them so that it does not build the double love of God and of our neighbor does not understand it at all. Whoever finds a lesson there useful to the building of charity, even though he has not said what the author may be shown to have intended in that place, has not been deceived, nor is he lying in any way.[50]

[49] Bede, *In Gen.* 4 (p. 213, line 709–p. 214, line 717): "Fermentum namque euangelicum mulier in farinae satis tribus abscondit ut totum fermentetur, cum sancta ecclesia, quam hoc in loco Sara significat, siue historiam in scripturis praedicet siue allegoriam reuelet seu ad superna contemplanda oculum suae expositionis attolat, semper ut dictis suis uirtutem siue dominicae seu fraternae caritatis instituit. Neque ullatenus se scripturam recte intellexisse quisquam putet, in qua institutionem caritatis inuenire non potuit."

[50] *De doctrina christiana* 1.36.40 (CCSL 32: p. 29, lines 1–7) "Quisquis . . . scripturas diuinas uel quamlibet earum partem intellexisse sibi uidetur,

Calvin B. Kendall

That is, a variety of interpretations may be possible. Those that promote the doctrine of Christian charity are correct. Those that do not are invalidated. But Augustine went on to stress that an interpretation that can be shown to be unintended by the Scriptures, even if it accords with the law of charity, should be corrected, lest the commentator fall into the habit of straying from the true path.[51]

Augustine and Bede would likely have agreed that the chief reason a commentator might mistake the intention of the Scriptures would be because he misunderstood the literal text. Bede's choice of words, in the passage I just quoted, is telling. The loaf is leavened, "whenever holy Church . . . either proclaims history in the Scriptures, or unveils allegory, or lifts up its interpretive eye to the contemplation of heavenly things. . . ." It was, of course, the commentator's job first to *proclaim* history on the literal level, then to *unveil* allegory on the typological level,

---

ita ut eo intellectu non aedificet istam geminam caritatem dei et proximi, nondum intellexit. Quisquis uero talem inde sententiam duxerit, ut huic aedificandae caritati sit utilis, nec tamen hoc dixerit, quod ille quem legit eo loco sensisse probabitur, non perniciose fallitur nec omnino mentitur." Trans. D. W. Robertson, Jr., *Saint Augustine: On Christian Doctrine* (New York, 1958), p. 30; cf. *De doctrina christiana* 3.27.38. It has been argued that Bede's knowledge of *De doctrina christiana* was limited to the excerpts of Eugippius: see Ray, "Who Did Bede Think He Was?," pp. 23–24 and n. 36, in the present volume. This passage is included among the excerpts (CSEL 9: p. 817, lines 14–20).

[51] Augustine, *De doctrina christiana* 1.36.41 (CCSL 32: p. 30, lines 21–25): "Sed quisquis in scripturis aliud sentit quam ille, qui scripsit, illis non mentientibus fallitur, sed tamen, ut dicere coeperam, si ea sententia fallitur, qua aedificet caritatem, quae finis praecepti est, ita fallitur, ac si quisquam errore deserens uiam eo tamen per agrum pergat, quo etiam uia illa perducit."

and finally to *lift up* his interpretive eye to the contemplation of heavenly things on the anagogical level. Bede's image makes the commentator a synecdoche for the Church. He was part of the allegory he was unveiling. It was, indeed, a heavy responsibility to speak in the true voice of the Church.

Bede's Neglected Commentary on Samuel

GEORGE HARDIN BROWN

BEDE'S *In primam partem Samuhelis* never gained the circulation of his other major exegetical works. Whatever the cause may be, it is not for lack of effort and artistry on Bede's part. Both in the prologue to the first book and to the third, he remarks how much labor and sweat, "sudor," went into this commentary.[1] As a major contribution it is not easily ignored: in his bibliography at the end of the *Historia ecclesiastica*, Bede records high on the list "On the First Part of Samuel, that is, up to the death of Saul, four books."[2] And it is a big work: at 272 pages in the modern edition, it ranks as Bede's longest Old Testament commentary. However, it survives in only eight medieval manuscripts, three of which

---

[1] Bede, *In Sam.* 1 Prol. (p. 10, line 55); 3 Prol. (p. 137, line 1). There are two traditional Latin and English titles for this book, 1 Samuel and 1 Kings (in Greek, 1 Kingdoms). Some Latin manuscripts of the Old Testament give the title 1 and 2 Kings to 1 and 2 Samuel and therefore what is now titled in the Revised Standard Version as 1 and 2 Kings is in those versions 3 and 4 Kings. The Codex Amiatinus and others seek to resolve the long-standing confusion by including both: thus, Amiatinus has "Incipit regum liber primus qui hebraice appellatur samuhel." See *Biblia Sacra iuxta latinam vulgatam versionem* (Rome, 1944), vol. 5: Liber Samuhelis, p. 71n. The Douay translation follows the usual Vulgate tradition in primarily listing the books as 1-4 Kings but also disambiguates with the heading "The First Book of Samuel, otherwise called the First Book of Kings": see *Holy Bible Translated from the Latin Vulgate* (Baltimore, 1899; reprinted, Rockford, Ill., 1971), p. 282.

[2] Bede, 5. 24 (p. 568): "In primam partem Samuhelis, id est usque ad mortem Saulis, libros IIII."

are early (ninth century), and the rest from the twelfth and thir-teenth.[3] This paucity stands in marked contrast to Bede's other biblical commentaries, most of which exist in numerous copies. Our era has not changed that state of affairs. Although one can find some scattered bibliographic references to the commentary, few scholars—even Bedan specialists—seem to have read the work in its entirety. A number of Bede's Old Testament commentaries are now available in English translations. Published are Arthur Holder's *On the Tabernacle*, Seán Connolly's *On the Temple* as well as *On Tobit* and *On the Canticle of Habakkuk*, Scott DeGregorio's *On Ezra and Nehemiah*, a number of briefer works contained in W. Trent Foley and Arthur Holder's *Bede: A Biblical Miscellany*, with another translation of Bede's *On Tobit*. Even Bede's Abbreviated Psalter has been translated.[4] But of Bede's great commentary on 1 Samuel as a whole we have no translation or critical interpreta-tion—as yet, although I hope to remedy that.

What is the problem with Bede's commentary on 1 Samuel? In *A Hand-List of Bede Manuscripts*, Max Laistner wrote: "Bede, as has often been remarked, in this commentary adopts the al-legorical method of interpretation in its most extreme form. To

---

[3] The early MSS are Lyons, 449, saec. IX1, New York, Pierpont Morgan Library, M. 335, saec. IX, and Paris lat. 12272, saec. IX. The later MSS are Cambridge, Trinity College 82, saec. XII, Douai, 325, saec. XII, London, British Library Add. 26714, saec. XIII1, Oxford, Jesus College 53, saec. XII, Salisbury, 136, saec. XII.

[4] Arthur G. Holder, trans., *Bede: On the Tabernacle*, Translated Texts for His-torians 18 (Liverpool, 1994); Sean Connolly, trans., *Bede: On the Temple*, Translated Texts for Historians 21 (Liverpool, 1995), and *Bede: On Tobit and On the Canticle of Habakkuk* (Dublin, 1997); Scott DeGregorio, trans., *Bede: On Ezra and Nehemiah*, Translated Texts for Historians 47 (Liver-pool, 2006); Trent Foley and Arthur G. Holder, trans., *Bede: A Biblical Miscellany*. Texts for Historians 28 (Liverpool, 1999); Gerald M. Browne, *The Abbreviated Psalter of the Venerable Bede* (Grand Rapids, Mich., 2002).

judge by the very small number of extant MSS, it would seem
as if even medieval scholars found his allegorizing excessive."[5]
But the overwhelming manuscript evidence of the enormous
popularity of extreme allegorical commentaries such as Pope
Gregory the Great's 1811-page *Moralia in Job* confounds such a
hypothesis.[6] And Bede's other highly allegorical Old Testament
commentaries are well represented by numerous manuscripts.
Most of them even include the term "allegorical" in their titles,
such as *In Ezram et Neemiam prophetas allegorica expositio, In Cantica Canticorum allegorica expositio,* and *Super Canticum Abacuc allegorica expositio.* The reason for all these, of course, is that Bede,
following St. Paul and the long patristic tradition from Origen,
Ambrose, Augustine, and especially Gregory, treats the whole
of the Old Testament as "in figura"—symbolic, typological,
and mysteriously instructive for our present life in the Church.
Bede's contemporaries would be well disposed to such an allegorical exposition. Although we may find reading page after
page of explicit allegoresis rather predictable and even laborious, meditative medieval clerics and literate lay people obviously found this procedure instructive and indeed stimulating. We
must look elsewhere, then, to discover the reason, if any, for the
relative obscurity of this particular hermeneutic text. A specialist
in Anglo-Saxon literature might object that eight manuscripts of
a work does not constitute obscurity, since most manuscripts in
Old English are unique, existing in but a single manuscript, but
compared with the Latin works of Bede, such as his commentaries on the Song of Songs, Luke, Mark, Acts of the Apostles,
and Apocalypse (each comprising more than a hundred extant
manuscripts), the manuscripts of his commentary on Samuel
are exiguous indeed. A further indicator of the paucity is how

[5] M. L. W. Laistner with H.H. King, *A Hand-List of Bede Manuscripts* (Ithaca,
N.Y., 1943), p. 65.
[6] The work is contained in CCSL 143, 143A and 143B.

few medieval libraries list the work in their catalogues: Laistner records two (Durham and Tournai) and my survey of medieval library catalogues has disclosed about a dozen more for the entire Middle Ages, both in England and on the Continent.[7] How little Bede's commentary on Samuel was known and used in the Middle Ages is strikingly illustrated by the fact that only two medieval authors, Hincmar of Rheims (c. 806–82) and Hugh of Fouilloy (c. 1100–1172/3), cite the work.[8]

In laying the allegorical path through 1 Samuel, Bede must have used whatever patristic materials were available to him. These seem confined to the *Homily on the Book of Kings* by Origen as translated by Rufinus[9] and Augustine's Book 17 of the

---

[7]Laistner, *Hand-List*, pp, 11, 13; *Registrum Anglie de libris doctorum et auctorum veterum*, ed. Richard H. and Mary A. Rouse, Corpus of British Medieval Library Catalogues 2 (London, 1991), Bede 7.12; *The Libraries of the Cistercians, Gilbertines, and Premonstratensians*, ed. David N. Bell, Corpus of British Medieval Library Catalogues 3 (London, 1992), Z19.107. Richard Sharpe, general editor of CBMLC, lists on his website (http://www.history.ox.ac.uk/sharpe/list.pdf) only four medieval library catalogues containing Bede's Samuel commentary (see p. 133); but when the CBMLC project is completed (to date eleven volumes of an expected seventeen have been published) the list will possibly be a little longer.

[8]Although Bishop Lull (d. 786), apparently working from Bede's own bibliography at the end of the *Historia ecclesiastica* 5.24, requested a copy of the commentary on 1 Samuel from Archbishop Koena of York, there is no evidence that he ever received the text: see Lull *Epistola* 125 (MGH, Epistolae selectae I, p. 263). A search through the databases of the PL and CLCLT (*Library of Latin Texts*) resulted in only two theologians who actually cite the commentary: Hincmar of Rheims, *De divortio Lotharii Regis* (PL 125:678D–679A), and Hugh of Fouilloy (Hugo de Folieto), *De claustro animae*, I.xv (PL 176:1043C–D, 1046C).

[9] PG 12, cols. 995–1012; also the edition, *Homélies sur Samuel*, ed. Pierre and Marie Thérèse Nautin, SC 328 (Paris, 1986).

City of God.[10] Unlike Isidore of Seville, who uses the same texts of Augustine in his *Questions on the Old Testament* by incorporating passages *en bloc* into his commentary, Bede in his usual artful way judiciously mixes bits of Origen and Augustine into his own original amalgam. As Adalbert de Vogüé astutely remarks,

> In contrast to Isidore's Questions, Bede's *In Primam Partem Samuelis* is a coherent commentary, though very succinct and sprinkled with brief omissions. The Saxon monk is further distinguished from Isidore by his more personal manner of using the earlier texts. His borrowings are limited sometimes to a word or to a characteristic citation. The locating of that which he owes to his predecessors demands great attention, inasmuch as he happens to combine the *Homily* of Origen and the *City of God* in a very subtle fashion.[11]

---

[10] Augustine, *De civitate Dei* 17.1–7 (CCSL 48: pp. 550–70). According to Adalbert de Vogüé, "Les plus anciens exégèses du Premier Livre des Rois: Origène, Augustin et leur epigones," *Sacris Erudiri* 29 (1986): 8, n. 9, Bede may also have borrowed a phrase or two from Augustine's *De diversis quaestionibus*.

[11] My translation de Vogüé's paragraph in "Les plus anciens exégèses," p. 8: "À la différence des *Questions* d'Isidore, l'*In Primam Partem Samuelis* de Bède est un commentaire suivi, encore que très succinct et parsemé de brèves omissions. Le moine saxon se distingue encore d'Isidore par sa manière plus personelle de remployer les textes antérieurs. Ses emprunts se bornent parfois à un mot ou à une citation caractéristique. Le repérage de ce qu'il doit à ses prédécesseurs demande donc une grande attention, d'autant qu'il lui arrive de combiner la Homilie d'Origène et la *Cité de Dieu* de façon très subtile." To de Vogüé's list of Bede's sources, one should add two more: lines 470–81 derived from Origen's homily, section 13, and lines 837–41 from Augustine's *De civitate Dei* 17.6 (CCSL 48: p. 566, lines 10–17), the latter noted by Paul Meyvaert, "In the Footsteps of the Fathers: The Date of Bede's *Thirty Questions on the Book of Kings* to Nothelm," in *The*

Since only a very few of the early exegetes comment on the whole of 1 Samuel, the loss of Bede's commentary to medieval biblical exegesis proved a massive lacuna.[12] Claudius of Turin (d. 827) includes citations from Origen and Augustine but the excerpts he uses from Bede come from Bede's other small work, *In Regum librum XXX quaestiones*,[13] and not from his complete commentary on 1 Samuel. Hrabanus Maurus (d. 856) in his commentary likewise shows no sign of knowing Bede's full commentary on 1 Samuel. Instead, his citations, marked "Ex Gregorio" and "Ex Beda," derive like Claudius of Turin's from other works of those authors that happen to refer to Samuel and the Book of Kings. Hrabanus Maurus's text on Kings became the standard commentary on Kings by its incorporation into the *Glossa Ordinaria*. So, even though Bede was the principal contributor to the commentaries in the *Glossa* on Tobit, Ezra-Nehemiah, the Acts of the Apostles, and the Canonical Epistles, his commentary on 1 Samuel does not appear in that popular chrestomathy or, indeed, in any other exegetical collection.

The relative oblivion of Bede's commentary on 1 Samuel cannot be charged to lack of interest in what Bede has to say on this biblical subject. His *In Regum librum XXX quaestiones*, which survives in some 44 manuscripts and found its way into various Carolingian and later commentaries, including the *Glossa Ordinaria*, should put that doubt to rest. Nor can it justifiably be objected that Bede's full commentary lacks interest. Rather, that commentary, fascinating and splendid in exegetical and literary material, represents a high mark in Bedan exegesis. It displays a

---

Limits of Ancient Christianity: Essays in Honour of R. A, Markus, ed. William F. Klingshirn and Mark Vessey (Ann Arbor, Mich., 1999), p. 269.

[12] Isidore's commentary (PL 83, cols. 391–422), which Bede does not use, participates in this textual lineage, inserting texts from Augustine and from Gregory's *Moralia in Job*, but not from Origen.

[13] This Bedan work is edited in CCSL 119, pp. 289–322.

concurrent concern for the historical, allegorical, tropological and anagogic meaning of the biblical text. Each element reinforces the other for a reader who can tolerate shifting equivalents as they work to enrich the understanding of the complexity of Christian mystery.

Bede's *In primam partem Samuhelis* is divided into four books that constitute thematic units, with roughly equal numbers of chapters in each book. Book 1, in seven chapters, deals with Samuel's career from childhood to judge and leader. Book 2, in eight chapters, tells of the Israelites' demand for a king, to which God reluctantly accedes, after which Samuel anoints Saul. Book 3, in seven chapters, recounts the actions of the deeply troubled Saul as leader and king threatened by the young hero David; and book 4, in nine chapters, extols the ascendant David, while the disfavored Saul falls in battle and dies.

A prologue precedes each of Bede's books. That is remarkable in itself, since, as Scott DeGregorio has called to my attention, it is the only exegetical work of Bede to have more than one prologue. The first prologue in 65 lines prepares the reader for all that follows by firmly establishing the authority for the allegorical treatment of the historical text. First he foregrounds three crucial texts in Scripture, two Pauline and one Petrine: "For what things soever were written, were written for our learning" (Rom. 15:4, Douai translation); "Now all these things happened to them in figure: and they were written for our correction, on whom the ends of the world have come" (1 Cor. 10:11); "And all the prophets, from Samuel and afterwards, who have spoken, have told of these days" (Acts 3:24). With that key reference to Samuel, Bede says he will carve out (exsculpere) the allegorical heart of the text, so that to the historical literal reading favored by the Jewish tradition he will with Christ's help add the spiritual symbolic meaning. After all, Bede says, the fact that Elcana had two wives can only have meaning for the celibate monk if those persons represent spiritual qualities or states. Bede, seeking the meaning of 1 Samuel for Christian times, neatly closes the prologue with a rhetorical envelope when he invokes the aid of St. Peter, whom he quoted at the beginning.

The prologue of the second book surprises us, because rather than furnish a summary of what went before and what will follow, as he does in his other commentaries and in the prologues to the third and fourth books of *In primam partem Samuhelis*, he declares that "instead of a proem, we are going to treat certain matters of chronology."[14]

Bede the historian temporarily displaces Bede the allegorist. The literal history is important for him. In ninety-five lines he earnestly attempts to sort out the chronological reigns of Saul, David, and Solomon by reckoning length of rules from Moses through Judges on the basis of the few temporal markers in the biblical text. This is a brave attempt by Bede, who never shirks a challenge when it comes to calendrical time reckoning. Modern biblical historians are still trying to figure out the chronology of these rulers. As the editors of the *New Oxford Annotated Bible* remark, "The length of Saul's reign is not known; David and Solomon are each said to have ruled for forty years, which is often used as a general and somewhat indefinite number...," and the editors add: "Problems of chronology of the kings of Israel and Judah permit no easy solution."[15] After surveying various opinions and giving his own, Bede concludes his attempt with the sentence, "But because this preface has proceeded at length,

---

[14] Bede, *In Sam.* 2 (p. 68, lines 1–7): "Quoniam in hoc libello, id est secundo, nostrae allegoricae expositionis in beatum prophetam Samuhelem de fine ducatus eiusdem Samuhelis et de initio regni Saul auxiliante domino sumus pro modulo nostro dicturi uisum est loco proemii de tempore quo quisque eorum Dei populo praefuerit aliqua tractare et quia scriptura sancta de hoc tacere uidetur quid ueri similius aestimari possit sollicita inquisitione scrutari."

[15] Bruce M. Metzger and Roland E. Murphy, eds., *The New Oxford Annotated Bible* (New York, 1994), p. 338 OT.

let us now proceed with the order of the Scripture text that we are investigating."[16]

With the brief third prologue we switch back onto the allegorical track. Here in a dedicatory address to Bishop Acca, Bede summarizes what he has accomplished in the first two books, "with not a little sweat" (*non pauco sudore*),[17] and what he will discuss in the third, in which Saul, who represents the rule of the Jews, will give way to the rule of Christ's church.

The fourth prologue is, like the second, a divagation, but this last one poignantly records a personal loss. In this one, Bede says that he was ready after a little rest to take on the last section, but the resignation of his abbot Ceolfrid and his departure as a pilgrim to Rome (and to the other life) gave him such a shock he was unable to continue for a time. But now with the new abbot, Hwætberht, chosen by the community, Bede will finish the commentary, taking up at the place where David defeats the Philistines at Celia (Keilah), namely 1 Sam. 23:1, and provide it with a "mystical" interpretation.[18]

Let us now consider in a little more detail Bede's allegorical method in this commentary to see whether it is more extreme or differs from his approach in his other Old Testament commentaries. He certainly is assiduous about what he is doing, telling us not just in the prologues but at opportune moments throughout the commentary that personages, etymologized names, events, and numbers hold valuable symbolic meaning for the sensitive Christian who recognizes providential exemplary acts in divinely guided history.[19] For the modern reader,

---

[16] Bede, *In Sam.* 2 (p. 70, lines 94–95): "Sed quia in longum praefatio processit ipsum iam quem scrutemur ordinem scripturae inchoemus."

[17] Bede, *In Sam.* 3 (p. 137, line 1).

[18] See Bede, *In Sam.* 4 (p. 212, lines 1–28).

[19] See Bede, *In Sam.* 1 (p. 29, line 769–p. 30, line 769; and p. 52, lines 1698–1722).

the allegory may seem arbitrary, because Bede can assign meaning for an individual passage and transfer it to a completely different context, and a figure such as Saul can at one moment
stand for the perfidy of the Jewish people and in the next for
Christ the Savior. For Bede, as for Origen and the Alexandrian
school, for Augustine and Gregory, and for much of the patristic tradition, the assignment of symbolic meaning is flexible as
long as, says Augustine in the *De doctrina christiana*, it conforms
finally to the overarching rules of faith and love.[20] But more
than that, Bede's allegory is consistent with a certain internal
logic. He understands that great biblical figures such as Saul
and David were at various times virtuous and at others wicked,
sometimes great and holy and exemplary as God's chosen favor-
ites, at other times mean, reprehensible, and odious to God. So
they allegorically symbolize both *in bono* and *in malo*.[21]

Thus, at the very beginning of the commentary, Bede identifies Elcana, who has two wives—Phennena and Anna—with
Jesus Christ who has two wives—the Jewish synagogue and the
Christian Church. The interpretation is felicitous, because the
wife who symbolizes the Jews was fruitful in the past whereas
the wife who prefigures the Gentiles was barren until, through
God's favor, she produced Samson and then multiple children

---

[20] Augustine, *De doctrina christiana* 3.2.2, 3.10.15–16, and 3.27.38–39 (CCSL
32: p. 78 line 17 – p. 78, line 6; p. 86, line 13 – p. 88, line 46; p. 99, line 13
– p. 100, line 9). D. W. Robertson, trans., *On Christian Doctrine* (New York,
1958), writes in his introduction: "Underlying the specific techniques of
both interpretation and exposition of Scripture the principle of first importance in St. Augustine's mind is charity" (p. x).

[21] Bede elsewhere presents double aspects of personages who represent
both good and bad qualities, as in his commentary on Tobit, where the
father Tobias (Tobit) "represents the Jews in a double aspect: one good
[the people Israel], one bad [proud Jews of the sixth age]," whereas "the
younger Tobias represents Christ's humanity, while the angel Raphael,
who journeys with and counsels the young Tobias, represents Christ's divinity": Foley, introduction to *On Tobias*, in *Biblical Miscellany*, pp. 55–56.

representing the converted nations. Because for Bede *nomen est omen* (i.e. every word in the Bible has significance and names are fraught with symbolic meaning), the interpretation is reinforced by the etymologies of the Hebrew names that Jerome furnished in his *Liber interpretationis hebraicorum nominum* (Book of the Interpretation of Hebrew Names).[22] Because Elcana means "possession of God" (*dei possession*),[23] it makes sense for him to prefigure God's Son. Anna, meaning "his favor" (*gratia eius*), provides an allegorical type as (1) *gentilitas* 'paganism' and (2) *ecclesia* 'church.'[24] Anna likewise prefigures Mary, and her canticle as a matter of historical fact forms the textual basis of Mary's *Magnificat*. Her prophet-son, Samuel, whose name means "his name is God" (*nomen eius deus*), grows up serving God as a type of the obedient Jesus.[25] Within this mode, there is no problem with Samuel first serving as a type of Christ and, later on in the narrative, with David also prefiguring Christ. For David, says Bede, "nearly always in the Scriptures mystically signifies the Lord Christ, but sometimes in his members and sometimes in himself."[26]

More ingenious is what Bede does when he encounters a plurality of names in a passage. He then takes what the names signify in Hebrew and forms an amalgam that results in a poetic conceit. Thus with the very first verse, "There was a man of Ramathaim-Sophim, of Mount Ephraim, and his name was Elcana," Bede draws on Jerome to define Ramathaim as "their height[s]" (*excelsa eorum*), Sophim as "a look-out, observation

---

[22] The work is printed in CCSL 72, pp. 57–161.

[23] Bede, *In Sam.* 1 (p. 11, line 16).

[24] Bede, *In Sam.* 1 (p. 13, line 98).

[25] Bede, *In Sam.* 1 (p. 20, line 366).

[26] Bede, *In Sam.* 4 (p. 213, lines 64–66): "Quia Dauid paene semper in scripturis dum mystice accipitur dominum Christum sed modo in suis membris modo in se ipso significat…" According to Jerome, as expounded on by Bede, David's name means "manu fortis siue desiderabilis": e.g., *In Sam.* 3 (p. 143, line 251; and p. 147, line 432).

post" (*specula*), Ephraim as "fruitful or growing" (*frugifer siue crescens*) and Elcana, as noted above, "God's possession." This results in an aggregate interpretation:

> There was therefore one man from their heights, that is, from the look-out of men, from the fruitful and crop-yielding mountain, and his name is the possession of God: "One Lord, one faith, one Baptism, one God" (Eph. 4:5–6), who holds his beloved always and consecrates his dwelling in the spiritual hearts of the faithful. Those hearts, having transcended the earthly way of life with the whole effort of their mind, desire to spy out the supernal light of wisdom, possessing that mount, which, with the pomp of worldly empire destroyed, has increased by the crop of believing peoples, and has filled the whole earth.[27]

You can imagine what Bede does with rest of 1 Sam. 1:1: "And his name was Elcana, the son of Jeroham, the son of Eliu, the son of Thohu, the son of Suph, an Ephrahimite" (*Et nomen, inquit, eius Helcana filius Hieroam filii Heliu filii Thau filii Suph Efratheus*), seeing that "the names of the fathers of Elcana express life, faith, virtues, and sublimity."[28]

---

[27] Bede, *In Sam.* 1 (p. 11, lines 16–25): "Fuit ergo uir unus de excelsa eorum, id est uirorum specula de monte frugifero et crescente, et nomen eius Dei possessio, *unus dominus una fides unum baptisma unus Deus*, qui dilectam sibi semper habet consecratque mansionem in spiritalibus fidelium cordibus quae transcensa conuersatione terrena toto mentis adnisu supernum sapientiae lumen speculari desiderant illum possidens montem qui destructa mundialis imperii pompa creuit fruge credentium populorum et impleuit omnem terram." Translations of *In Sam.* are mine throughout.

[28] Bede, *In Sam.* 1 (p. 12, lines 57–58): "Nomina patrum Helcanae uitam fidem uirtutes et sublimitatem pandunt...." Bede, following Jerome, understands Hieroam to mean "merciful," Heliu "my God of him," Thau "sign," Suph "observer," and Ephrahim "rich or dusty," from which names

Significantly, what Bede does in interpreting 1 Samuel is not different from what he resolutely does in his other Old Testament commentaries, which survive in more manuscripts. In these commentaries, Bede is "following the footsteps of the Fathers," who similarly allegorize biblical personages.[29] We are all familiar with the traditional patristic allegorical interpretation of the Song of Songs, in which the Bridegroom signifies Christ and the bride, the Church. In his commentaries, even while engaging in traditional figural allegoresis, Bede discloses, often in sensitive and sometimes surprising metaphors, fresh points of comparison, new insights that delight and edify. For example, commenting on 1 Sam. 3:15, he does a charming exegesis on the meaning of the young Samuel asleep in the Temple as a type of Christ:

> The Lord remained in secret repose with the Father, with whom he does not cease to dispose and govern all things invisibly, awaiting the moment when with the night of vices repulsed, he might open up the doors of the virtues, when with the shadow of the Law fading away, he might unlock the entrance of evangelical truth; and where, with the sun of justice breathing in the heart of each one, he gazed at the risen radiance of faith. He, opening the ampler gifts of his Spirit, immediately promised the hoped for entrance of the eternal home in the heavens. That occurred not only at that time among the Jews but also happens today among us to this day. For whoever either has not yet received

---

Bede constructs quite a scenario in *In Sam.* 1 (p. 12, line 56 – p. 13, line 96). Note also how Bede plays with the names Bethel, Galgal, Masfat in *In Sam.* 1 (p. 66, line 2289 – p. 67, line 2306).

[29] Bede's frequent affirmation that he is "following the footsteps of the Fathers" (*sequens uestigia patrum*) signals that he is following patristic orthodoxy, not that he is slavishly and unoriginally simply copying their comments; as the noted above (see Introduction, p. 8), he is "following their tracks," not "*in* the their tracks." See further the essays in this volume by Roger Ray, Alan Thacker, and Joyce Hill.

the grace of Christ or, having received it, rejects it by the merits of sins, for such a one situated in the night of blindness, Christ, who always watches over his holy ones, sleeps, and has closed the entrance of his heavenly kingdom to him. But when the person receives the light of hoping for and seeking forgiveness, quickly "the Lord aroused as from sleep" (Ps. 77:65) opens the doors of the virtues, which during the oppressive evening of perfidy the person had closed off. Very beautifully concurring wih this sense, though with another trope, is the fact that while the Lord sleeps in the boat, the sailors are endangered; when he awakes, they are freed (Matt. 8:24–26).[30]

By counterpoising Samuel as a figure of Christ in the Old Testament and Christ himself in the New Testament, Bede conjoins type and anti-type.

In commenting on the following chapter, in which the Israelites are put to flight and the ark is captured by the Philistines, Bede first treats the battle in allegorical terms as a struggle between Judaism and the Gentiles, and then moves to a tropologi-

---

[30] Bede, *In Sam.* 1 (p. 38, lines 1114–31): "Manebat dominus in secreta quiete cum patre cum quo inuisibiliter omnia disponere et gubernare non cessat expectans quando depulsa nocte uitiorum uirtutum ostia panderet quando legis umbra decedente ueritatis euangelicae limina reseraret et statim ubi in corde cuiuspiam adflante sole iustitiae fidei conspiciebat iubar exortum aperiens ampliora sui spiritus dona perpetuae domus in caelis sperandum promittebat ingressum. Quod non solum tunc in Iudaeis sed et in nobis usque hodie geritur quicumque enim gratiam Christi aut nondum accepit uel acceptam culparum meritis abiecit huic in nocte caecitatis posito Christus qui semper in sanctis uigilat dormit caelestisque ei regni iam aditus occlusit; at dum lucem sperandae petendaeque ueniae recipit confestim *excitatus tamquam dormiens dominus* ostia uirtutum quae incumbente perfidiae uespera clauserat aperit. Cui sensui quamuis sub alio tropo pulcherrime concinit quod ipse dominus in naui dum dormit nautae periclitantur dum euigilat liberantur."

cal or moral interpretation, saying, "You should not think these events are only to be interpreted allegorically about the ancient state of the people of God so that they are not also suitable tropologically for you personally."[31] After urging the reader not to rely on his own merits but on the rock of God, he says: "Beware lest you turn your back to the blows of the enemy by sinning, but rather, according to the admonition of the apostle James, 'Resist the devil, and he will fly from you' (James 4:7)."[32] At the end of this extensive passage on moral conduct, he concludes with a pretty metaphor: "Now, having been preoccupied with this moral exposition, let us return to the order of the text, and seek in the ancient grove of the letter [the literal], fresh new fruits of spiritual allegory."[33]

Here we see how Bede, as elsewhere in the commentary, maintains the distinction between the allegorical mode that applies to the Church and the whole people of God and the tropological that pertains to individual moral behavior. Although he spends most of his efforts on the allegorical, he inserts the tropological at important junctures, usually with a direct address in the second person singular.

Bede directly addresses the reader, "lector," in the second (and sometimes third person) at critical points. No doubt this device derives from late antique models, particularly St. Jerome, who in the prologue to his Vulgate version of 1 Samuel, pleads: "I beg you, reader, not to consider my labor a rejection of the

---

[31] Bede, *In Sam.* 1 (p. 41, lines 1228–30): "Neque haec ita allegorice super antiqui Dei populi statu interpretata putes ut non etiam tibi tropologice conueniant."

[32] Bede, *In Sam.* 1 (p. 41, lines 1235–7): "Caue autem ne terga mentis ferientibus peccando uertas hostibus sed potius iuxta quod ammonet apostolus Petrus resiste diabolo et fugiet a te."

[33] Bede, *In Sam.* 1 (p. 41, lines 1262–4): "Verum his morali expositione praeoccupatis redeamus ad ordinem lectionis et in antiquissimo litterae nemore noua spiritalis allegoriae poma quaeramus."

ancients."[34] The address to the reader presages later writers' admonitions, such as Dante's addresses to the reader in the *Divine Comedy*. In chapter 6, Bede directs a caveat at the reader about the sinful behavior of the sons of Heli. Specifying their wickedness on both the literal and allegorical levels, he ends with the remark: "We have discussed these matters more meticulously so that you, reader, may be mindful of what you should avoid in detail."[35] Sometimes Bede makes his address to the reader in the form of a challenge. For example, "Do you want proof for what I'm saying?"[36]

In his commentary on 1 Samuel, Bede embellishes his text with a number of rhetorical figures, but, as always, he uses these with sobriety and restraint. For instance, here is a typical passage, in which he engages in wordplay (*repetitio, conduplicatio*) and transferred meaning arising from allegorical interpretation:

> "*Caput* autem Dagon et duae *palmae manuum* eius *abscissae* erant super *limen*" (1 Sam. 5:4). *Caput* omnis peccati superbia diaboli et opus idolatriae quod quasi duabus *palmis* impietatis professione laudum et uictimarum caerimoniis agebatur a cognato corpore, id est a cohaerentibus sibi turbis seductorum, *abscissum* iam iamque *foras*que mittendum Christi augescente triumpho parebat. Qui quasi *caput* et *manus* Dagon *trunci* in *limine* iacere monstrabat cum ait: "Nunc iudicium est mundi, nunc princeps huius mundi eicietur *foras*." (John 12:31)

> "*Porro* Dagon truncus manserat in loco suo" (1 Sam. 5:5). *Porro* populus idolotriae abiecta et *elimin*ata professione atque operatione daemonica inter eos qui in fide praecesserant quasi

---

[34] *Prologus sancti Hieronymi in libro Regum*, in *Biblia sacra iuxta Latinam Vulgatam versionem ad codicem fidem*, vol. 5 (Rome, 1944) p. 9, line 5: "Obsecro te lector, ne laborem meum reprehensionem aestimes antiquorum."

[35] Bede, *In Sam.* 1 (p. 29, line 768 – p. 30, line 769): "Haec enucleatius diximus ut per singula lector quid caueas memineris."

[36] Bede, *In Sam.* 1 (p. 53, lines 1735–6): "Vis probari quae dicimus?"

iuxta arcam Dei humilis submissusque remanere quam cum diabolo *foras* mitti, id est ab ecclesâe memberis anathematizari, malebat."[37]

Notice that not only are the words repeated and played upon but also their clausal relationships are parallel (e.g., the initial positions of *caput...caput; porro...porro*).

In a passage a little further on, glossing the verse "and the cart came into the field of Josue a Bethsamite, and stood there" (1 Sam. 6:14), Bede says that the Church prepares to make a resting place wherever there are hearts prepared to receive Christ, for "*Talis* semper ecclesiae profectus, *talis* eius erat in nationes aduentus, *talis* erit et reditus ad Israhel."[38] Such moderate play with syntax, tense, and word repetition is characteristic of Bede's commentaries.

Bede is a great stylist, so in this commentary we are not surprised to find devices such as chiasmus and envelope structure. For instance, interpreting the verse "And all the house of Israel

---

[37] Bede, *In Sam.* 1 (p. 47, line 1508 – p. 48, line 1522): "'The *head* of Dagon and both the *palms* of his hands were *cut off* upon the *threshold*' (1 Sam. 5:4). The *head* of all sin is the devil's pride and the work of idolatry which is done by the kindred body as if with two *hands* by the profession of impiety and by ceremonies of praises and sacrificial victims; that work appears now as *cut off* and *cast out* from the related body, that is, from the adherent throngs of seducers, as the triumph of Christ augurs. He intimates as it were that the head and hands of Dagon's trunk lie on the *threshold* when he says: "Now is the judgment of the world, now will the prince of this world be *cast out*" (John 12:31).' '*Then* only the trunk of Dagon remained in its place' (1 Sam. 5:5). *Then* the people, with their profession of idolatry abandoned and the diabolical work among them eliminated who had gone forth in faith, that people preferred to remain next to the ark of God humble and obedient rather than be *cast out* with the devil, that is, be excommunicated from the members of the Church."

[38] Bede, *In Sam.* 1 (p. 53, lines 1764–6): "Such is the progress of the Church, such was its advent among the nations, such will be its return to Israel."

rested following the Lord" (*Et requieuit omnis domus Israhel post dominum*: 1 Sam. 7:2), Bede writes: "Extremam conuersae in fine Iudaeae felicitatem typice designat" ("The verse allegorically indicates the utmost felicity in the end of converted Judaea"), where *extremam* reaches across to modify *felicitatem*, surrounding *conversae* and its referent *Iudaeae*, all meaningfully enclosing the central kernel *in fine*.[39] No one has as yet done a systematic analysis of Bede's use of *cursus* (the system of rhythmical clause endings), but it is strikingly classical. To take just a couple instances from the first prologue, we find at the end of a thirteen-line question, the conclusion "...sensum qui nos uiuaciter interius *castigando erudiendo consolando reficiat*," ("...the allegorical sense of Scripture which restores us by chastising, educating, consoling"),[40] a *cursus* that also exhibits *parechesis* (repetition of sounds). This prologue then concludes with the aurally satisfying *cursus*, which compares the remark of St. Peter (Acts 3:24) "qui cuncta quibus diebus sint aptanda perdocuit qualiter singula sint eisdem diebus *aptanda quaeramus*" ("who taught that all the things were to be applied in his days as we should seek to apply each of them in our own").[41]

So, since Bede's allegorical treatment of 1 Samuel is original even while following traditional paths, and since its literary qualities are equal to those in his other works, what are we to conclude about its loss of prominence historically? Let us reconsider the possible reasons given at the beginning of this essay. One supposition might be that it was just considered unimportant by contemporaries. That will not do, because the commentary deals with a major historical biblical book, one that Bede also partly explored in the popular *In Regum librum XXX quaestiones*. Bede's biblical commentaries were prized and sought after during and immediately after his lifetime. We have

---

[39] Bede, *In Sam.* 1 (p. 59, lines 1995–6).

[40] Bede, *In Sam.* 1, Prol. (p. 9, line 34).

[41] Bede, *In Sam.* 1, Prol. (p. 10, line 64).

the letters of Anglo-Saxon missionaries on the Continent, such as Boniface and Lull, begging for copies of Bede's works.[42] Alcuin and the Carolingians honored and read his writings and because of them bestowed on Bede the title of "Father of the Church," elevating his authority to that of Ambrose, Augustine, Jerome, and Gregory.[43]

What then is the reason for its neglect? Is it its hard Latin and its length? This commentary on 1 Samuel, composed at the height of Bede's hermeneutic career, is written in a clear but erudite Latin that admittedly demands much of the reader. It employs a very extensive vocabulary with recondite verbs, such as *ingruere* ("to advance threateningly"), *exinterare* (to disembowel"), *impertire* ("to impart"), *delibare* ("to skim off"). Its prose is challenging. But the difficult Latinity is not a sufficient explanation for its neglect; for, if that were a hindrance, how could we account for Aldhelm's wildly popular tour-de-force, that *opus geminatum* (twinned work) in both prose and verse, *De virginitate*, with its excruciatingly recherché vocabulary?[44] Those works may lack Bede's finesse but the prose version especially with its convoluted prose style is more than comparable in linguistic difficulty. Then is it the length of Bede's work that is the problem? This commentary indeed extends to 272 pages

[42] Boniface, *Epistolae* 75, 76, 91 (MGH, Epistolae selectae I, pp. 158, 159, 207); Abbot Cuthbert, *Epistola* 116 (MGH, Epistolae selectae I, p. 251); and Lull, *Epistola* 125, 126, 127 (MGH, Epistolae selectae I, pp. 263–5).

[43] For Bede's reputation as a Doctor of the Church, see the essays in this volume by Roger Ray, Alan Thacker, and Joyce Hill.

[44] For information about Aldhelm and his Latin style see my article and bibliography in *Medieval England: an Encyclopedia*, ed. Paul Szarmach, M. Teresa Tavormina and Joel T. Rosenthal (New York, 1998), pp. 15–17, to which should be added Andy Orchard, *The Poetic Art of Aldhelm*, Cambridge Studies in Anglo-Saxon England 8 (Cambridge, 1998): and Michael Lapidge, *The Anglo-Saxon Library* (Oxford, 2006), pp. 93-105, 178-91.

in four books—not light and easy reading surely; but it is only twenty pages longer than the next contender, the historically well-represented *In Genesim*; and it is considerably shorter than his even more popular New Testament commentary on Luke. So none of these factors seem enough to explain the paucity of medieval manuscripts of the work.

My own suggestion for a solution to this quandary is that manuscripts of Bede's *In primam partem Samuhelis* did not find their way into the right Carolingian libraries at the right time in the ninth century in order to be included in the commentary collections formed during that period, as the absence of Bede's text in the commentaries of Claudius of Turin and Hrabanus Maurus indicates. The text may not have arrived in a timely fashion on the Continent because the scriptorium of Wearmouth-Jarrow, heavily burdened with requests for the works of its famous house-author, found it difficult even with Bishop Lull's specific request for this commentary to furnish copies of this long work. The lengthy *In primam partem Samuhelis* had to compete with the demand for Bede's commentaries on popular books of the Bible such as Genesis and Luke. "The pressure of such demands from the continent," Malcolm Parkes has written, "together with demands which had arisen from within England itself, seems to have produced something approaching a crisis at Wearmouth-Jarrow." Abbot Cuthbert encountered all sorts of problems, especially labor problems, caused by the winter cold.[45] Bede's *In primam partem Samuhelis* had to wait its turn for copying, though Cuthbert assured Lull he would meet the Bishop's request, "if we live."[46] Whatever copy or copies of the commentary reached the Continent apparently did not get to the right scholars in time.

Once it was left out of the canon of commentaries that formed the basis of exegetical study in the Middle Ages, this

---

[45] See Malcolm Parkes, *The Scriptorium of Wearmouth-Jarrow* (Jarrow Lecture, 1982), p. 15.

[46] Quoted by Parkes, *Scriptorium*, p. 15; see also p. 16.

commentary never gained acceptance. It may be difficult for us who live in an age of great university and national libraries filled with printed books, of interlibrary loan, of databases and the internet, to comprehend how capricious the distribution of manuscripts was in the early Middle Ages. Although Bede had access to one of the finest libraries of his age, it lacked many of what we consider standard classical, educational, exegetical, and patristic works. Its shelves held no works by Cicero, or later rhetoricians such as Marius Victorinus or Atilius Fortunatianus. There was nothing of Boethius and very little of Origen. It did not have Cassiodorus's *Institutiones* and his rhetorical treatises. It featured only Eugippius's excerpts from Augustine's *De doctrina christiana*, with the whole fourth book excluded.[47] If a generation later such works are available to Alcuin in the library of York Minster, other works are missing from that roster.[48] The presence and survival of a manuscript of any work was chancy. Bede's *In primam partem Samuhelis* was apparently just not available to Carolingian compilers for inclusion in the exegetical and homiletic compendia and *catenae* (collections of excerpts from the writings of biblical commentators) that constituted the basis for medieval hermeneutics into the twelfth century.

---

[47] See Roger Ray's essay above p. 23. The edition by Pius Knöll of Eugippius, *Excerpta ex operibus S. Augustini*, CSEL 9.1 (Vienna, 1885), has been widely and justly criticized but not replaced. See CPL, no. 676: "Opus tanti momenti ad textum Augustini emendandum, proh dolor pessime edidit P. Knöll" [This work of such great importance for the emendation of Augustine's text has alas been miserably edited by P. Knöll]. Bede also used Eugippius's excerpts for his *Collectio ex opusculis sancti Augustini in epistulas Pauli apostoli*; see Fransen, "D'Eugippius à Bède le Vénérable." Bede's Latin text remains unedited, but David Hurst published a translation from five early manuscripts: see *Excerpts from Augustine on the Letters of Paul*, trans. David Hurst, Cistercian Studies Series 183 (Kalamazoo, Mich., 1999).

[48] Alcuin, *Versus de sanctis Euboricensis* (p. 122, line 1538–p. 126, line 1562).

Hence, unlike some of Bede's other commentaries, this work of his is lacking in the *Glossa Ordinaria.* This circumstance helps provide an explanation why Bede's *In primam partem Samuhelis* was the least known and cited of all his major works.

Footsteps of His Own:
Bede's Commentary on Ezra–Nehemiah

Scott DeGregorio

A T THE FOREFRONT of Bede's achievements as an exegete stands his ground-breaking work on Ezra-Nehemiah.[1] A massive work in three books, this Bedan commentary is the only complete exegesis of this portion of the Old Testament to come down to us from either the patristic or medieval era. The existence of the work adds weight to Roger Ray's claim in his contribution to this volume that Bede "wrote as if he were blazing—not following—trails."[2] However much Bede declared himself to be pursuing the Fathers' footsteps, none had been left behind for him to trace in this instance.[3] The absence of a

---

[1] This work, edited by Hurst in CCSL 119A, is Bede's fifth longest Old Testament commentary, behind his treatments of the tabernacle, Genesis, the Song of Songs, and 1 Samuel. According to Max Laistner's *A Hand-List of Bede Manuscripts* (Ithaca, N.Y., 1943), pp. 39–41, it survives in thirty-two manuscripts, placing it third in terms of sheer numbers amidst Bede's ten Old Testament commentaries.

[2] See above Ray, "Who Did Bede Think He Was?" p. 24. The same point has been made about Bede's commentaries on the tabernacle and first temple, which were also firsts of their kind: see Arthur G. Holder, "New Treasures for Old in Bede's *De tabernaculo* and *De templo*," *Revue Bénédictine* 99 (1989): 237–9.

[3] Prior to Bede, Origen appears to have written some sermons on Ezra, as we know from Cassiodorus, who had one of these translated from Greek into Latin: see *Institutiones* 1.6, ed. R. A. B. Mynors, (Oxford, 1937), p. 27. But none of these works have survived. Moreover, Origen and earlier

prior exegetical tradition on Ezra-Nehemiah makes the references to Jerome in the commentary's prologue all the more interesting.[4] Jerome commented prolifically on the prophets and was the major authority on those books.[5] But nowhere did he work out anything like a complete allegorical interpretation of Ezra-Nehemiah, a task that would fall to Bede.

The mention of this "famous translator and teacher of Holy Scripture"[6] at the outset of the work therefore tells us more about Bede's own studied sense of self-presentation than it does

Fathers in general appear to have preferred the Septuagint's Esdras A to the canonical account, which is the subject of Bede's commentary: on this point, see Thomas Denter, *Die Stellung der Bücher Esdras im Kanon des Alten Testamentes. Eine kanon-geschichtliche Untersuchung*, Diss. Freiburg (Marienstatt, 1962), pp. 53–81; and P.-M. Bogaert, "Les livres d'Esdras et leur numerotation dans l'histoire du canon de la Bible latine," *Revue Bénédictine* 110 (2000): 6–7, 19.

[4] Bede, *In Ezram* Prol. (p. 237, lines 1–21). After quoting a passage dealing with Ezra in a letter of Jerome, Bede concludes his prologue as follows: "In quo nimirum opere maximo nobis adiumento fuit praefatus ecclesiae magister Hieronimus in explanatione prophetarum qui eadem quae Ezras et Neemias facta scribunt ipsi sub figura Christi et ecclesiae fienda praedixerant." [In this work the greatest help to us was the aforementioned teacher of the Church, Jerome, in his explanation of the prophets, who themselves had foretold that the same events which Ezra and Nehemiah wrote about would be carried out under the figure of Christ and the Church.] Trans. Scott DeGregorio, *Bede: On Ezra and Nehemiah*, Translated Texts for Historians 47 (Liverpool, 2006), p. 2. All subsequent translations are from the latter.

[5] See J. N. D. Kelly, *Jerome: His Life, Writings, and Controversies* (London, 1975), pp. 290–5; and Pierre Jay, *L'exégèse de Saint Jérôme, d'après son Commentaire sur Isaïe* (Paris, 1985),pp. 11–18.

[6] Bede, *In Ezram* Prol. (p. 237, line 1): "Eximius sacrae interpres ac doctor scripturae…". Trans. DeGregorio, *On Ezra and Nehemiah*, p. 1.

about his actual "use" of sources.[7] Though breaking new ground, he nonetheless portrays himself as adapting a pre-existing tradition, as following the weighty *auctoritas* of a venerated Church Father, Jerome. It was a shrewd move, consistent with Bede's authorial positioning elsewhere, and no doubt loaded with the same rhetorical intention.[8] Yet such purposeful self-effacement should in no way blind us to the daring originality of the work or the high quality of its exegesis.[9] For Bede in this commentary demonstrates a command of the genre commensurate with that of those eminent expositors of the Sacred Page he so revered, even if the tug of *humilitas* required he say otherwise.

Ezra-Nehemiah and the Parameters of Allegorical Interpretation

The main source for the history of Israel under Persian rule, Ezra-Nehemiah tells the story of the rebuilding of the second temple and the restoration of its cult and community.[10] While

---

[7] Henry Mayr-Harting, *The Venerable Bede, the Rule of St. Benedict, and Social Class* (Jarrow Lecture, 1976), p. 19, was therefore right to observe that Bede's commentary "...probably does not depend on Jerome as heavily as the preface implies."

[8] See above, pp. 17, for Roger Ray's insightful remarks on *captatio benevolentiae.*

[9] On Bede's originality as an exegete, see further Holder, "New Treasures and Old," p. 249; Roger Ray, "What Do We Know about Bede's Commentaries?," *Recherches de théologie ancienne et médiévale* 49 (1982): 11; Bernard Robinson, "The Venerable Bede as Exegete," *Downside Review* 112 (1994): 221; and Scott DeGregorio, "The Venerable Bede on Prayer and Contemplation," *Traditio* 54 (1999): 5–8.

[10] For general accounts of Ezra-Nehemiah and its place in Jewish history, see Leon Wood, *A Survey of Israel's History* (Grand Rapids, Mich., 1986), pp. 330–45; and Lester Grabbe, *Ezra-Nehemiah*, Old Testament Readings (London, 1998), pp. 11–68.

modern English bibles print the text as two individual books, entitled Ezra and Nehemiah respectively, they exist as a single work in their Hebrew and Greek forms.[11] Structurally, the narrative as a whole may be divided into three neat units, each involving a return from exile and projects of restoration and reform. Ezra 1–6 describes the first return of Jewish exiles to Judah in 538 BC, authorized by Cyrus the Great (559–530 BC) in order to promote the rebuilding of the temple in Jerusalem. Led by Zerubbabel and the high priest Jeshua, the exiles erect an altar upon arriving and lay the temple foundations, but in the face of Samaritan opposition they do not complete the temple itself until 516 BC, in the sixth year of Darius I (522–486 BC). Next, Ezra 7–10 relates the mission of Ezra, who fifty-eight years later is permitted by Artaxerxes I (465–425 BC) to lead back a second group of exiles. A priest and scribe of God's Law, Ezra returns with the explicit aim of rebuilding the Jewish community in accordance with the teaching of the Torah, witnessed above all in his efforts to reform the people and their leaders by dissuading them from intermarriage with foreigners. Nehemiah

---

[11] In the Hebrew Bible, the work is known as "Ezra-Nehemyah," while in the Greek of the Septuagint it is referred to as "Esdras B," in contrast to another version, "Esdras A," which is not deemed canonical and so not reckoned a part of the Hebrew canon. For a recent review of these textual issues, see Bogaert, "Les livres d'Esdras," esp. pp. 5–12. The division into two books, first attested in Origen's list of Old Testament books preserved in Eusebius, *Historia ecclesiastica* 6.25.2 (SC 41: pp. 125–6), did not become standard until long after Bede's time. In the preface to his Vulgate translation of Ezra-Nehemiah, Jerome states that he has based his work on a single book that he had in the Hebrew: see *Praefatio sancti Hieronymi in libro Ezrae*, in *Biblia sacra iuxta Latinam Vulgatam versionem ad codicem fidem*, vol. 8 (Rome, 1950), p. 4, and cf. *In Ezram* Praef. (p. 237, line 5), which, quoting Jerome's *Epistola* 53 (CSEL 54: p. 461, line 20), likewise states that the materials "are recounted in a single book" (*in uno uolumine narrantur*).

1–13 forms the third and final section, the events of which take place some thirteen years later either in the reign of the same Artaxerxes or a subsequent ruler of this name.[12] Dismayed that much of Jerusalem still lies in ruin, Nehemiah, cupbearer at the Persian court, is granted permission to return to the city to organize the reconstruction of its damaged walls. After overcoming foreign opposition and seeing the project through to completion, he too shifts his attention to problems plaguing the Jewish community, and the story concludes with Nehemiah initiating a series of reforms, targeting unjust taxation, mixed marriages, and lax Sabbath observance.

In the Prologue to the commentary, Bede announces his intention to approach these events allegorically. As Book 1 opens he wastes no time acclimating his audience to the allegorical mode. Using the first hundred lines like a second prologue, he provides a handy summary of the story's symbolic terrain. In the spiritual sense, says Bede, Scripture equates the temple not only with Christ but equally with the Church understood as the whole body of the righteous.[13] Solomon's building the first temple in seven years and finishing it in the eighth thus signifies the fact that now, in the present age, Christ is building a Church to which all believers will be gathered in the eighth or final age of heavenly rest.[14] Its subsequent destruction by the Babylonians and the captivity of the Jewish people meanwhile symbolize the fall of the baptized through temptation and their resulting imprisonment in sin.[15] By contrast, their

---

[12] Bede of course knew nothing of the view of some modern scholars that the historical Ezra may in fact have lived later than Nehemiah; see for example George Anderson, *A Critical Introduction to the Old Testament* (London, 1964), pp. 220–2.

[13] *In Ezram* 1 (p. 241, lines 1–4).

[14] *In Ezram* 1 (p. 241, lines 21–27).

[15] *In Ezram* 1 (p. 242, lines 42–48).

release from captivity, as well as such events as the return to Jerusalem, the rebuilding of the temple, and even the recovery of the holy temple vessels, designate the "return of penitents to the Church" through repentance and good works.[16] Summing up his main purpose in the work, Bede concludes this opening summary as follows:

> But since the prophet Ezra sufficiently explains how all these things came to pass, I want to relate some episodes from this book and, so far as the Lord will grant, to expound them according to the spiritual sense so that it may be more clearly disclosed how those who have perished due to negligence and error should be brought back to repentance, by how much grace of God and by how much effort of their own pardon ought to be sought and procured for the sins they have committed, and how these same penitents together with those who have recently come to the faith should build one and the same house of Christ and together look forward to the ceremonies of its dedication in the future.[17]

In addition to providing a helpful summary of the whole, these opening remarks make it clear that Bede's treatment of the second temple will depart in some obvious ways from his discussions of the Solomonic Temple and its predecessor, namely the Mosaic Tabernacle.

To be sure, *De templo* and *De tabernaculo* do share many methodological, stylistic, and thematic parallels with his treatment of Ezra-Nehemiah, and certainly it is reasonable to surmise that he conceived them as a group, a trilogy on the history of the temple in its successive phases. Even so, we should take care to

---

[16] *In Ezram* 1 (p. 242, line 73 – p. 243, line 78).

[17] *In Ezram* 1 (p. 243, lines 78–88): "Verum quia de his omnibus propheta Ezras quomodo sint facta sufficienter explicat libet de uolumine eius aliqua commemorare et prout dominus dederit spiritali sensu exponere quo manifestius patefiat qualiter his qui per neglegentiam uel errorem

attend to some important differences that set his work on Ezra-Nehemiah apart.

First, as the passage just quoted indicates, and as the ensuing exegesis makes clearer, the bulk of the story told in Ezra-Nehemiah is not primarily about the reconstruction of material buildings.[18] By contrast, the subject of the tabernacle and temple commentaries remains those material structures themselves, how each and every one of their parts betokens some aspect of the Church, conceived simultaneously as an earthly and heavenly reality.[19] Because Ezra-Nehemiah contains far less in the way of architectural description, Bede evidently saw that it was not suited to the same mode of analysis. Instead of copious lists of architectural features, he would encounter a narrative wherein the temple's material reconstruction constitutes a relatively small part. Its chief interest is the reconstruction of something human and spiritual—the faith of the Jewish people themselves.[20] With its controlling images of exile and repatriation, of destruction and reconstruction, of loss and recovery, the saga of their journey back to a state of spiritual integrity before Yahweh could thus be aligned by Bede with a particular spiritual condition experienced by the Christian—namely, the condition of being separated from the community of the Church through sin and returning to it through repentance.

perierant sit ad paenitentiam redeundum quanta Dei gratia quanto ipsorum conatu sit admissorum poscenda uel impetranda uenia quomodo idem paenitentes una cum eis qui nuper ad fidem uenerant unam eandemque Christi domum aedificent ac pariter in futuro dedicationis illius sollemnia expectent." Trans. DeGregorio, *On Ezra and Nehemiah*, p. 9.

[18] For example, only a handful of verses from the ten chapters comprising the Book of Ezra are devoted to descriptions of the temple or to its rebuilding.

[19] See Arthur G. Holder, "Allegory and History in Bede's Interpretation of Sacred Architecture," *American Benedictine Review* 40 (1989): 115–31, esp. pp. 117–19.

[20] On this point, see Wood, *Survey of Israel's History*, p. 337.

Scott DeGregorio

According to the Mystical Sense: Sin and Repentance

The decision to correlate the narrative sequence of Ezra-Ne-hemiah with the spiritual experience of sin and repentance was Bede's own; none of this comes from Jerome. Throughout the commentary, Bede develops the parallel on simultaneous levels and with varying degrees of specificity. The first of these levels, targeting the whole body of the elect, is the most pervasive, its development beginning right away with Bede's treatment of the first two verses of Ezra. There we read of the proclamation issued by the Persian conqueror Cyrus the Great allowing the Jews who have long been exiled in Babylonia to return to Jerusalem to rebuild the temple. After moving through various details associated with the literal-historical sense of these verses, Bede reads them *iuxta mysticos sensus*, that is, "according to their mystical senses."[21] Cyrus here represents Christ, the returning Jews, those whom He frees from sin and leads to salvation:

> So the Lord made Cyrus like his only-begotten Son, our God and Lord, Jesus Christ, because just as Cyrus freed God's people when he destroyed the kingdom of the Chaldeans, sent them back to their homeland, ordered that the temple destroyed by fire in Jerusalem be rebuilt, and even took care to publicize this edict in writing in order that Jeremiah's words might be fulfilled in which he predicted that this would happen, so in the same way the mediator of God and men, having destroyed the devil's reign over the world, reclaims his elect who have been scattered by the devil's tyranny and gathers them into his Church.[22]

[21] See the essay in this volume by Calvin Kendall for discussion of Bede's views on Scripture's manifold senses; for additional comment, see Charles Jones, "Some Introductory Remarks on Bede's *Commentary on Genesis*," *Sacris Erudiri* 19 (1970): 151–66; and Robinson, "Bede as Exegete," pp. 202–4.

[22] *In Ezram* 1 (p. 245, lines 178–87): "Assimilauit ergo Cyrum dominus unigenito filio suo Deo et domino nostro Iesu Christo quia sicut ille de-

Later in Books 2 and 3, this Christ-like mission of redeeming the elect is passed on to the figures of Ezra and Nehemiah, who equally assume the role of saviors of their people.[23]

The focus of this first allegorical level, however, remains steadily on the need for repentance itself, on that progression from the destruction and captivity of sin to the safety of salvation. The two central movements of the first half of the story, the journey from Babylon to Jerusalem and the reconstruction of the temple, are treated by Bede as potent figures of that progression. The journey back to Jerusalem, for instance, teaches us that "…what occurred once for a single people takes place on a daily basis amidst all those who repent after committing sins: those who through negligence have fallen into the temptations and snares of the devil rise again with divine help through the exercise of penance."[24] Similarly, the reason the second temple took longer to build than the first is that "it takes great effort for someone who by sinning shows his contempt for the sacraments of the faith he has received to win back his former worthiness, because to him easy purification through the water of baptism cannot be given again, but the foul crime must be washed away

structo Chaldeorum imperio populum Dei liberauit ac patriam remisit templumque quod erat incensum in Hierosolimis reaedificari praecepit et hoc ipsum edictum etiam per litteras manifestare curauit ut implerentur uerba Hieremiae quibus hoc futurum esse praedixit, ita mediator Dei et hominum destructo per orbem diaboli regno electos suos qui erant dispersi ab eius tyrannide reuocatos in suam congregat ecclesiam." Trans. DeGregorio, *On Ezra and Nehemiah*, p. 13.

[23] On Ezra and Nehemiah as figures of Christ, see *In Ezram* 2 (p. 309, line 858 – p. 310, line 912; p. 336, line 1957 – p. 337, line 1997); and *In Ezram* 3 (p. 339, lines 5–17, 28–32).

[24] *In Ezram* 1 (p. 261, lines 785–9): "Quod ergo de uno populo semel factum est hoc de omnibus post peccata paenitentibus cotidie solet actitari dum hi qui per neglegentiam in temptationes et laqueos inciderunt diaboli per industriam paenitentiae diuinitus adiuti resurgent." Trans. DeGregorio, *On Ezra and Nehemiah*, p. 37.

through the long labour of penance, copious streams of tears, and the unremitting toil of continence."[25] Only through the miraculous aid of Christ and His sacraments, Bede is continuously at pains to emphasize, is it possible for the temple's completion and dedication—i.e. the Church's completion in heaven—to reach fulfillment.[26]

Connected to the foregoing is a further level of signification. Working alongside Christ in this providential economy are those here on earth chosen to execute the work of rebuilding, namely those whom He selects to the priestly calling.[27] For "when after baptism we again incur death by sinning, we must

[25] *In Ezram* 2 (p. 305, lines 699–704): "...sed multi laboris est eum qui accepta fidei sacramenta peccando contemnit pristinam recipere dignitatem quia non huic facilis emundatio per aquam baptismi denuo dari potest sed infectum scelus longo paenitentiae labore largis lacrimarum fluentis districtiore continentiae sudore eluendum est." Trans. DeGregorio, *On Ezra and Nehemiah*, p. 106.

[26] See Sister Mary Thomas Aquinas Carroll, *The Venerable Bede: His Spiritual Teachings*, Catholic University of America Studies in Medieval History 9 (Washington, D.C., 1946), pp. 99–144, for a discussion of the sacraments as Bede treats them in his writings.

[27] For supplemental discussion of Bede and pastoral care, see Alan Thacker, "Monks, Preaching and Pastoral Care," in *Pastoral Care before the Parish*, ed. John Blair and Richard Sharpe (Leicester, 1992), pp. 137–70. esp. 152–60; Thomas Eckenrode, "The Venerable Bede and the Pastoral Affirmation of the Christian Message in Anglo-Saxon England," *The Downside Review* 99 (1981): 258–78; Sarah Foot, "Parochial Ministry in Early Anglo-Saxon England: The Role of the Monastic Communities," in *The Ministry: Clerical and Lay. Papers read at the 1988 Summer Meeting and the 1989 Winter Meeting of the Ecclesiastical History Society*, ed. W. J. Sheils and Diana Wood, Studies in Church History 26 (Oxford, 1989), pp. 43–54; and Judith McClure, "Bede's *Notes on Genesis* and the Training of the Anglo-Saxon Clergy," in *The Bible in the Medieval World: Essays in Memory of Beryl Smalley*, ed. Katherine Walsh and Diana Wood, Studies in Church History, *Subsidia* 4 (Oxford, 1985), pp. 17–30.

come to life again through this same faith by repenting and be returned once more to the fellowship of the faithful *through the reconciliation of priests of the Church* (my emphasis)."[28] Bede makes it clear that this is a select group: just as only some were sent back to Jerusalem to rebuild the temple, so "it is not the duty of everyone but only of the perfect to labor in the building up of this Church even by preaching to others."[29]

Since the work of repentance owes so much to this select body of preachers, Bede devotes ample space to the nature of their office. He returns to three themes again and again. First of all, he stresses that

> whoever has decided to teach others should first teach himself, and that he who aims to instruct his neighbors to fear and love God should first make himself worthy for the office of teacher by serving God more eagerly, lest by chance he should hear from the Apostle: *You, then, who teach others, do you not teach yourself? You who preach against stealing, do you steal?*[30]

---

[28] *In Ezram* 1 (p. 276, lines 1390–3): "et cum post baptisma denuo mortem peccati incurrimus per eandem necesse est fidem paenitendo reuiuiscamus ac per reconciliationem sacerdotum ecclesiae rursus fidelium coetui reddamur." Trans. DeGregorio, *On Ezra and Nehemiah*, p. 60.

[29] *In Ezram* 1 (p. 248, lines 276–8): "...non tamen omnium sed perfectorum solummodo est in aedificationem eiusdem ecclesiae etiam aliis praedicando laborare." Trans. DeGregorio, *On Ezra and Nehemiah*, pp. 16–17.

[30] *In Ezram* 1 (p. 272, lines 1240–8): "Sic autem et in spirituali aedificatione sic omnimodis necesse est ut quisquis alios docere decreuerit prius se ipsum doceat qui proximos ad timorem uel ad amorem Dei instituere intendit primo se ipsum instantius Deo seruiendo dignum doctoris officio reddat ne audiat ab apostolo: *Qui ergo doces alium te ipsum non doces qui praedicas non furandum furaris;* unde et ipse de se apostolus: *Castigo,* inquit, *corpus meum et seruituti subicio ne forte aliis praedicans ipse reprobus efficiar.*" Trans. DeGregorio, *On Ezra and Nehemiah*, p. 54. Arthur G. Holder,

If they are to administer the sacrament of penance to others, those called to the sacerdotal office must remain pure in both deed and doctrine, never forgetting "the sacred state by which they were consecrated to the Lord through the Holy Spirit on the day of redemption, and which they prepare their hearers to receive as well."[31] Otherwise they must be ejected from the priesthood, like those returnees in Ezra 2:61–63 who, despite their priestly descent, were banished from altar service because of their impure origins.[32] In addition to priestly purity, Bede makes much of the need for teachers to go beyond verbal instruction by setting righteous examples for their audience. Those in positions of authority must strive to surpass their subjects in the performance of good works, for in this way "their subjects are incited by their good examples and, now devout, they carry out the duties appropriate to their station in life and, admonished by their pious exhortations, they delight to pour forth copious tears for the errors they have committed."[33] In Bede's view, the work of repentance is as much a matter of good example as it is of sound doctrine. Thus he acknowledges that it is Ezra's mourning over the people's sins that moves them to

"The Venerable Bede on the Mysteries of Our Salvation," *American Benedictine Review* 42 (1991): 154–5, has noted the prominence of this theme in *De tabernaculo* and *De templo* as well.

[31] *In Ezram* 2 (p. 321, lines 1358–61): "Oportet enim ut doctores ecclesiae numquam obliuiscantur sanctimoniae qua ipsi sunt domino consecrati per spiritum sanctum in die redemptionis ad quam suscipiendam etiam suos auditores instituant." Trans. DeGregorio, *On Ezra and Nehemiah*, p. 130.

[32] *In Ezram* 1 (p. 256, lines 611–18).

[33] *In Ezram* 3 (p. 367, line 1145 – p. 368, line 1151): "Cum enim praesules quantum honore praestant tantum etiam bonis operibus subditos anteire satagunt tunc et idem subditi bonis eorum incitati exemplis suae gradum uitae iam deuoti exsequuntur eorumque piis exhortationibus ammoniti lacrimas pro admissis erratibus…crebras fundere delectantur." Trans. DeGregorio, *On Ezra and Nehemiah*, pp. 194–5. For further dis-

guilt and penance, and later interprets Nehemiah's lament over the ruined city walls as signifying any believer's need to bewail the destruction wrought by sin.[34] Finally, in Book 3 especially, Bede's attention turns to the theme of the heavenly rewards that await good priests.[35] Like the choir of singers who enter the rebuilt city in Neh. 12:37, priests who have endeavored to repair the souls of the faithful will enter heaven to receive the payment for their endeavors. As a result of the more sacrosanct manner of life to which they have committed themselves here on earth, "so at that time they will surpass the general rewards of those people through the gift of a higher remuneration... For however many people each person now instructs to life whether by his word or example, for the same number will each be honored and appear more glorious at the time when that life is attained."[36]

According to the Literal Sense: Church Reform

On these first two interpretative levels, then, Bede's uses the Ezra-Nehemiah story to narrate the sojourn of the Holy Church Universal throughout this world as it endures the exile of sin

cussion of this theme, see DeGregorio, "Bede on Prayer," pp. 5–13; and Alan Thacker, "Bede's Ideal of Reform," in *Ideal and Reality in Frankish and Anglo-Saxon Society: Studies Presented to John Michael Wallace-Hadrill*, ed. Patrick Wormald, Donald Bullough, and Roger Collins (Oxford, 1983), pp. 130–1.

[34] *In Ezram* 2 (p. 328, lines 1626–9) and 3 (p. 341, lines 89–94).

[35] On this theme, cf. Holder, "Mysteries of Our Salvation," pp. 159–61.

[36] *In Ezram* 3 (p. 381, lines 1687–91, 1697–9): "...ascenduntque filii sacerdotum super domum Dauid dum sancti praedicatores siue martyres sicut nunc generalem iustorum uitam uel ministerio uerbi uel agone martyrii transeunt ita tunc generalia eorum praemia sublimioris dono remunerationis antecedent... . Quantos enim nunc quisque uerbo uel exemplo suo erudit ad uitam pro tantis tunc in perceptione uitae gloriosior apparens honorificabitur." Trans. DeGregorio, *On Ezra and Nehemiah*, p. 213.

and, thanks to the grace of Christ and the hard work of His preachers, experiences the return to blessedness. In the course of his remarks, he no doubt covers a wide range of correlative topics common to the works of many previous Fathers, thus demonstrating not only his debt to but also his command of that tradition.[37] But it is on yet another, very different level of signification that his truly bold and original reading of Ezra-Nehemiah takes its shape. For alongside the two previous levels he places a third, this one concerned not with the timeless realities of Christian revelation and their traditional exegetical interpretations but with the social *realia* of his own Northumbrian world.[38] In the literal sense of the Ezra-Nehemiah story, in other words, Bede finds not only theological truths but a series of episodes, themes, and personages that he believed could be directed to the concerns he had about the repentance and reform of his own native Northumbrian church. That Bede had such concerns is well known from his last extant work, the *Epistola ad Ecgberhtum Episcopum*. Composed in November 734, just months before his death, this brief letter written to his bishop friend Ecgberht lists a whole series of corruptions plaguing Nor-

---

[37] For similar conclusions about Bede's adept handling of the patristic tradition, see J. N. Hart-Hasler, "Bede's Use of Patristic Sources: The Transfiguration," *Studia Patristica* 28 (1993): 197–204; Benedicta Ward, "'In medium duorum animalium': Bede and Jerome on the Canticle of Habakkuk"; and Joseph Kelly, "Bede on the Brink," *Journal of Early Christian Studies* 5 (1997): 85–103.

[38] I have discussed this aspect of the commentary in two previous articles, "Bede's *In Ezram et Neemiam* and the Reform of the Northumbrian Church," *Speculum* 79 (2004): 1–25, and "Bede's *In Ezram et Neemiam*: A Document in Church Reform?," in Stéphane Lebecq, Michel Perrin, and Olivier Szerwiniack, *Bède le Vénérable: entre tradition et postérite* (Lille, 2005), pp. 97–107, which should be consulted as supplements to the remarks I offer here.

[39] The brother of the Northumbrian king Eadberht, Ecgberht served as a bishop from 732–5 before becoming archbishop of York from 735–66.

thumbrian religious life and urges their reform.[39] Scholars long assumed that Bede confined such objectives to the *Epistola* and his other non-exegetical writings, but it is now indisputable that he chose to air them in his exegesis as well, and above all in his work on Ezra-Nehemiah.[40] The *Epistola* makes clear that Bede was extremely anxious about the proliferation of so-called family minsters—that is, monasteries founded on land bequeathed in perpetuity from one family member to another, often with the backing of royal support, and staffed by secularized quasi-monastic thanes unconcerned with true religious discipline.[41] His critique in the *Epistola* on such institutions and those who support and inhabit them is scathing in the extreme:

> There are others, laymen who have no love for the monastic life nor for military service, who commit a graver crime by giving money to kings and obtaining lands under the pretext of building monasteries, in which they can give freer reign to their libidinous tastes. . . They do not gather monks there but rather they find those vagrants who have been expelled from monasteries in other places for the sin of disobedience, or whom they have lured away from other monasteries, or for sure, those of their own followers whom they can persuade to take the tonsure and promise monastic obedience to them.[42]

Bede's letter to him has not been studied with the close attention it deserves, although see the recent discussion of it by John Blair, *The Church in Anglo-Saxon Society* (Oxford, 2005), pp. 100–17; also DeGregorio, "Reform of the Northumbrian Church," pp. 6–9.

[40] On this point, see Scott DeGregorio, "*Nostrorum socordiam temporum*: The Reforming Impulse of Bede's Later Exegesis," *Early Medieval Europe* 11 (2002): 107–22.

[41] Blair, *Church in Anglo-Saxon Society*, pp. 84–91, 100–8, offers a fresh account of the problem.

[42] *Epistola* 12 (p. 415–16): "At alii grauiore adhuc flagitio, cum sint ipsi laici, et nullo uitae regularis uel usu exerciti, uel amore praediti, data regibus pecunia, emunt sibi sub praetextu construendorum monasterio-

Scott DeGregorio

While it all seems a far cry from the Jerusalem of Ezra and
Nehemiah, the biblical narrative actually provided Bede with
just the right occasion to touch upon this contemporary Northumbrian issue. Commenting on Ezra 6:18, which tells of the
appointing of priests and Levites to serve within the rebuilt temple, he writes:

> The order of devotion required that, after the building and
> dedication of the Lord's house, priests and Levites be straight-
> away ordained to serve in it: for there would be no point in hav-
> ing erected a splendid building if there were no priests inside
> to serve God. This should be impressed as often as possible on
> those who, though founding monasteries with splendid work-
> manship, in no way appoint teachers in them to exhort the
> people to God's work but rather those who will serve their own
> pleasures and desires there.[43]

This allusion to monasteries ornate on the outside but corrupt on the inside is the only such one in all of Bede's exegesis.
Both thematically and linguistically, it intersects with the more

---

rum territoria in quibus suae liberius uacent libidini… non monachos
ibi congregant, sed quoscunque ob culpam inobedientiae ueris expulsos
monasteriis alicubi forte oberrantes inuenerint, aut euocare monasteriis
ipsi ualuerint; uel certe quos ipsi de suis satellitibus ad suscipiendam tonsuram promissa sibi obedientia monachica inuitare quiuerint." Trans. Judith McClure and Roger Collins, in *Bede: Ecclesiastical History of the English
People* (Oxford, 1994), p. 351.

[43] *In Ezram* 2 (p. 302, line 597 – p. 303, line 604): "Ordo poscebat deuotio-
nis ut post aedificatam ac dedicatam domum domini mox sacerdotes ac
leuitae qui in ea ministrarent ordinarentur ne sine causa domus erecta
fulgeret si deessent qui intus Deo seruirent. Quod saepius inculcandum
eis qui monasteria magnifico opere construentes nequaquam in his stat-
uunt doctores qui ad opera Dei populum cohortentur sed suis potius
inibi uoluptatibus ac desideriis seruiunt." Trans. DeGregorio, *On Ezra
and Nehemiah*, p. 102.

expansive treatment he devotes to the problem in the *Epistola*. Such overlap, accordingly, aligns his remarks in the commentary with the more patently reformist preoccupations of the *Epistola*.[44] From the *Epistola* we learn also that episcopal taxation was a further abuse in the Northumbrian church that had Bede incensed to the core. In a key passage, he describes the situation:

> For we have heard, and it is indeed well known, that there are many of the villages and hamlets of our people located in inaccessible mountains or in dense forests, where a bishop has never been seen over the course of many years performing his ministry and revealing the divine grace. But not one of these places is immune *from paying taxes that are due to that bishop* (my emphasis).[45]

On two occasions, specific details within Ezra-Nehemiah allowed Bede to target this deeply corrosive problem. First, in Neh. 5:1–4, a great outcry emanates from the Jewish community as some of the wealthier brethren impose costly taxes on those

[44] In addition to the thematic parallel, there is linguistic overlap between the *Epistola*'s "suis tantum inibi desideriis... deseruiunt" (p. 415) and *In Ezram*'s "suis potius inibi uoluptatibus ac desideriis seruiunt" (p. 303, lines 603–4).

[45] *Epistola* 7 (p. 410): "Audiuimus enim, et fama est, quia multae uillae ac uiculi nostrae gentis in montibus sint inaccessis ac saltibus dumosis positi, ubi nunquam multis transeuntibus annis sit uisus antistes, qui ibidem aliquid ministerii aut gratiae caelestis exhibuerit; quorum tamen ne unus quidem *a tributis antistiti reddendis* esse possit immunis." Trans. McClure and Collins, p. 347. The phrase "paying taxes that are due to that bishop" (*tributis antistiti reddendis*) may mean something like churchscot, i.e. obligatory payments of grain by each household to the church for the support of the clergy. Note, however, that at *Epistola* 7 (p. 411) Bede criticizes those bishops who demand money (*pecunia*) from the people, implying that monetary payment of church dues could also stand behind his remarks in the commentary. For more on this, see Blair, *Church in Anglo-Saxon Society*, pp. 153–60.

working to repair Jerusalem's city walls. Bede begins his comments on this passage with a re-statement of the historical level of meaning, and then quickly moves to develop a parallel to his own local situation:

> In the same way, we see this occurring among us today. For how many are there among God's people who willingly desire to comply with divine commands but are hindered from being able to fulfill what they desire not only by a lack of temporal means and by poverty but also by the examples of those who seem to be endowed with the garb of religion, but who exact an immense tax and weight of worldly goods from those who they claim to be in charge of while in return giving nothing for their eternal salvation either by teaching them or by providing them with examples of good living or by devoting effort to works of piety for them? Would that some Nehemiah (i.e. a 'consoler from the Lord') might come in our own days and restrain our errors, kindle our breasts to love of the divine, and strengthen our hands by turning them away from our own pleasures to establishing Christ's city![46]

Later, in his exegesis of part of Neh. 12:44, which reads "For Judah was pleased with the ministering priests and Levites," Bede returns to the topic, this time using the image of genuine priestly solicitude as an occasion to admonish those guilty of clerical avarice in the present:

> But woe to those priests and ministers of holy things who are happy to exact from the people the payment owing to their

[46] *In Ezram* 3 (p. 359, line 825 – p. 360, line 837): "Quod apud nos cotidie eodem ordine fieri uidemus. Quanti enim sunt in populo Dei qui diuinis libenter cupiunt obtemperare mandatis sed ne possint implere quod cupiunt et inopia rerum temporalium ac paupertate et exemplis retardantur eorum qui habitu religionis uidentur esse praediti cum ipsi ab eis quibus praeesse uidentur et immensum rerum saecularium pondus ac uectigal

office but are not at all willing to labor for their salvation, nor to offer them any holy guidance by living uprightly, nor to sing of the pleasantness of the heavenly kingdom by delightfully preaching to them. Instead, they are shown not to open the doors of the heavenly city for them by having citizenship in heaven, but rather to shut these doors by acting wickedly. The people when they are confessing or praising the Lord are by no means made happy by the works of these priests and ministers, but are pressed into affliction all the more.[47]

It is impossible to read these as general reflections only, given what we know from the *Epistola* about Bede's attitude to the problems of his own local situation. Indeed, the knowledge that undue taxation of the laity by avaricious Northumbrian churchmen ranks high on the *Epistola*'s list of contemporary evils cannot but work to localize his exasperation here, directing it forcefully at the guilty ecclesiastics of his own day, obviously in an attempt to urge the need for repentance and reform.

As a final example of Bede's deploying the Ezra-Nehemiah story as a gloss on the ills of his own contemporary world, let us

exigunt et nihil eorum saluti perpetuae uel docendo uel exempla uiuendi praebendo uel opera pietatis impendendo conferunt. Atque utinam aliquis in diebus nostris Neemias, id est consolator a domino, adueniens nostros compescat errores nostra ad amorem diuinum praecordia accendat nostras a propriis uoluptatibus ad constituendam Christi ciuitatem manus auertens confortet." Trans. DeGregorio, *On Ezra and Nehemiah*, p. 184.

[47] *In Ezram* 3 (p. 386, lines 1866–74): "Sed uae illis sacerdotibus ac ministris sanctorum qui sumptus quidem suo gradui debitos sumere a populo delectantur sed nil pro eiusdem populi student salute laborare non aliquid sacri ducatus ei recte uiuendo praebere non de suauitate regni caelestis ei quippiam dulce praedicando canere sed nec ianuas ei supernae ciuitatis aperire municipatum in caelis habendo uerum potius occludere peruerse agendo probantur in quorum operibus nequaquam confitens siue laudans dominum populus laetari sed multo magis cogitur affligi." Trans. DeGregorio, *On Ezra and Nehemiah*, p. 218.

consider his treatment of the figure of Ezra. Unlike Nehemiah, who is a secular figure,[48] Ezra is described as both a priest and a scribe, two roles that made him particularly adaptable to Bede's contemporary concerns. For these roles, Bede recognized, could be readily merged with those of eighth-century Northumbrian clergy, making the biblical figure an especially potent model for present emulation. Yet it is the strikingly concrete way the commentary develops these correspondences that makes them so compelling.

Concerning Ezra's status as "a scribe swift in the Law of Moses" (Ezra 7:6) and "a most learned scribe of the Law of the God of heaven" (Ezra 7:12), Bede emphasizes that Ezra's task was not only the preservation and transmission of Holy Writ but also its learned dissemination through preaching and teaching it to the people. Thus, before explaining that it was Ezra who rewrote "the whole sequence of sacred Scripture" that had been destroyed along with the first temple, Bede clarifies in a crucial passage just what these textual endeavors were meant to accomplish:

> But because when the temple had been burned down and the city of Jerusalem had been demolished, the holy writings kept there were likewise burnt through enemy devastation, it was proper that, when the Lord showed mercy and returned to His people, these writings should also be restored, so that having restored the buildings that had been destroyed they would also have writings from which they would receive encouragement *and learn how they might be inwardly restored* in faith and love of their Creator (my emphasis).[49]

---

[48] Neh. 2:2 describes him as the cupbearer to King Artaxerxes; later in the narrative, he serves as a governor of Judah: see Neh. 5:14.

[49] *In Ezram* 3 (p. 307, lines 772–8): "Verum quia templo incenso atque urbe Hierosolima subuersa scripturae quoque sanctae quae ibidem seruabantur simul fuerant hostili clade perustae et has miserante domino atque

Ezra restores the Law, that is to say, in order to move the people to repentance, to reform their heart and minds. As a scribe, then, he does not just prefigure Christ, who restored the Mosaic Law through the New Covenant; nor is he merely a copyist. Rather, Bede's Ezra is also portrayed as a teacher, an exegetical *doctor* who, much like Bede himself, is concerned to reform others through sacred texts and their interpretation.[50] In Bede's own words, stated near the end of Book 2, "Indeed, we can relate the person of Ezra in a figurative way not only to the Lord Christ but also to any leader or teacher in the Church . . ."[51]

Linked with this scribal imagery is Ezra's role as *sacerdos*, priest. As such, his job in the Old Testament story is to rebuild not the physical temple but the worshipping Jewish community. He accomplishes this by installing priests and Levites in the temple, by expelling the foreign women whom some had taken as wives, and by teaching the Law to the people. Bede of course finds much here to treat allegorically, but again he is keen to direct his remarks toward more contemporary aims as well. Hence in Bede's scheme, Ezra is not just *sacerdos*, as the canonical book calls him, but also *pontifex*, "high priest," as the term is usually translated. Now in the biblical account Ezra is nowhere called high priest, though the genealogy given in Ezra 7:1–5 does place him in a priestly line of descent that goes back to the high priest Aaron. So was Bede mistaken? What else could his description of Ezra as *pontifex* mean?

ad suum populum reuerso reparari oportebat ut quia aedificia eruta restaurauerant haberent unde ipsi ammoniti restaurari intus in fide et dilectione sui creatoris discerent." Trans. DeGregorio, *On Ezra and Nehemiah*, p. 108.

[50] Cf. my remarks below, n. 53.

[51] *In Ezram* 2 (p. 318, lines 1239–41): "Possumus sane personam Ezrae non solum ad dominum Christum sed etiam ad aliquem praesulem siue doctorem ecclesiae figuraliter referre . . ."

A close reading of the commentary shows, I believe, that this label is not intended to signal Ezra's high priestly status. Bede clearly acknowledges that the high-priestly office was in fact assigned to others and, in doing so, he often employs a different terminology, namely *summa sacerdos*.[52] By contrast, the term *pontifex*, as Bede applies it to Ezra, appears to function as a deliberate form of type-casting. Its purpose is to distinguish Ezra as a special priest whose outstanding zeal and authority to command and correct other priests made him an ideal paradigm for contemporary episcopal authority. These associations emerge most clearly in Book 2 of the commentary. In a stunning passage, Bede there deliberately equates Ezra's pontifical role as a corrector of priestly wrongdoing with that of a modern archbishop. Commenting on the account of the trouble with the foreign women in Ezra 9, Bede observes that, though some of the priestly leaders had sinned, others were outraged and quick to report the crime to Ezra. Drawing out the meaning for the present, Bede comments as follows:

> And it should be carefully noted and used as an example of good works that while some leaders sinned and caused the common people who were entrusted to them to sin, other leaders who

---

[52] *In Ezram* 2 (p. 331, lines 1743–7): "Eliasib erat summa sacerdos temporis illius. Siquidem post Iesum filium Iosedech Ioachim filius eius et post eum Eliasib filius ipsius summi sacerdotii gradu functus est ut et sequentia huius sacrae historiae et Iudaica Iosephi probat historia." [Eliashib was the high priest at that time. For after Jeshua son of Josedech, his son Joachim occupied the office of high priest, and Joachim's son Eliashib served after him, as both the following part of this sacred narrative and Josephus's *History of the Jews* attest.] Trans. DeGregorio, *On Ezra and Nehemiah*, p. 144. See also *In Ezram* 1 (p. 271, lines 1210–11); and *In Ezram* 2 (p. 336, line 1929). For *sacerdos magnus*: *In Ezram* 1 (p. 271, line 1221; p. 278, line 1475); *In Ezram* 2 (p. 316, line 1158); and *In Ezram* 3 (p. 344, line 215; p. 376, line 1494).

were of more wholesome view for their part did their best to correct those sins; but because they cannot do this themselves they refer the matter to their *pontifex* (i.e. their archbishop) through whose authority so grave, so manifold, and so long-lasting a sin can be expiated.[53]

Merging past and present roles, Bede's phrase *pontifex, id est archiepiscopus* is most revealing. For it translates the meaning of Ezra's actions into a definite Northumbrian register, providing a map of sorts for the reforming actions of religious leaders in his own time. Just as Ezra rises up to set straight those under his charge, so too, as Bede implies in writing to Bishop Ecgberht, are Northumbrian episcopal authorities obligated to correct priestly waywardness and secular wrongdoing. Thus, as much as he stands as a type of Christ, the biblical figure of Ezra has more immediate and local applications for Bede. In this Jewish priest and scribe, Bede discerned a combination of qualities that resonated strongly with the special needs of the Northumbrian church—Ezra is both scribe, i.e. a teacher and exegete, and *pontifex*, i.e. an archbishop and religious authority. Such qualities made him especially germane to Bede's reforming purposes.

Conclusion: Vestigia Bedeae

In a move unique to his long list of biblical commentaries, Bede concludes the third and final book of *In Ezram* with a prayer in the first person:

[53] *In Ezram* 3 (p. 327, lines 1583–9): "...notandumque diligenter atque in exemplo operis trahendum quod ea quae principes peccauerunt et plebem sibi commissam peccare fecerunt aeque principes alii qui sanius subponebant corrigere satagunt; uerum quia per se ipsos nequeunt referunt ad pontificem, id est archiepiscopum, suum causam cuius auctoritate flagitium tam graue tam multifidum tam diutinum expietur." Trans. DeGregorio, *On Ezra and Nehemiah*, pp. 139–9.

And you, highest father of lights, by whom every excellent thing is given and from whom every perfect gift descends, you who have given me, the humblest of your servants, both the love and the aid to consider the wonders of your law, and have manifested to me, unworthy though I am, the grace not only to grasp the ancient offerings in the treasury of this prophetic book *but also to discover new ones beneath the veil of the old* and to bring them forth for the use of my fellow servants—*Remember me with favor, oh my God* (my emphasis).[54]

It is a revealing conclusion to the work.[55] Here, at the end of a commentary devoted to portions of Scripture no prior exegete had attempted to cover, we have—in Bede's own words—noth-

[54] *In Ezram* 3 (p. 392, lines 2108–15): "Et tu summe pater luminum a quo omne datum optimum et omne donum perfectum descendit qui mihi humillimo seruorum tuorum et amorem dedisti et auxilium considerandi mirabilia de lege tua quique in thesauro prophetici uoluminis non solum uetera amplectendi uerum et noua sub uelamine ueterum donaria inueniendi atque in usus conseruorum meorum proferendi indigno mihi gratiam praestitisti *memento mei Deus meus in bonum*." Trans. DeGregorio, *On Ezra and Nehemiah*, p. 226. Note the biblical allusions here: James 1:17 for the "father of lights" from whom perfect gifts descend; Psalm 119:18 for the "wonders of your law"; Matt. 13:52 for the bringing forth old and new things from the treasury; and finally Neh. 13:10 for the petition, "Remember me with favor, oh my God." The Matthew verse, a favorite of Bede's, works to identify Bede himself as a scribe, suggesting yet another parallel between himself and Ezra, who of course is so depicted in the famous miniature in the Codex Amiatinus. Cf. *De tab.* 2 (p. 65, lines 925–9), which also employs the verse with similar implications, as Holder, "New Treasures and Old," p. 248, has noted.

[55] Such an end would be even more fitting if the speculations I have offered elsewhere about the date of this commentary are correct. See my "Reform of the Northumbrian Church," pp. 20–23, as well as the introduction (pp. xxxvii–xlii) to my translation of the commentary, where I suggest that Bede may have continued to work on *In Ezram* into the

ing less than a repudiation of the compiler's role so often hung upon him. In treating Ezra-Nehemiah, he envisaged his task as consisting not in recycling old meanings but in discovering "new ones." Going where none had ventured previously, Bede succeeded in bringing Ezra-Nehemiah into the patristic mainstream by subjecting it to allegorical interpretation, making this neglected text speak, as it were, the language of the Fathers. Hardly the work of a novice, for this achievement Bede would rise to the status of an *auctor*, as the *Glossa Ordinaria* records. In that compendious volume of authoritative commentary, the entirety of the gloss on Ezra-Nehemiah derives from one commentator, Bede.[56]

But Bede's achievement here goes beyond even this. Indeed, as we have seen, the meaning of Ezra-Nehemiah was for him not simply a question of allegory. For here was a text laden with implications for his world, and he did not hesitate to read it accordingly. In the actions of Ezra and Nehemiah, in the high standards of priestly purity and ministry in the restored temple, and in other elements of the story besides, he detected the very models that needed to be set in place in order to save eighth-century Northumbria from spiritual ruination. The presence

early 730's, in which case it just may be his latest extant commentary; for an opposing view, see Paul Meyvaert, "The Date of Bede's *In Ezram* and His Image in the Codex Amiatinus," *Speculum* 80 (2005): 1087–1133, whose claims for an early date I have addressed in the introduction to my translation, pp. xxxviii–xli. Suggestively, the only other Bedan work to conclude with a first-person prayer is the *Historia ecclesiastica*, which we know Bede worked on into the early 730's. If *In Ezram* is Bede's latest commentary, the prayer would be all the more striking, revealing a very different self-understanding of his life-work than that offered by the more familiar tags of *uestigia patrum sequens* and *famulus Christi*, the most common descriptors of his career.

[56] For the text of the gloss on Ezra-Nehemiah, see *Biblia Latina cum Glossa Ordinaria*, 2:261– 305. In addition, see Hill's essay in this volume for more on Bede's perceived *auctoritas* in later centuries.

of such themes in a biblical commentary thus underscores the degree to which his exegesis could grow out of, and respond to, the same matrix of social, political, and religious concerns that prompted him to write the prose *Vita sancti Cuthberti,* the *Historia ecclesiastica,* and above all the *Epistola ad Ecgberhtum.* The commentary's topical thrust indeed makes it one of his most innovative creations, proof of the range his exegetical abilities could take no less than of the cultural work he believed the genre of biblical commentary itself could effectively accommodate. Accordingly, further study of the work should strengthen the sense shared by scholars today that, as an exegete, Bede did far more than follow the footsteps of others. His devotion to the Fathers who preceded him did not prevent him from moving in his own direction and, in doing so, from leaving footsteps of his own.

Christ as Incarnate Wisdom in Bede's Commentary on the Song of Songs

ARTHUR G. HOLDER

FOR THE VENERABLE BEDE, the Song of Songs was an allegorical drama prefiguring "the mysteries of Christ and the
Church . . . under the figure of a bridegroom and a bride."[1] In
this interpretation he was, of course, following well-established
patterns of Christian interpretation. However, unlike many other exegetes both before and after, Bede understood those mysteries of Christ and the Church in a distinctly historical manner.
For Bede, the Song of Songs presents an elaborately detailed
theology of history, with its centerpoint in the Incarnation of
Jesus Christ—the coming in human flesh of God's own divine
Wisdom and Word.

With this in mind, my purpose in this essay is twofold. First, I
want to illustrate the determinative influence that Bede's theology of history exercised on his exegesis; in order to do so, I will
examine his use of sources in the Song commentary, with particular reference to some very interesting passages that speak of
the incarnate Christ as a nursing mother. Second, I want to suggest some ways that Bede's commentary on the Song of Songs
may help us appreciate what he is doing in the *Historia ecclesiastica* and the other works of hagiography and history, particularly
in his famous treatments of the Northumbrian saints Cuthbert
and Hild. Although at first glance it may seem that source analysis and considerations of intertextuality hardly represent dra-

[1] Bede, *In Cant.* 1 (p. 190, lines 1–3): "mysteria Christi et ecclesiae...sub
figura sponsi et sponsae."

169

matically new directions in Bede studies, I hope to demonstrate the need for more consistent and sophisticated application of these familiar interpretive tools.

In the Song commentary, as in so many others, Bede explicitly claims to be "following the footsteps of the Fathers."[2] But which Fathers, precisely? There has been a considerable amount of scholarly confusion about the answer to this question, which I have attempted to address in more detail elsewhere.[3] In brief, I conclude that Bede knew neither Origen's commentary on the Song nor that of Gregory the Great. In a long polemical preface, and elsewhere throughout his commentary, Bede was refuting a lost treatise by Julian of Eclanum, a Pelagian author who had interpreted the Song as a celebration of human sexuality; understandably, Julian's influence appears to have been mostly that of a foil. The last book of Bede's work is a compendium of fifty-three extracts from various writings by Gregory of Great; Bede explicitly says that he did not have access to the similar collection compiled by Paterius.[4] But the single most important influence on Bede's exegesis of the Song was the massive commentary produced by a writer named Apponius, who was probably abbot of an Italian monastery early in the fifth century.[5] Apponius acknowledged Origen among his own sources, so by using Apponius Bede was influenced by Origen, albeit indirectly and unwittingly. Most significantly, it was from Apponius that Bede drew his overall interpretive scheme, in which the Song of Songs appears as a progressive narrative of salvation history focused on the incarnation of the Word of God.

---

[2] Bede, *In Cant.* Prol. (p. 180, line 503): "patrum uestigia sequentes."

[3] Arthur Holder, "The Patristic Sources of Bede's Commentary on the Song of Songs," *Studia Patristica* 34 (2001): 370–5.

[4] Bede, *In Cant.* 6 (p. 359, lines 17–24).

[5] Apponius's commentary on the Song of Songs is edited in CCSL 19: 1–311.

What was distinctive or unusual about Bede's reading of the Song in comparison with that of other early Christian interpreters? To begin with matters of form, it is worth noting that Bede did make it all the way through the Song of Songs, and that his commentary on all eight chapters has been preserved. That is more than we can say for most of his predecessors, or for many who came after. Origen's commentary and homilies both stop before the end of the second chapter, and of course we only have them in Latin translation. The commentary of Gregory the Great covers only the first eight verses of chapter one. And, in the twelfth century, Bernard of Clairvaux notoriously took eighty-six sermons just to get to the beginning of chapter three, and then he died. On the other hand we have Apponius, who did get to the end, with a sprawling commentary that runs to 310 pages in the critical edition. Bede's commentary is shorter by a third, or even by a half—if we choose not to count the preface against Julian or the concluding compendium of passages from Gregory. Like all of Bede's exegesis, it is both succinct and edifying, never discursive or pedantic. As Benedicta Ward wrote, "This treatise . . . was for the use of preachers as well as the meditations of monks."[6] In both cases, what was needed was straightforward exposition of the text rather than flights of fancy or academic argumentation.

In his commentary, Bede usually understands the bride of the Song to represent the whole body of the faithful, the catholic Church, whereas later commentators such as Bernard often identified the bride primarily with the individual Christian soul. Not that this was a twelfth-century innovation, for the so-called "tropological" or "moral" level of interpretation is clearly present much earlier—in Origen and Gregory, and indeed in Bede as well. In the patristic and earlier medieval writers, however, the moral reading is usually subordinate to the "allegorical"

[6] Benedicta Ward, *Venerable Bede* (London, 1990), p. 77.

reading properly so called—that is, to the level of interpretation referring to Christ and the Church.[7] Thus Bede will occasionally introduce a line of interpretation by identifying the Bride as "Holy Church or every elect soul."[8] Phrases of this sort do not signal that he is about to give two different interpretations, one for the Church as a whole and another for individual souls. Rather, he means that every elect soul participates in the Church's espousal to Christ by virtue of membership in the body. The company of faithful souls *is* the Church; the moral sense of the text is simply the allegorical sense writ small.

Since I have mentioned the famous fourfold scheme of medieval biblical interpretation, it is perhaps appropriate to note the use that Bede makes (or does not make) of it in his commentary on the Song of Songs. In words echoing John Cassian's classic definition, Bede names the four senses (literal, allegorical, moral, and anagogical) when he is explaining how the "honeycomb" of Sg. 4:11 drips honey just as Holy Scripture exudes wisdom when squeezed by the interpreter.[9] Near the end of the commentary, however, when he is dealing with the problematic reference in Sg. 8:1 to "my brother who is sucking the breasts of my mother," he is careful to explain—in words that reflect the influence of Apponius, and through him the indirect influence of Origen—that the Song has no carnal or literal meaning, but the whole of it must be understood spiritually and typologically.[10] Thus the words about "my brother who is sucking the

---

[7] See Calvin Kendall's essay in this volume for extensive discussion of the terminology Bede applied to the spiritual senses of Scripture.

[8] Bede, *In Cant.* 1 (p. 210, lines 788–9): "ecclesia sancta uel anima quaeque electa."

[9] Bede, *In Cant.* 3 (p. 260, lines 618–25).

[10] Bede, *In Cant.* 5 (p. 337, lines 1–4): "Et in multis enim et in omnibus et in hoc maxime loco testatur hoc carmen quia nil carnale et iuxta litteram resonet sed totum se spiritualiter ac typice uelit intellegi." Cf. Apponius, *In Canticum canticorum* 1 (CCSL 19: p. 4, lines 38–41): "In quo utique nihil de carnali amore, quem gentiles cupidinem appellant, qui insania

breasts of my mother" are spoken by the Synagogue representing the Hebrew people of old as they long for Jesus to come as
their brother in the flesh.

Unlike some other commentators, Bede makes no attempt to
locate the Song in the context of events in the life of Solomon,
such as his betrothal or wedding. To employ the terms Bede
himself used in his treatise *De schematibus et tropis* he understands
the Song of Songs as an allegory in words, not in deeds.[11] For
Bede, the verse in question was never spoken by a literal person in ancient Israel whose brother was sucking at the mother's
breast; nor does it even refer to the literal breasts of "the glorious Mother of God," the Virgin Mary. Rather, he takes this verse
as having been spoken by the Synagogue of old, who longed for
Christ to be born and nourished from "the substance of human
nature," who is the mother of us all.[12] Once again, the spiritual
meaning of the Song of Songs—which is its only meaning—has
to do with the Incarnation of Christ. For Bede, the Incarnation included the Savior's entire life and ministry—his birth,
teaching, healing, suffering, death, resurrection, ascension, and
sending of the Holy Spirit. All of this was once the Synagogue's
expectation; now it has become the Church's fulfillment, and
her joy.

The Synagogue and the Church, the Old Testament and the
New, are thus united in their devotion to Christ. At the very
beginning of the Song, the Synagogue longs for Christ to kiss
her with the kisses of his mouth by coming to teach her in person and no longer through intermediaries such as angels and
prophets. And it is she who goes on to say, this time directly
to Christ: "For your breasts are better than wine." The breasts

potius intellgi potest quam amor, sed totum spiritale, totum dignum
Deo, totumque animae salutare." Apponius was in part dependent here
on Origen, *Commentarius in Canticum* Prol. (GCS 33: p. 66, line 29; p. 68,
line 5).

[11] Bede, *DST* 2.2 (p. 164, line 218 – p. 166, line 235).
[12] Bede, *In Cant.* 5 (p. 338, lines 21–31).

of Christ, Bede explains, are the first principles of New Testament faith, which are better than the wine of the Old Testament law.[13] We are perhaps most likely to think of breasts in a love song as objects of erotic desire. And indeed, they function as objects of desire for Bede as well—not, however, because they carried for him any connotations of nudity or sexual activity. Instead, throughout his commentary, Bede consistently interpreted references to "breasts" as symbolic of the mother's ability to nourish her children with milk—in this case, the milk of true doctrine. As he noted, this was in accordance with St. Paul's reminder to the Corinthians that he had fed them with milk, not solid food.[14]

In this very first verse of the Song, however, Bede encounters a peculiar problem that leads him to some very creative exegesis. This verse is supposed to have been spoken by the Synagogue to Christ the bridegroom, but how is it possible for a male bridegroom to have breasts?[15] Bede first explains that this apparent anomaly is no accident, but is deliberately placed here, right at the beginning of the Song, in order to show us from the start that we are dealing with a text that must be interpreted figuratively.[16] We ought not to be surprised, Bede says, that Christ is spoken of as having feminine body parts, for there are in fact other such passages in the Bible. He then cites four of them: one from the Book of Revelation in which the Vulgate describes the Son of Man as "girded with a golden sash across the paps" (Rev. 1:12-3); two verses from the sixty-sixth chapter of

---

[13] Bede, *In Cant.* 1 (p. 191, lines 50–1).

[14] 1 Cor 3:2.

[15] The origin of this conundrum in Greek and Latin translations of the unpointed Hebrew text of the Song, along with an overview of patristic and early medieval interpretation, is to be found in G. Joy Ritson, "Eros, Allegory and Spirituality: The Development of Heavenly Bridegroom Imagery in the Western Christian Church from Origen to Gregory the Great," 2 vols. (Ph.D. diss., Graduate Theological Union, 1997).

[16] Bede, *In Cant.* 1 (p. 191, line 70 – p. 192, line 82).

Isaiah, in which the Lord speaks of himself as giving birth (Isa. 66:9) and as being like a mother caressing her child (Isa. 66:13); and finally that passage in Matthew's gospel where Jesus says to the unbelieving city of Jerusalem: "How often would I have gathered your children together, as a hen gathers her chicks under her wings, and you would not!" (Matt. 23:37). All four of these passages seem to have been chosen because in Bede's estimation they metaphorically refer to Christ as possessing female anatomy. But we should note that Christ is also identified with the personification of Lady Wisdom in Bede's commentary on the eighth chapter of Proverbs; and further on in the Song commentary, he does not hesitate to refer to Christ the Teacher as *magistra ueritas*, or "Mistress Truth."[17]

In our own time, feminist biblical scholars and proponents of inclusive language in the churches have provoked considerable controversy by calling attention to scriptural passages that accord feminine attributes to God. But many such passages were obviously well known to Bede, and readily accepted. One wonders, though, how he came to compile this particular set of testimonies in support of a feminine Christ. Did he perhaps find them already linked together for this purpose in the work of some other writer? Jerome cites the Matthew passage in his explication of the maternal imagery in Isa. 66:13, but he makes no special apology for the feminine symbolism,[18] and I do not

---

[17] Bede, *In prou. Sal.* 1 (p. 59, line 1 – p. 65, line 96); *In Cant.* 3 (p. 284, lines 517–8). For a reference to the Holy Spirit as also possessing feminine characteristics, see *In Cant.* 4 (p. 310, lines 434–7): "Potest aptissime uocabulo matris et genetricis ecclesiae gratia spiritus sancti per quam ipsa ecclesia renata Deo et constructa est designata intellegi quia uidelicet spiritus Hebraice genere feminino *ruha* nuncupatur." [The grace of the Holy Spirit, through whom the Church herself has been born in God and knit together, can very aptly be understood as being designated by the term "mother of the Church and the one that bore her," because in Hebrew the Spirit is called *ruha*, a word in the feminine gender.]

[18] Jerome, *In Esaiam* 18 (CCSL 73A: p. 780, lines 12–15).

know of another patristic author who cites these particular texts for this purpose. The comparison of wine to law and milk to gospel is right out of Apponius, as is the imagery of the nursing Christ. But Apponius's explication focuses on the two breasts of Christ as symbolic representations of the two heralds of the gospel who were named John—John the Baptist who acknowledged him as the suffering Lamb of God, and John the Evangelist who proclaimed him as the Word by whom all things were made.[19] In Apponius there is no apology or scriptural warrant for the feminine Christ, or even any indication that it might present a problem. Bede thought that this imagery might trouble the reader, so he apparently consulted the concordance of his memory to bring forth other biblical passages using similar language. It is a fine piece of creative biblical scholarship, and a startling allusion to the "Jesus as Mother" theme that is so much better attested both earlier (in Clement, Ambrose, Augustine, and others), and later (in Anselm and the Cistercians, and in Lady Julian of Norwich).[20] But it is not the only such passage in Bede's commentary, or even the most remarkable.

In her important essay on "Jesus as Mother," Caroline Walker Bynum claimed that what distinguished twelfth-century writers like Bernard and Aelred from earlier authors who referred to God or Christ as mother was that "the tendency of these Cistercian authors to associate in the same discussion God's motherhood and the pastoral burdens of clergy or abbots is in marked contrast to patristic authors, who do not connect Jesus' mothering with the mothering of earthly men."[21] Insofar as this assertion applies to Apponius and Bede, it needs to be revised. We

---

[19] Apponius, *In Canticum canticorum* 1.20 (CCSL 19: p. 14, lines 299–311).

[20] Ritamary Bradley, "Patristic Background of the Motherhood Similitude in Julian of Norwich," *Christian Scholar's Review* 8 (1978): 101–13.

[21] Caroline Walker Bynum, *Jesus as Mother: Studies in the Spirituality of the High Middle Ages* (Berkeley, 1982), p. 148.

have already seen that Apponius expounds the breasts of Christ as the two Johns who were heralds of the gospel, and elsewhere he says that Christian pastors are breasts when they nourish the Christian people with biblical teaching.[22] As for Bede, we find him explaining that the breasts of Sg. 4:5 belong this time not to the bridegroom but to the Church as bride, whose teachers are "quite aptly referred to as breasts, since they supply the milk of the life-giving word to those who are still infants in Christ."[23] Later, in reference to Sg. 4:10, he goes on to develop this imagery at considerable length by showing that pastors who nourish the faithful with the milk of doctrine are thereby imitating the mothering Christ in whose ministry they share:

> Since an infant is not able to eat bread very well, the mother in a certain manner makes the very bread she eats into flesh and feeds the infant from that bread through the lowliness of breasts and the taste of milk. "In the beginning was the Word, and the Word was with God, and the Word was God" (John 1:1); this is the eternal food that refreshes angels because they are satisfied with the sight of his glory. And "the Word became flesh and dwelt among us" (John 1:14), so that in this way the Wisdom of God which consoles us as a mother may refresh us from that very same bread and lead us through the sacraments of the Incarnation to the knowledge and vision of divine splendor. But holy teachers also take the bread with which they are fed in a sublime manner and convert it into milk with which they nourish little children, so that the more exalted their contemplation of eternal joys in God, the more

[22] Apponius, *In Canticum canticorum* 7.25–6 (CCSL 19: p. 164, line 326 – p. 165, line 357).

[23] Bede, *In Cant.* 3 (p. 251, lines 268–70): "ubera autem etiam aptissime nuncupantur quia paruulis adhuc in Christo lac uerbi salutaris infundunt."

humbly are they at the same time taking pity on their neighbors' weakness.[24]

None of this is particularly original to Bede. The image of Christ taking flesh in order to act as a mother who converts divine wisdom into more easily digestible milk is found in Augustine,[25] and we have already noted how Apponius spoke of the maternal function of apostles and teachers. But Bede develops the theme throughout his commentary with both enthusiasm and a pleasing elegance.

Thus we see that, for Bede, it is impossible for Christians to interpret the Song of Songs apart from the great narrative of salvation history set forth in both biblical testaments and continued in the Church's ministry throughout the ages. We are better able to appreciate both his perspective and his achievement if we take the trouble to analyze his use of sources. With any medieval author, and especially with an author as learned and inventive as Bede, effective source analysis must consider

---

[24] Bede, *In Cant.* 3 (p. 258, lines 543–55): "Quia enim minus idoneus est infans qui pane uescatur ipsum panem edendo quodammodo mater incarnat et per humilitatem mammillae ac lactis sucum de ipso pane pascit infantem. *In principio erat uerbum, et uerbum erat apud Deum, et Deus erat uerbum,* hic est cibus sempiternus quo reficiuntur angeli quia uisa eius gloria satiantur; *uerbum autem caro factum est et habitauit in nobis,* ut sic etiam sapientia Dei quae nos sicut mater consolatur de codem ipso pane reficeret ac per sacramenta incarnationis ad agnitionem uisionemque diuinae claritatis traiceret. Sed et doctores sancti panem quo sublimiter ipsi saginantur conuertunt in lac quo paruulos nutriant dum quo altius aeterna in Deo gaudia contemplantur eo infirmitati proximorum humilius compatiuntur."

[25] Augustine, *Tractatus in Iohannem* 98.6 (CCSL 36: p. 579, lines 4–10); on God as both father and mother to the faithful, see *Enarrationes in Psalmos* 26.18 (CCSL 40: p. 164, lines 2–5).

not only *which* sources are being employed, but *how* they are used, and *to what end.*[26]

We have seen how it is that a sense of history helps us unpack the meaning of Bede's commentary on the Song; now let us consider how that commentary itself may help us understand the *Historia ecclesiastica* and his other historical works. As scholars from a wide variety of disciplines are increasingly coming to realize, anyone wishing to understand Bede must read and re-read all of Bede—the exegesis along with the histories, the grammatical works along with the poetry and hymns.[27] An acquaintance with the breadth of Bede's corpus is necessary in order to get a sense of his telescopic perspective, which focuses our attention sometimes on the big picture, and sometimes on the local details; first on the universal, and then on the particular. Reading Bede is something like using one of those CD-ROM programs with a zoom in/zoom out feature. For the big picture, click on the treatise on *The Reckoning of Time* which traces the history of the cosmos from creation, through the six ages of world history, to final judgment and beyond. To zoom in on a close-up of the years of Christ's Incarnation, click on the *Homilies on the Gospel.* Want a super close-up of one Northumbrian monastery in the late seventh and early eighth centuries? Click on *The History of the Abbots of Wearmouth and Jarrow.* But as we

---

[26] This point (which bears frequent repetition) was made years ago by Paul Meyvaert in his essay on "Bede the Scholar" in *Famulus Christi: Essays in Commemoration of the Thirteenth Centenary of the Birth of the Venerable Bede,* ed. Gerald Bonner (London, 1976), p. 42: "It is always more important to note what Bede is doing with his sources than how much and from whom he may be borrowing."

[27] For recent examples of such approaches, see Scott DeGregorio, "Bede's *In Ezram et Neemiam* and the Reform of the Northumbrian Church," *Speculum* 79 (2004): 1–25; and Erik Knibbs, "Exegetical Hagiography," *Revue Bénédictine* 114 (2004): 233–52.

jump around from one time period to another, and from place to place, we must always remember Bede's overall perspective: in time, the centerpoint is the Incarnation (which explains his preference in the *Historia ecclesiastica* for dating events according to the *annus Domini*);[28] in space, Bede's cosmic center lies on an axis that runs between Jerusalem and Rome. In the Song commentary, what I have been calling Bede's theology of salvation history gives us the larger picture within which we are meant to place the story of the Anglo-Saxon church traced in the *Historia ecclesiastica*.

A study of the Song commentary can also help to deepen our appreciation of the methods of composition employed by Bede the historian as he sorted through his various sources and authorities. When he concludes his commentary with an impressive collection of excerpts from Gregory the Great, are we not reminded of his careful transcription of the Gregorian correspondence at the end of Book 1 of the *Historia ecclesiastica*? In both cases, the great pontiff's sanctity and esteemed reputation warranted having his words set apart and quoted verbatim. On the other hand, Bede's use of Apponius, though extensive, was much freer and more critical. Occasionally he acknowledges his dependence on Apponius, but more often he does not. Sometimes he incorporates material from his source, sometimes he corrects Apponius silently, often he ignores him altogether. But the result throughout is an apparently seamless literary product whose complex interweaving of sources we discover only through laborious and patient investigation. The same is true, of course, with the *Historia ecclesiastica*—the difference being that the work

---

[28] But Bede by no means abandoned the practice of *annus mundi* dating. As Faith Wallis explains in the introduction to her translation of *De temporum ratione*: "The historiographical intention in the *Reckoning of Time* is, then, quite different from that of the *Historia ecclesiastica*. The theme of the latter is the particular providence of God with regard to the English; that of the former is the continuity and pattern of general providence

has been so carefully studied by so many scholars over the years that the critical editions and the best translations identify the sources Bede used and assess his treatment of them.

Still another way in which an acquaintance with Bede's exegesis can enhance our reading of his historical works is by illuminating some of the themes and images he employs. For example, recent scholarship has emphasized the way in which Bede's portraits of St. Cuthbert in the metrical and prose lives, and again in the *Historia ecclesiastica*, hold up the ideal of a monastic pastor who perfectly balances contemplation and action. The seminal scholarly treatment of this theme appeared in 1983 with Alan Thacker's article on "Bede's Ideal of Reform" in which he observed that Bede viewed Cuthbert through a lens borrowed from Gregory the Great, which led him to treat the saint as an exemplary figure who was by turns a monastic preacher, a reformer, a contemplative, and a bishop.[29] Subsequent studies of Bede's presentation of Cuthbert have given us several different variations on Thacker's theme: Clare Stancliffe discerned a "polarity between pastor and solitary"; Simon Coates found "tension" and "ambivalence" in Bede's attempt to affirm the Gregorian mixed life without giving up the desert ascetic ideal represented by Antony and Martin of Tours; and John Eby has argued that the structure of Bede's prose *Life of Cuthbert* sets

---

throughout time. Bede uses *annus mundi* throughout the chronicle because it underscores this continuity; he uses *annus Domini* reckoning in the *Historia ecclesiastica* because its action takes place within the Sixth Age of the world, and because the Dionysian *computus* associated with *annus Domini* era plays such an important part in his overall story." Faith Wallis, trans., *Bede: The Reckoning of Time*, Translated Texts for Historians 29 (Liverpool, 1999), pp. lxx–lxxi.

[29] Alan Thacker, "Bede's Ideal of Reform," in *Ideal and Reality in Frankish and Anglo-Saxon Society: Studies Presented to J. M. Wallace-Hadrill*, ed. Patrick Wormald, Donald Bullough, and Roger Collins (Oxford, 1983), pp. 136–42.

forth a series of transformations, from secular childhood to pastoral vocation to spiritual maturity.[30]

How are we to adjudicate among these various (and somewhat different) interpretations? Granted that Bede sees Cuthbert as a worthy example of both action and contemplation, are we to think of the two ideals as being presented in succession, or in polarity, or in ambivalent tension, or in a trajectory of transformation? None of the three scholars who have followed Thacker in addressing this theme has emulated his assiduous attention to the author's works in other genres.

However, as Scott DeGregorio has shown, Bede's own position on the relation of contemplation and action is implicit in his histories and hagiographies, but it becomes quite explicit throughout the homilies and commentaries.[31] For example, in the Song commentary we find many passages such as the interpretation of Sg. 5:2: "I sleep and my heart keeps watch," which Bede understands as spoken by the Church as she "longs to cling to the Lord in secret and silent contemplation." He continues:

> Surely Holy Church says these things in the person of those
> who desire to serve the Lord in the serenity of this temporal
> life by psalms, fasts, prayers, alms, and this temporal life's other
> more peaceful activities. But since this life is one of labor, not
> of rest, she soon hears the Lord's voice arousing her and ex-

---

[30] Clare Stancliffe, "Cuthbert and the Polarity between Pastor and Solitary," in *Saint Cuthbert: His Cult and His Community to A.D. 1200*, ed. Gerald Bonner, David Rollason, and Clare Stancliffe (Woodbridge, 1989), pp. 21–44; Simon Coates, "The Bishop as Pastor and Solitary: Bede and the Spiritual Authority of the Monk-Bishop," *Journal of Ecclesiastical History* 47 (1996): 601–19; John Eby, "Bringing the *Vita* to Life: Bede's Symbolic Structure of the Life of St. Cuthbert," *American Benedictine Review* 48 (1997): 316–38.

[31] Scott DeGregorio, "The Venerable Bede on Prayer and Contemplation," *Traditio* 54 (1999): 3–39.

horting her to the sweaty toil of preaching so that she will remember that in the time of this exile she has not been denied
an inner foretaste of the peace she desires, but neither is she
allowed to enjoy it forever in its fullness.[32]

Here, in a nutshell, we have Bede's teaching on contemplation. As DeGregorio notes, Bede does not share Gregory the
Great's fascination with the psychology of the mystic vision.[33] For
Bede, contemplation itself is usually described in rather practical terms, as it is in this passage. Contemplation is equated with
devotion in prayer, with meditation on Scripture, even with the
giving of alms! For Bede, contemplation is not so much a state
of consciousness as a particularly delightful form of worship
and communion. Such contemplation is by definition brief, oc-
casional, unpredictable, and always a gift of grace. The purpose
of this gift is twofold: to provide pastors and teachers with the
wisdom and insight they need to perform their ministry, and to
whet the Church's appetite for future bliss.

In Bede's view, throughout the time of this mortal life every
pastor and teacher, and especially a saintly bishop like Cuthbert,
must necessarily oscillate between the fleeting delights of reflection on divine mysteries and what Bede calls "the sweaty toil of
preaching." Contemplation is always mediated and partial; action is always on behalf of the neighbor's health and salvation.
Both are essential to the Christian life on earth, but neither will
carry over into the life that is to come. As Bede explains with
reference to Sg. 2:17, the alternation of contemplation and

---

[32] Bede, *In Cant.* 3 (p. 274, line 137 – p. 275, line 144): "Haec quidem
ecclesia sancta dicit in eis qui in serenitate uitae temporalis psalmis ieiuniis
et ceteris uitae temporalis orationibus et elemosinis quietoribus actibus
domino seruire cupiunt. Verum quia laboris est haec uita non requiei
mox excitantis se domini sentit uocem atque ad sudorem praedicandi
cohortantis ut meminerit sibi in tempore huius exilii desideratae quietis
nec abnegatum penitus gustum nec perfruitionem aeternaliter datum."
[33] DeGregorio, "Bede on Prayer," pp. 29–30.

good works will continue only "until the day breathes and the shadows retire." "For at that time," he goes on to say, "we will no longer labor in good works, nor, since we are to be made perfect suddenly and in a instant, will we contemplate heavenly things 'through a mirror and in obscurity' (1 Cor. 13:12), but for eternity the whole Church at once will see the King of heaven in his beauty."[34] The phrase about seeing the King of heaven in his beauty is an allusion to Isa. 33:17, which becomes particularly poignant if we remember that this verse was reported to have been on Bede's own lips just before he died, when he interrupted his final work of dictation just long enough to declare that he was content to be released from the body since it meant that he would at last be able to see Christ the King in all his beauty.[35] For Bede, there is no great fundamental polarity between active ministry and contemplative prayer. The tension in his presentation of Cuthbert and the other saints results rather from the fact that, for Bede, neither action nor contemplation can ever be complete on this side of eternity. Both find their fulfillment only in heaven, when zealous action gives way to love's consummation, and contemplative intimations are exchanged for the direct and unmediated vision of God.

Another theme that appears in both the Song commentary and the *Historia ecclesiastica* is the theme of apostolic motherhood. We have seen in the commentary how Bede compared both Christ and his pastors to nursing mothers who transformed the robust bread of divinity into milk more palatable for infants.

---

[34] Bede, *In Cant.* 2 (p. 229, lines 705–8): ". . . quia tunc uidelicet nec ullo boni operis labore adficimur nec *per speculum et in enigmate* perfectiores quique raptim et ad momentum caelestia contemplantur sed ipsum caeli regem in decore suo tota simul aeternum ecclesia uidebit."

[35] Cuthbert, *Epistola de obitu Bedae* (p. 584).

[36] Bede, *HE* 4.23 (pp. 410–12). On the use of this epithet by Bede and other early medieval writers, see Clarissa Atkinson, *The Oldest Vocation: Christian*

Perhaps this can help us understand the ministry of Hild, who is twice referred to as "mother" by Bede.[36] Clare Lees and Gillian Overing have argued that Bede actually downplays Hild's role as a teacher and political leader, in favor of those "more learned men" at Whitby who were in his opinion better suited for the exercise of pastoral ministry by reason of their gender.[37] From a feminist perspective, these scholars contend that Bede called Hild a "mother," making her "a reproducer, but not a producer in her own right," because he disapproved of women's active participation in the affairs of church and state.

It is certainly not my intention to rehabilitate Bede as a proto-feminist on the basis of his commentary on the Song of Songs. Indeed, that work contains several passages clearly reflective of a male monastic bias, such as a critique of women who entrap men with their embellished bodies and soft words, or the observation that the bride in the Song is behaving just like a woman when she constantly desires to tarry indoors in the house with her beloved, so that the bridegroom is always having to call her outdoors to work in the vineyards or gardens.[38]

But even though we must acknowledge Bede's patriarchal attitudes, we should be cautious about accepting the account that Lees and Overing provide of his attitude toward Hild. Catherine

---

Motherhood in the Middle Ages (Ithaca, N.Y., 1991), pp. 64–100. For the Anglo-Saxon historical context, see Mary Dockray-Miller, *Motherhood and Mothering in Anglo-Saxon England* (New York, 2000).

[37] Clare Lees and Gillian Overing, "Birthing Bishops and Fathering Poets: Bede, Hild, and the Relations of Cultural Production," *Exemplaria* 6 (1994): 35–65. For the *doctioribus uiris* in whose presence Caedmon was examined, see Bede *HE* 4.24 (p. 416). The patriarchal attitudes implicit in Bede's treatment of women are also uncovered in Stephanie Hollis, *Anglo-Saxon Women and the Church: Sharing a Common Fate* (Woodbridge, 1992), pp. 179–270, and in Dockray-Miller, *Motherhood and Mothering*, pp. 1–41.

[38] Bede, *In Cant.* 2 (p. 225, line 568 – p. 226, line 573); and 1 (p. 209, lines 732–8).

Karkov has recently suggested that Bede's apparent "silencing" of Hild may actually reflect a dearth of source material available to him as a result of the eclipse of her reputation at Whitby during the time of Abbess Ælfflæd and her successors there.[39] Here I want to raise a rather different literary and theological question about the way that Lees and Overing have interpreted the gendered force of Bede's treatment of Hild's spiritual motherhood, and in order to do so I once again call attention to intertextual relations between the *Historia ecclesiastica* and Bede's work in the field of biblical exegesis.

Since the mothering imagery used in the Song commentary is specifically in reference to the teaching ministry of Christ and his apostles, it seems quite likely that Bede would have seen Hild's "motherhood" at Whitby as having been exercised not only in her nurturing of six monks who later became bishops, but also in her own active ministry. There is no reason to limit Bede's conception of "spiritual motherhood" to the exercise of those functions completely separated from what Lees and Overing call "the means of cultural production."

After all, in his commentary on Ezra and Nehemiah, Bede did not hesitate to identify the "female singers" (*cantrices*) of Ezra 2:65 as the many persons of the feminine sex who "not only by the way they live but also by preaching enkindle the hearts of their neighbours to the praise of their Creator."[40] Similarly, Bede

---

[39] Catherine Karkov, "Whitby, Jarrow and the Commemoration of Death in Northumbria," in *Northumbria's Golden Age*, ed. Jane Hawkes and Susan Mills (Stroud, 1999), p. 130: "Bede cannot be held responsible for silencing Hild, or reducing her to the role of spiritual mother, although overall his treatment of women is, as many have noted, problematic...If we learn nothing of her words, actions, or cult, it may be because she had already been relegated to obscurity by the time of Bede."

[40] Bede, *In Ezr.* 1 (p. 257, lines 650–3): "Bene autem cantoribus etiam cantrices iunguntur propter sexum uidelicet femineum in quo plurimae repperiuntur personae quae non solum uiuendo uerum etiam

speaks of the inspiring example of Hild's holy life, but he also depicts her as a pastor when he describes how even in her illness "she never ceased . . . to instruct the flock committed to her charge both in public and in private."[41] We find her presiding over her monastery with great industry, establishing a strict monastic rule, teaching her nuns and monks to continue in peace and charity above all else, and providing counsel to kings and princes in their difficulties.[42]

Such works of active ministry are not exceptions to Hild's spiritual motherhood, but expressions of it. By extension, we might even see her apostolic maternity vicariously at work when she encourages the poet Caedmon to ruminate on the sacred history "like some clean animal chewing the cud" so that he might turn it into melodious verse for the edification of the people.[43] Here the imagery changes a bit, but the result is the same. Caedmon himself is not an apostolic mother—that role is reserved for Hild—but perhaps there is a suggestion that he is being compared to a dairy cow in her herd, transforming doctrinal mysteries into more easily digestible milk at her command.

Bede's commentary on the Song of Songs is interesting in its own right as a great work of Christian spirituality, and we have seen that a close reading of this commentary can be instructive for students of the *Historia ecclesiastica* as well. Benedicta Ward has suggested that Bede may have intended the five books of that history as complement to the five books of Moses in the Old Testament.[44] Henry Mayr-Harting would have us see Bede's account of the foundations of the English church as parallel to

---

praedicando corda proximorum ad laudem sui creatoris accendant." Trans. Scott DeGregorio, *Bede: On Ezra and Nehemiah*, Translated Texts for Historians 47 (Liverpool, 2006), p. 32.

[41] Bede, *HE* 4.23 (p. 412).

[42] Bede, *HE* 4.23 (p. 408).

[43] Bede, *HE* 4.24 (p. 418).

[44] Ward, *Venerable Bede*, p. 114.

his commentary on the building of Solomon's temple.[45] Calvin Kendall believes that the *Historia ecclesiastica* is a continuation of the Acts of the Apostles.[46]

These insightful juxtapositions are by no means mutually exclusive. I find myself agreeing with them all; indeed, we might say that for Bede there is but one sacred story recapitulated over and over again in Scripture and in the Church's experience in every age.

So I do not mean to refute these other helpful comparisons, but to embrace them, when I conclude that while Bede's *Historia ecclesiastica* is indeed the story of a chosen people coming to a promised land, and a blueprint for constructing a holy temple, and the extension of the apostolic mission to the ends of the earth, it is at the same time a song of love in which a bridegroom calls and a bride answers, in which a mother feeds and children are nourished, in which Divine Wisdom takes flesh and human souls sigh with longing for a vision of their God.

[45] Henry Mayr-Harting, *The Venerable Bede, the Rule of St. Benedict, and Social Class* (Jarrow Lecture, 1976).

[46] Calvin Kendall, "'The Manifest Truth of History': Method and Meaning in Bede's Triple Narrative of the Conversion of King Edwin" (paper presented at a conference on "Bede as Writer and Thinker," Center for Medieval Studies, University of Minnesota, April 1998).

Bede's Originality in his Use of the Book of Wisdom in his *Homilies on the Gospels*

Lawrence T. Martin

I N THE PREFACE TO HIS *Expositio Actuum Apostolorum,* and in several other places as well, Bede characterized himself as a traditionalist, "following in the footsteps of the Fathers,"[1] and his exegetical works often include frequent and lengthy quotations from earlier writers. Consequently, many earlier scholars faulted Bede for his heavy dependence on the thoughts and even the very words of his predecessors. This criticism was applied not only to Bede's exegetical commentaries, but to his *Homilies on the Gospels* as well. For example, Edwin Charles Dargan's classic two volume work, *A History of Preaching,* gives Bede's homilies only a few sentences, dismissing Bede as "largely a compiler," and describing his homilies as "monkish and dry, and full of extracts from the Fathers, especially Gregory the Great."[2] Cyril Smetana describes Bede's *Homilies* that were included in the homiliary of Paul the Deacon as "a mosaic of biblical and patristic sourc-

---

[1] *Exp. Act.* Praef. (p. 3, lines 9–10). For further instances of this phrase in Bede's writings, see Roger Ray's essay above, p. 11, n. 2.

[2] Edwin Charles Dargan, *A History of Preaching,* 2 vols. (New York, 1968), 1: 187 and 147. It is interesting to compare Dargan's dismissive attitude toward Bede's homilies with that of O. C. Edward Jr., who, in his recently published *A History of Preaching* (Nashville, Tenn., 2004), devotes considerable attention to Bede and emphasizes the great influence Bede's homilies had on the rich tradition of monastic preaching in the Middle Ages (pp. 143–9).

Lawrence T. Martin

es."[3] In his article "Bede the Scholar," Paul Meyvaert presents
a survey of such scholarly viewpoints which deprecate Bede's
supposed lack of originality, and then defends Bede against this
charge. Meyvaert does not deny that Bede's exegetical works are
full of borrowings from earlier writers, but he argues that Bede's
scholarship consists in "the way in which Bede has developed
this [borrowed] material, by the structure he has given it. It has
somehow become more coherent in his hands; the sum is greater than its parts. It takes a kind of genius to do this sort of thing
well, a kind of genius which Bede undeniably possessed . . ."[4]
In Meyvaert's view, Bede is not simply a compiler handing on
the work of others. However, despite Meyvaert's use of the label
"genius," the Bede he describes remains a solid traditionalist,
not an original thinker or innovator. Meyvaert's article concen-
trates on Bede's textbooks and exegetical commentaries, making no reference to Bede's homilies, an unfortunate omission,
since the homilies offer rich examples of Bede's creativity and
innovation in his use of traditional sources, both patristic and
biblical.

In contrast to the frequency of direct quotations from the
Fathers in Bede's exegetical commentaries, his homilies have
almost no direct quotations from patristic sources. There are,
however, plenty of echoes from the works of the Fathers in
Bede's homilies, and indeed at times Bede simply seems to para-
phrase his patristic source, interpreting the same biblical passage in essentially the same way as did his predecessor. At other
times, however, the earlier writer's ideas are freely adapted by

[3] Cyril L. Smetana, "Paul the Deacon's Patristic Anthology," in *The Old
English Homily and its Backgrounds*, ed. Paul Szarmach and Bernard
Huppé (Albany, N.Y., 1978), p. 80. It should be noted that some of the
selections from Bede in Paul the Deacon's homiliary are actually extracts
from Bede's commentaries, presented as homilies.

[4] Paul Meyvaert, "Bede the Scholar," in *Famulus Christi: Essays in Commemoration of the Thirteenth Centenary of the Birth of the Venerable Bede*, ed. Gerald
Bonner (London, 1976), p. 62.

Bede in a highly innovative way to his own homiletic themes
and purposes regarding the spiritual life of his monastic listeners and readers. For example, in his homily for the feast
of the Purification, Bede draws on passages from Augustine
and Jerome concerning the symbolism of pigeons and doves.
But Bede uses the passages to develop one of his rich themes
of monastic spirituality, "sobriety, simplicity and compunction
of heart," whereas the context of the passage from Augustine
concerned the controversy with the Donatists about whether
baptism could be repeated, and the passage from Jerome dealt
with the evaluation of marriage and the question of remarriage
for widows.[5]

Bede's homilies are also characterized by numerous quotations from books of Sacred Scripture beyond the gospel text
directly under consideration. Bede often seems to be led from
a word, phrase or theme in the gospel pericope to another
place in the Scriptures where the same word, phrase or theme
functions in a particularly rich way with respect to the spiritual life. This practice of "concordance exegesis" was well established in patristic tradition, and Jean Leclercq suggests that
it was rooted in rabbinic exegesis.[6] However, the way in which
Bede interrelates biblical texts is often highly creative, and for
the listener/reader, it can be extremely demanding as well as
rewarding. Quite often, instead of merely making a brief allusion to another scriptural passage, Bede takes considerable
time to explore the riches of the two passages that he connects,
relishing certain words and phrases, repeating them in fugue-
like patterns of allusion, and using them as a sort of bridge

[5] For a fuller discussion of Bede's innovative adaptation of patristic material in his homily for the Purification, see the introduction to *Bede
the Venerable: Homilies on the Gospels*, trans. Lawrence T. Martin and David Hurst, 2 vols., Cistercian Studies Series, 110–11 (Kalamazoo, Mich.,
1991), 1: xvii–xxii.

[6] Jean Leclercq, *The Love of Learning and the Desire for God*, trans. Catharine
Misrahi (New York, 1962), p. 82.

between the historical world of the gospel story and the present world of his listeners' or readers' own spiritual experience.[7] The homilies are intended "both to explain the sacred text and to move [the listeners], to produce appreciation and delight as well as understanding."[8] Indeed, it seems quite likely that Bede envisioned his homilies as offering ever greater riches and new sorts of connections each time they were encountered in the organized pattern of prayerful private reading which monastic writers refer to as *lectio divina*, or in public reading in Chapter or the Night Office.[9] It is perhaps this intention that sometimes guided Bede both in his selection of biblical texts beyond the gospel story itself, and in his manner of treatment of these biblical texts.

In his homilies Bede was especially inclined to draw upon passages from the wisdom books of the Old Testament in order to build a bridge linking his audience to events of the gospel story. It is not possible here to consider Bede's use of all seven of the books of wisdom. I will not attempt any discussion of

[7] Lawrence T. Martin, "The Two Worlds in Bede's Homilies: The Biblical Event and the Listeners' Experience," in *De Ore Domini: Preacher and Word in the Middle Ages*, ed. Thomas L. Amos, Eugene A. Green, and Beverly Mayne Kienzle (Kalamazoo, Mich., 1989), p. 35; cf. Philip West, "Liturgical Style and Structure in Bede's Christmas Homilies," *American Benedictine Review* 23 (1972): 431.

[8] Lawrence T. Martin, "Bede's Structural Use of Wordplay as a Way to Teach," in *From Cloister to Classroom: Monastic and Scholastic Approaches to Truth*, ed. E. Rozanne Elder (Kalamazoo, Mich., 1986), p. 31.

[9] A modern monastic author, writing about *lectio divina*, observes: "The repetitive character of *lectio divina* means that we pass through the same territory several times during life. Each time we will find ourselves aware of different aspects of what we are reading. As our perspective changes with experience, we will become more perceptive of the deeper meanings of the text that were previously hidden from us." Michael Casey, *Sacred Reading: The Ancient Art of Lectio Divina* (Liguori, Mo., 1996), p. 47.

Bede's enormous use of the Psalms, which are, in any case, different from the rest of the wisdom books in many ways.[10] I must also rule out consideration of the Song of Songs because of the complexity of the exegetical tradition concerning that book, a tradition to which Bede himself contributed a commentary.[11] Bede only quotes Ecclesiastes once and, perhaps surprisingly, he makes relatively little use of the Book of Job. The two wisdom books which (except for the Psalms) Bede most often quotes in his homilies are the Book of Proverbs and the Book of Wisdom (also known as the Wisdom of Solomon). I will concentrate in the present essay on Bede's use of the Book of Wisdom because this book offers particularly rich and interesting examples of Bede's complex rhetorical use of biblical allusion to link his audience to the gospel story.

The Book of Wisdom is perhaps the latest book in the Old Testament. In fact, because of its late date and because it was written in Greek, it did not enter the Hebrew canon, and today it is considered one of the books of the Apocrypha. In the Latin Vulgate, however, it is placed among the wisdom books, between the Song of Songs and the Book of Ecclesiasticus (or Sirach).[12] The main purpose of the Book of Wisdom was to strengthen the faith of Jews in Egypt, who were facing many challenges from the religious and philosophical ideas circulating in the Helle-

---

[10] For a wide-ranging treatment of Bede and the Psalms, see Benedicta Ward, *Bede and the Psalter* (Jarrow Lecture, 1991).

[11] On this work, see, in addition to Holder's essay in this volume, Ann Matter, *Voice of My Beloved: The Song of Songs in Medieval Western Christianity* (Philadelphia, 1990), and Rosanna Guglielmetti, "'Super Cantica canticorum': Nota sulla tradizione dei commenti di Ruperto di Deutz, Bernardo di Clairvaux, Guglielmo di Saint-Thierry, Beda e Alcuino," *Studi Medievali* 43 (2002): 277–86.

[12] For a more detailed account of these matters, see James Reese, "Wisdom of Solomon," in *The Oxford Companion to the Bible*, ed. Bruce M. Metzger and Michael D. Coogan (Oxford, 1993), p. 803.

nistic world.[13] To achieve this purpose, the author borrows the language and themes of Greek philosophical reflection, and the resulting image of wisdom in this book is consequently often rather abstract and less connected to the practical value of wisdom for everyday life that characterizes the other wisdom books. The Book of Wisdom has, however, had an important place in Christian tradition, not only because certain passages have been given Christological or Mariological interpretations, but also because the book places considerable emphasis on the doctrine of the immortality of the soul, an idea which otherwise lacks very much Old Testament support.

According to my reckoning, there are seventeen echoes of the Book of Wisdom in Bede's homilies. Interestingly, however, it was not the teaching on the immortality of the soul or the traditional Christological or Mariological readings of particular passages that seem to have drawn Bede to this book. Instead, certain fairly specific themes and distinctive locutions from this book appear again and again in Bede's homilies, functioning as a sort of motif that enriches Bede's homiletic focus on a fundamental contrast between two sorts of basic attitudes toward life. Many of Bede's allusions to the Book of Wisdom are from two poems found early in the biblical book. The opening poem of the Book of Wisdom is addressed to rulers, directing them to "love justice" (*Diligite iustitiam qui iudicatis terram*) and to seek the Lord in "simplicity of heart" (*in simplicitate cordis*: Wisd. 1:1). The poet goes on to warn his aristocratic audience against the corrupting potential of power, because, he says, "Wisdom will never enter the soul of a malevolent person" (*Quoniam in malivolam animam non intrabit sapientia*: Wisd. 1:4), and "the spirit of discipline flees the deceitful" (*spiritus disciplinae effugiet fictum*: Wisd. 1:5). It is the contrast between these two life orientations, "simplicity of

---

[13] Addison G. Wright, "Wisdom," in *The New Jerome Biblical Commentary*, ed. Raymond E. Brown, Joseph A. Fitzmyer, and Roland E. Murphy (Englewood Cliffs, N.J., 1990), p. 511.

heart" versus "malevolence" or "deceit" that occurs again and again as a major theme in Bede's homilies.

First, let us consider Homily 12 of Book 1, for the Feast of the Epiphany. The gospel reading is the story of Jesus' baptism, from chapter 3 of Matthew's gospel. Bede takes this story as "a noble example of perfect humility" (*magnum perfectae humilitatis exemplum*), both because of Jesus' willingness to be baptized by a mere human being, and because of John's protestations of his unworthiness.[14] In Matthew's account, Jesus says that his baptism by John is proper "to fulfill all justice" (*implere omnem iustitiam*: Matt. 3:15). This perhaps provided for Bede, by a sort of concordance exegesis, a hook to the opening poem in the Book of Wisdom, the first words of which are *Diligite iustitiam*. If so, the link is not explicit, since Bede does not quote the first part of Wisd. 1:1. He does, however, draw heavily on the following verses of the poem for his contrast between "simplicity of heart" and "malevolence" or "deceit." In the gospel story, when Jesus was baptized, "He saw the Spirit of God descending like a dove and coming down on him" (Matt. 3:16). Bede observes that the dove is "a very simple bird" which he takes as symbolizing the simplicity of Jesus' nature, and also as a call to all Christians to be "simple and clean of heart,"[15] an echo of Wisd. 1:1. Indeed, Bede here inserts a quotation made up of phrases from the first five verses of the Book of Wisdom, contrasting this quality of

---

[14] Bede, *Hom.* 1.12 (p. 80, lines 2–19); trans. Lawrence T. Martin and David Hurst, *Bede the Venerable: Homilies on the Gospels*, 2 vols., Cistercian Studies Series, 110 and 111 (Kalamazoo, Mich., 1991),1:113–14; all subsequent translations are taken from the latter. Bede's *Homilies on the Gospels* are arranged in two books, with twenty-five homilies in each book. The homilies of Book 1 are in vol. 110, and those of Book 2 are in vol. 111.

[15] Bede, *Hom.* 1.12 (p. 83, lines 117–24): "Bene autem Spiritus reconciliator in columba quae multum simplex est auis apparuit ut et suae uidelicet naturae simplicitatem per huius speciem animalis ostenderet, *Spiritus enim sanctus disciplinae effugiet fictum*, et eum in quem descendit man-

"simplicity of heart" with the "malevolence" of a soul which wisdom will not enter (Wisd. 1:4), and with the "deceit" which the Holy Spirit of discipline or instruction flees (Wisd. 1:5). Bede underscores the contrast by juxtaposing the dove as a symbol of simplicity of heart with the serpent which deceived Eve in the story of the fall in the third chapter of Genesis. Bede also alludes here to the story of Simon Magus in the eighth chapter of Acts, Simon the magician being an example of the sort of "malevolent soul" into which true wisdom will not enter. Later in the same homily Bede returns to the theme of the contrast between "the fraudulent tooth of a serpent" and "the simple eye of a dove, which the Lord . . . loves very much in his Church."[16] In a long passage, Bede discourses, in a fashion reminiscent of the bestiary tradition, on the natural characteristics of doves—for example, the dove "does not nourish itself or its young with tiny mice or grubs, as almost all smaller birds do,"[17] but the dove's diet is limited to "the fruits and seeds of the earth" (*terrae fructibus et semine*) with which it nourishes not only its own young but also the young of strangers.[18] Bede explores the richness of what he calls "seven examples of virtue concerning the nature of the dove"[19] and its symbolic significance, for which he uses

suetum mitemque ac misericordiae supernae praeconem ministrumque doceret mundo esse futurum. Simul et omnes qui sua gratia essent renouandi simplices ac mundi corde ammoneret ingredi..." Trans. Martin and Hurst, 1:117.

[16] Bede, *Hom.* 1.12 (p. 85, lines 194–6): "...serpentino potius dente fraudulenti quam simplici oculo columbino..." Trans. Martin and Hurst, 1:120.

[17] Bede, *Hom.* 1.12 (p. 85, lines 203–5): "...ne minimas quidem musculas uel uermiculos quibus minores paene omnes auiculae se suosque pullos nutriunt." Trans. Martin and Hurst, 1:120.

[18] Bede, *Hom.* 1.12 (p. 85, lines 209–11); trans. Martin and Hurst, 1:121.

[19] Bede, *Hom.* 1.12 (p. 86, lines 243–44): "Haec de natura columbae septem uirtutis exempla commemorasse sufficiat." Trans. Martin and Hurst, 1:122.

the terms *mysterium, sacramentum, moraliter interpretanda, mystico, figura,* and the foreshadowing (*umbra*) being in agreement with the fulfillment (*veritas*),[20] and he makes many connections to passages referring to the dove in the Song of Songs, and to the story in the eighth chapter of Genesis concerning Noah's sending out a dove at the end of the Flood—passages which were seen as pregnant with significance in the tradition of allegorical exegesis of the sort which Bede practiced in his own commentaries on Genesis and on the Song of Songs.[21]

Bede left us no commentary on Matthew's gospel, but it is interesting to compare the homily on Matthew's story of Jesus' baptism with the corresponding sections of Bede's commentaries on Mark and Luke, since the portion of the pericope under discussion (the descent of the dove) is essentially identical in all three of the synoptic gospels.[22] Bede's *In Marcum* includes a very brief use of some of the same material concerning the allegorical significances of the nature of the dove as that found in Bede's homily,[23] but in the commentary he makes no use of the opening poem from the Book of Wisdom. In his *In Lucam,* Bede's discussion of this passage is fairly short and lacking in dove-lore, but he does make a brief connection between the dove of the baptism story and the opening poem of the Book of Wisdom. He does not, however, directly mention "simplicity" in connection with the dove or quote the "simplicity of heart" portion of the Book of Wisdom poem, although he does quote "the spirit of discipline or instruction flees deceit" portion of the poem.[24] The theme of the contrast between "simplicity of heart"

---

[20] Bede, *Hom.* 1.12 (p. 86, lines 230, 236, 246, 247, 248; p. 87, line 265); trans. Martin and Hurst, 1:121–3. See Calvin Kendall's essay in this volume for an illuminating discussion of Bede's use of these terms for the "divine meaning" of a biblical text.

[21] See the source notes in Martin and Hurst, 1:120–2.

[22] Compare Matthew 3:16 with Mark 1:10 and Luke 3: 21–22.

[23] Bede, *In Marcum* 1 (p. 444, lines 272–6).

[24] Bede, *In Lucam* 1 (p. 84, lines 2566–7).

and "malevolence" or "deceitfulness" is, in any case, much more fully developed in Bede's homily, where it dominates his entire treatment of the gospel story.

John's gospel does not include the story of Jesus' baptism. There is, however, a passage in the first chapter of John's gospel where John the Evangelist quotes John the Baptist concerning his relationship to Jesus, and the Baptist here refers to seeing the Spirit coming down like a dove on Jesus. This Johannine text is, in fact, the pericope for another of Bede's homilies, for one of the Sundays after Epiphany. Here again Bede takes the dove as symbolic of "innocence and simplicity" (*innocentiam simplicitatemque*) and he again quotes the opening verse of the Book of Wisdom, "Seek the Lord in simplicity of heart,"[25] but simplicity of heart is a minor theme in this homily, and Bede does not here develop the contrast between simplicity and its opposite, "malevolence" or "deceit." Bede's idea of the dove as a symbol of simplicity is perhaps derived from St. Augustine's tractate on this Johannine reading. However, for Augustine *simplicitas* has to do with the singleness, i.e., the unique, unrepeatable character of Christian baptism as opposed to the Donatist heretics, who advocated rebaptism of the lapsed. For Bede, *simplicitas* is instead the quality of soul set forth in the poem in the opening chapter of the Book of Wisdom.

In another homily on a different Johannine text, Bede develops a similar contrast between simplicity and "guile" (*dolus*), and here again he draws on the opening poem from the Book of Wisdom. The gospel story in this homily is Jesus' calling of Phillip and Nathaniel to be apostles (John 1:43–51). In the story Jesus refers to Nathaniel as "an Israelite in whom there is no guile" (*in quo dolus non est*: John 1:47). Bede, probably following Augustine, explains the necessary distinction between "sin"

---

[25] Bede *Hom.* 1.15 (p. 107, line 92 – p. 108, line 96); trans. Martin and Hurst, 1:151.

(*peccatum*) and "guile" (*dolus*), for, Bede says, it is impossible for any human being to be without sin,[26] and in support of this he quotes Ecclesiastes (Eccl. 7:21), Bede's only use in his homilies of that most pessimistic of the wisdom books. However, it is possible for human beings to be without guile, says Bede, for to be without guile is simply to "have conducted themselves with simple and clean hearts" (*simplici et mundo corde conuersati esse*) and for this definition he cites the authority of Wisd. 1:1, "Seek the Lord in simplicity of heart," a call which, Bede affirms, is addressed to all of the faithful. He also quotes Jesus' exhortation to his apostles in Matthew's gospel to be "simple like doves" (*estote . . . simplices sicut columbae.* Matt. 10:16).[27] Here Bede does not seize the opportunity to talk about the nature of doves, and instead he provides his listeners with Old Testament models of simplicity, including Job, who in the first verse of the wisdom book which bears his name is introduced as "a man simple and righteous."[28]

In yet another homily, from one of the Sundays after Easter, Bede once more utilizes his theme of the contrast between the virtue of "simplicity of heart" (Wisd. 1:1) and its opposite vice, the "deceit" (*fictum*) referred to in Wisd. 1:5. The text of this homily is John 16:5–15, which is part of Jesus' farewell discourse in which he promises to send the Paraclete. Near the beginning of the homily, Bede explains that Jesus refers to the Holy Spirit as "the Paraclete" because that term means "the Consoler," and Jesus' followers, saddened by his departure, would be consoled by the coming of the Spirit. The coming of the Spirit will, however, be not a consolation but a terrifying judgment to those who refused to believe in Jesus, says Bede, pointing to Jesus' words in the gospel story, still promising the coming of

[26] Bede *Hom.* 1.17 (p. 123, lines 148–51); trans. Martin and Hurst, 1:171.

[27] Bede, *Hom.* 1.17 (p. 123, 151–6); trans. Martin and Hurst, 1:171.

[28] Bede, *Hom.* 1.17 (p. 123, lines 156–61); trans. Martin and Hurst, 1:171.

the Spirit, but referring to the effect this coming will have on the sinful: "And when he comes, he will convict the world of sin and of righteousness and of judgment" (John 16:8). By "the world," Bede explains, Jesus meant "the adherents of the world" who were to be convicted when the Spirit came, "of the sin of its unbelief."[29] Bede here emphasizes the fact that virtue has a flip side or a negative opposite, viz., the absence of the virtue in question—in this case, the virtue of belief and the vice of unbelief. To underscore this idea Bede introduces another line from the opening poem of the Book of Wisdom: "Virtue that has been tested reproves the unwise" (*probata autem virtus corripit insipientes*: Wisd. 1:3).[30]

Later, in the concluding exhortation of this same homily, Bede returns to Wisdom 1:5.[31] In this homily on the sending of the Paraclete, of course, unlike the earlier cases, the verse from the opening poem of the Book of Wisdom is used partly because it appears to be an Old Testament explicit reference to the Holy Spirit, i.e., a trinitarian text. However, this text also functions in this homily, as in the earlier examples, to carry the universal theme which appears to have been close to Bede's heart, viz., the fundamental contrast between the attitude described as "simplicity of heart" and that called "deceit" (or perhaps "pretense" is a better English rendering of *fictum*), the same opposite of *simplicitas* which is called "guile" (*dolus*) in the homily concerning Nathaniel.

Another of Bede's homilies for the Sundays after Easter is based on the portion of John's gospel that immediately follows the pericope of the homily which has just been discussed. The reading continues Jesus's farewell discourse and, as in the ear-

---

[29] Bede, *Hom.* 2.11 (p. 255, 65–67): "Claret namque quod ipse filius Dei dominus noster Iesus Christus cum esset in mundo arguebat mundum, id est sectatores mundi, de peccato suae incredulitatis…" Trans. Martin and Hurst, 2:100.

[30] Bede, *Hom.* 2.11 (p. 255, line 93); trans. Martin and Hurst, 2:101.

[31] Bede, *Hom.* 2.11 (p. 259, lines 216–17); trans. Martin and Hurst, 2:106.

lier text, Jesus contrasts his followers with "the world," saying, "Amen, Amen, I say to you, you will be weeping and wailing, but the world will rejoice" (John 16:20). At this point Bede pauses to give a fuller description of the meaning of the Johannine term "the world": "those who loved the world, those whom, on account of their base thoughts the Lord called 'the world,' rejoiced when they condemned him who was troubling for them even to look at to a shameful death."[32] This rather elaborate sentence ends with a concatenation of two verses from a poem in chapter two of the Book of Wisdom. The phrase "condemned to a shameful death" is from verse twenty, and "him who was troubling for them even to look at" is from verse fifteen.

The poem from which these two verses are lifted takes up the entire second chapter of the Book of Wisdom. It is a sort of Browningesque dramatic monologue, dripping with irony, put in the mouth of the "wicked" (*impii*), and those whose "thoughts are twisted" (*cogitantes non recte*, Wisd. 1:16–2:1). These anonymous speakers lay out their perverse plans to oppress the poor, the aged, the weak, and especially the virtuous man "for he is of no use to us and he is contrary to our doings" (Wisd. 2:12). The phrases that Bede borrows to characterize "those who love the world" are taken from this part of the ironic poem, where the wicked speakers rage against the virtuous man: "He is grievous unto us, even to behold, for his life is not like other peoples," and his ways are very different" (Wisd. 2:15), and a few verses later, "Let us condemn him to a most shameful death" (Wisd. 2:20).

Bede's application of these verses to the specific "lovers of the world" who condemned Jesus to death shows that Bede was thinking of the ironic poem of the second chapter of the Book of Wisdom as a whole in order to draw his parallel. He reverses

---

[32] Bede, *Hom.* 2.13 (p. 268, lines 50–52): "Gaudebant mundi amatores quos ob infimas cogitationes mundum uocat dominus cum morte turpissima condemnarent illum qui grauis erat eis etiam ad uidendum." Trans. Martin and Hurst, 2:119.

the order of the two verses (which are separated by five verses in the poem), and he reworks the syntax in order to achieve a dramatic ending to his homiletic statement. The effect he is seeking here is not New Testament fulfillment of Old Testament prophecy, but rather the increase in the homiletic impact achieved by drawing on the ironic monologue of the earlier writer. Only those listeners who caught the allusion and recalled its ironic setting would, of course, have fully appreciated Bede's art here. The point that Bede is making in his homily does not absolutely depend on recognition of the allusion and its context, but such recognition adds an element of delight for the listener or reader who does perceive the allusion to the poem from the biblical book and knows its ironic context. In other words, this passage illustrates an important generalization that can be made about Bede's homilies—that they were intended to be accessible to all but to offer special delights here and there that would reward the more learned or those who returned to them time and again as the Church year brought them back as sacred readings for the Divine Office or daily Chapter.

Bede's History in a Harsher Climate

Walter Goffart

IN A MEMORABLE APPRECIATION of Bede, the late Sir Richard Southern spoke of being awed by Jarrow, the site of the monastery in which Bede lived and worked.[1] The Jarrow that I visited inspired more regret than elation. There was a church lying amidst the decay of industrialism, with pylons and high-tension wires providing the only uplift. Since then, there have been changes for the better, but South Tyneside seems immune to improvement. Hopeful organizers have now created a small theme park called "Bede's World."

Jarrow is a few miles downstream from Newcastle (a twelfth-century town) and not far from Hadrian's Roman wall. With Wearmouth, its twin, about fifty miles to the south, Bede's home was among the earliest monasteries in Northumbria. It had been

[1] R. W. Southern, "Bede," in *Medieval Humanism and Other Studies* (1970; reprinted, Oxford, 1984), p. 1. His comment that "whatever beauty there may be is distinctly austere," suggests that, at a simple level, his eyes and mine made out the same spectacle. Southern grew up near Jarrow. My remarks in what follows are based mainly on my chapter "Bede and the Ghost of Bishop Wilfrid," in *The Narrators of Barbarian History (A.D. 550-800): Jordanes, Gregory of Tours, Bede, and Paul the Deacon* (Princeton, N.J., 1988; reprinted, Notre Dame, 2005), pp. 235–328. It is supplemented by my "The *Historia ecclesiastica*: Bede's Agenda and Ours," *Haskins Society Journal: Studies in Medieval History* 2 (1990): 29–45, and "L'Histoire ecclésiastique et l'engagement politique de Bède," in *Bède le Vénérable entre tradition et postérité. Actes du colloque international Bède le Vénérable: bilan et perspectives*, ed. Stéphane Lebecq, Michel Perrin, and Olivier Szerwiniack (Lille, 2005), pp. 149–58 (which overlaps with the present study).

founded by a rich, restless nobleman named Benedict Biscop. The English Benedict tirelessly traveled to the Continent and Mediterranean, acquiring sumptuous furnishings for his foundations and a library of some 200 books.[2] He made Wearmouth and Jarrow treasure-houses for these artifacts from an advanced civilization. At no time before (even in the days of Roman Britain) had so much written culture been accumulated so far to the north. Bede was the most learned and productive scholar of the eighth century. He probably has no rival even in glamorous, remote Byzantium. The missionary and pedagogic activity of Anglo-Saxons in the Carolingian empire gave his name and exegetical writings wide currency beyond the homeland he himself never left. While living, Bede was neither hidden away nor obscure. By middle age he was the Northumbrian equivalent of a celebrity. Dignitaries from Canterbury far to the south dealt with him on serious matters, notably the contents of the history he was composing; and when he wrote admonitions to the bishop of York, he could expect a hearing.[3]

Monks were not normally ordained; Bede, however, was made a priest in 703. This marked his start as an ecclesiastical writer, a preacher on parchment. He died thirty-two years later. Biblical commentaries were the staple of his production, but he also wrote historical works. In 725 he composed a chronicle, or compact history of the world. Precisely when he started the *Historia ecclesiastica gentis Anglorum* is not certain. Nevertheless he was old when this long, ambitious work was launched. He had not written anything of the kind before.[4]

The *Historia ecclesiastica* has five books. Starting with a description of the British Isles and their population, and with a glance at the Roman period, the history traces the gradual Christianization of England and ends with a brief account of conditions at

---

[2] Peter Hunter Blair, *The World of Bede* (1970; reprinted, Cambridge, 1990), pp. 155–83.

[3] Goffart, *Narrators,* pp. 241 n. 33, 274–5, 296–8.

[4] Goffart., pp. 241–42, 246–49.

the time of writing. These final lines are concerned only with Northumbria, and the same holds for more than half the entire history. Bede does not disregard England, but his work is not about all the lands conquered by the Anglo-Saxons. His slant is overwhelmingly Northumbrian. The chronological scope is also uneven. We hear much in books one and two about the Gregorian mission that started in 596, and most of the seventh century is well taken care of. But that is all. Just when Bede could have relied on his personal observations, his narrative virtually stops. The twenty-five years down to the time of writing are largely disregarded.

Bede's history is remarkably sunny. One admirable and endearing hero or heroine after the other parades before us. O happy island to have origins like these! None of the so-called "barbarian histories"—Jordanes, Paul the Deacon, Widukind, and others—comes anywhere close to being so positive and glowing. The extraordinary charm of Bede's England is unlikely to be a simple and direct reflection of what early England really was. Others before me have been well aware of this sobering thought. At a conference on early medieval historiography in 1993, Henry Mayr-Harting deplored a recent development in Bede studies: a generation of Bede lovers—Peter Hunter Blair, J. N. L Myres, Dorothy Whitelock, J. M. Wallace-Hadrill—had departed from the scene. Their passing left Bede exposed in a harsher climate of Collinses, Kirbys, and Goffarts. I don't know how Roger Collins and David Kirby earned their anathemas; my sins are obvious. Even James Campbell, once a reliable Bede lover, had dared to bring the word "humbug" into Bede's vicinity.[5] Today's surly iconoclasm seems to be defacing even St. Bede.

[5] Henry Mayr-Harting, "Bede's Patristic Thinking as an Historian," in *Historiographie im frühen Mittelalter*, ed. Anton Scharer and Georg Scheibelreiter, Veröffentlichung des Instituts fur Österreichische Geschichtsforschung 32 (Vienna, 1994), p. 367. In my case he was referring to the Bede chapter of *Narrators*. For Campbell and "humbug," also see Mayr-Harting, p. 367.

Walter Goffart

When the Center for Medieval Studies at the University of Minnesota–Twin Cities invited me to speak at its conference on "Bede as Writer and Thinker" in 1998, I was asked whether there might have been a deep shift in my thinking about Bede in the ten years since I published *The Narrators of Barbarian History*. Did I still believe that Bishop Wilfrid, a prominent Northumbrian who died in 709, was "a concern central to Bede's project?" I had to answer with apologies that my research had moved to other subjects, but that I had tried to keep track of how my Bede chapter has fared.

A disappointing aspect of its reception has been what looks to me like a *reductio ad Wilfridum*. Roger Collins, for example, declares: "[Goffart's] thesis, that Bede was reacting to the post-humous influence of Wilfrid, may seem a little narrow."[6] What is narrow here is Collins's arbitrary encapsulation of my argument. My Bede chapter covers much ground. The longest subsection, called "the genesis of Northumbrian church history," tries to subvert the cherished idea that Bede's history is isolated and unique.

At least one reviewer generously pointed out that, in this section, I "bring the *Historia ecclesiastica* into a dynamic relationship with the rest of the literature of the Northumbrian Golden Age," and Averil Cameron flatteringly associates these same pages with Clifford Geertz's anthropology by referring to a "thick Northumbrian context."[7] I mention Wilfrid in the chapter title and pay much attention to Bede's attitude to him. But, *pace* Roger Collins and those who, like him, confuse the contents with the title, my account of the *Historia ecclesiastica* is more concerned

[6] Judith McClure and Roger Collins, "Introduction," in *The Ecclesiastical History of the English People. The Greater Chronicle. Bede's Letter to Egbert*, ed. McClure and Collins, Oxford World's Classics (Oxford, 1994), p. xx, n. 19.

[7] David Pelteret, "Year's Work in Old English Studies," *Old English Newsletter* 23 (1989), p. 81; Averil Cameron, review of Goffart, *Narrators of Barbarian History*, in *American Historical Review* 95 (1990): 1172.

with the Northumbrian kingdom and church of Bede's adulthood than with Wilfrid alone.

My *Narrators of Barbarian History* approaches the four historians of its title with an explicit program, the proper name for which, as Nancy Partner has helpfully told me, is "intentionalist." "If a single theme runs through this book," I say early in the Preface, "it is that, like us, Jordanes, Gregory, and the others meant to write what they did and were well aware of what they said and why."[8] There is more explanation in chapter 1:

> The four authors...undertook, for a variety of reasons, to record and interpret the past. Though more often honest and high-minded than not, their endeavors were never innocent, nor should anyone wish them to be. Their portrayals were conscious and deliberate, and worthy of sustained attention for precisely this reason.[9]

My intentionalism was not meant to be revolutionary or combative. But clouds gather thickly over the head of anyone who dares suggest that Bede might have been anything but innocent, spotless, and without sin. Some commentators portray Bede as a remote scholar, detached from the world, wholly caught up in books. My Bede is *engagé* and interventionist, too much so to remain unstained by what he was doing. Henry Mayr-Harting unrepentingly sides with innocence: "Bede's real world, I persist in thinking, was the world of books." Mayr-Harting said so in 1972 and does again in 1993. A Bede of this kind avoids entanglement in the dirty world.[10]

[8] Goffart, *Narrators*, p. ix

[9] Ibid., pp. 16–17.

[10] Mayr-Harting, "Bede's Patristic Thinking," p. 373 (he adds: "my own perception of Bede as a scholar, historian, and human being is of a totally different character"; I respect that dissent). For his earlier formulation of this idea, see *The Coming of Christianity to Anglo-Saxon England* (London, 1972), p. 40.

The source passages I am about to quote give an example of the intentionalist approach to Bede. Doing so may illustrate what Mayr-Harting calls a "harsher climate." The two quotations can be entitled, "Young Wilfrid decides to visit the Holy See." I begin with the account of Wilfrid's biographer, Stephen of Ripon, and continue with Bede's adaptation of Stephen's story:

> "After the lapse of a few years, it came into the heart of this same young man, by the promptings of the Holy Spirit, to pay a visit to the see of the Apostle Peter, the chief of the Apostles, and to attempt a road hitherto untrodden by any of our race. By so doing he believed that he would cleanse himself from every blot and stain and receive the joy of the divine blessing.[11]

> My vows have been rendered to the Lord and I will fulfill them…to visit the Apostolic See, and to learn the rules of ecclesiastical discipline, so that our nation may grow in the service of God."[12]

[11] Stephen, *Vita Wilfridi* 3 (p. 8): "Deinde post circulum annorum, suggerente spiritu sancto, apellare et videre sedem apostoli Petri et apostolorum principis, adhuc inattritam viam genti nostrae temptare in cor adolescentis supradicti ascendit et ab ea omnem nodum maculae solvendum sibi credens et beatitudinem benedictionis accipiendam." Trans. Colgrave, *Life of Wilfrid*, p. 9.

[12] Stephen, *Vita Wilfridi* 4 (p. 10): "Sunt vota mea Domino, quae reddam,…ut visitem sedem apostolicam et ecclesiasticae disciplinae regulas didicerim in augmentum gentis nostrae ad serviendum Deo." Trans. Colgrave, *Life of Wilfrid*, p. 11. Wilfrid's biographer is now called Stephanus or (as here) Stephen of Ripon. The traditional identification that Colgrave subscribed to is withering away (and not, I am happy to say, only by my doing). For the evidence, see Kirby, "Bede, Eddius Stephanus and the 'Life of Wilfrid'," pp.102–3; Goffart, *Narrators*, pp. 281–3. William Trent Foley, *Images of Sanctity in Eddius Stephanus* Life of Bishop Wilfrid, *An Early English Saint's Life* (Lewiston, N.Y., 1992), despite its title, contains nothing that bears on the issues I discuss.

Stephen tells us about the youthful Wilfrid, while he was at Lindisfarne learning to be a monk at what may then have been the sole monastery in Northumbria. Wilfrid decides to visit Rome; he aims to enter the record books as the first Englishman to make this arduous journey. What he will get for his pains— that is, by reaching the tomb of St. Peter—is the fullest possible forgiveness for his sins. Stephen's account has innocent charm. Its attention to St. Peter's forgiving sins (and to the adolescent Wilfrid's believing that he needed forgiveness) is entirely believable. In the next passage, the bishop of Lyons offers Wilfrid inducements to stay in Frankish Gaul. Wilfrid demurs, giving a new reason for going to Rome: it is the source for the rules of ecclesiastical discipline; by learning them, he will profit his fellow-countrymen in the worship of God. It seems as though Wilfrid, once on the Continent, had become aware of the diversity of church usages and had decided to learn the right ones, as he would in Rome. Stephen introduces a major theme of his hero's life. A thorough grounding in Roman ecclesiastical practices would be very important to Wilfrid's career.

Bede had Stephen's story before him but did not summarize it literally:

> After [Wilfrid] had served God in that monastery for some years, being a youth of shrewd understanding, he gradually came to realize that the way of virtue taught by the Irish was by no means perfect; so he resolved to go to Rome to see what ecclesiastical and monastic practices were observed in the apostolic see.[13]

---

[13] Bede, *HE* 5.19 (pp. 518–19): "In quo videlicet monasterio cum aliquot annos Deo serviret, animadvertit paulatim adulescens animi sagacis minime perfectam esse virtutis viam, quae tradebatur a Scottis, proposuitque animo venire Romam, et qui ad sedem apostolicam ritus ecclesiastici sive monasteriales servarentur videre." I do not follow Colgrave's translation of *virtutis viam, quae tradebatur a Scottis* as "the traditional way of virtuous life followed by the Irish." The contrast of this passage with the *Vita Wilfridi* is not observed by Charles Plummer

Benign interpreters might say that Bede's abbreviation simply made explicit what Stephen implied. If we assume that Bede
knew what he was doing, it looks as though he went well beyond
abridgement. He conjures up Wilfrid as a quick-witted youth,
who, while still underage, sniffs out defects explicitly labeled
Irish. Stephen calls nothing Irish; he does not know about "defects." Bede's lines, though inspired by Stephen's *Life*, are his invention. He moves to Wilfrid's youth the hostility to Irish usages
that crucially advanced his later career. This exercise in trans-
posing Wilfrid's later attitudes to a much earlier date deserves
notice as being an authorial initiative. As I said in *The Narrators
of Barbarian History*, Bede deliberately did what he did, even if
distortion was needed to do so.

This intentionalist approach to Bede has been pioneered by
others. The basic issue is whether or not the *Historia ecclesiastica*
is mimetic. Does it supply an exact image of what once was, or is
it an artistic design, having the man-made truth of literary creation? Was early England exceptionally beautiful and enchant-
ing, as it looks in the *Historia ecclesiastica*, or did Bede simply give
it that guise? Are we dealing with nature or cosmetics? Elegant
précis of the *Historia ecclesiastica* are often written, combining
admiration, praise, piety, and love. Patriotic Englishmen deal
reverently with a national treasure. But some have also cast critical looks at the *Historia ecclesiastica* and recognized that, however
lovable and attractive the world of the *Historia ecclesiastica* may
be, the image is not realistic. The very judicious James Campbell is an example of such discernment.[14] What we look into
is a distorting mirror, not a simple reflection. The removal of

in his fundamental commentary, *Venerabilis Baedae opera historica,* 2 vols.
(1896; reprinted, 2 vols. in 1, Oxford, 1946), vol. 2, p. 321, or in *Bede's
Ecclesiastical History of the English People : A Historical Commentary,* ed. J. M.
Wallace-Hadrill, Thomas Charles-Edwards, Patrick Wormald and others
(Oxford, 1988), p. 192.

[14] James Campbell, "Bede I," in *Essays in Anglo-Saxon History* (London,
1986), p. 25.

makeup from so endearing and cherished a text as the *Historia ecclesiastica* attracts vehement responses.

The editors of the new and welcome World's Classics edition of Bede's history outline the second major aspect of what I do in *The Narrators of Barbarian History*: "Only relatively recently has it come to be appreciated that some explanation is needed for Bede's undertaking of the [*Historia ecclesiastica*]; one, moreover, that takes account of his particular methods of working and of the special concerns which he displays for various themes, topics, and personalities. Goffart...has led the way here."[15] The goal I announce in *Narrators* is to explore "the immediate and local circumstances that gave rise to the *History*." I continue, "In the life of early Northumbria, the composition and issuance of a work so largely concerned as Bede's is with local developments was itself a historical event."[16] David Kirby's Jarrow Lecture for 1992, on "the Contemporary Setting" of Bede's history is, to quote Paul Remley, "one of the first continuous responses to arguments set out in [Goffart's] treatment of Bede." Kirby in fact anticipated me in drawing attention to Bede's immediate context. He wrote as early as 1983, "The key to unlocking the process of writing the *Historia ecclesiastica* may still lie concealed in the tensions of the time in which Bede wrote."[17]

Most of the *Historia ecclesiastica* was not drafted contemporaneously with the persons and events written about. The time of composition, ca. 730, has to be kept clearly distinct from the earlier period that was Bede's main subject—mainly the seventh century, down to 705. To us, the problems of the 1920s are mere

[15] McClure and Collins, "Introduction," *Ecclesiastical History*, p. xx, n. 19.

[16] Goffart, *Narrators*, p. 236.

[17] D. P. Kirby, *Bede's Historia ecclesiastica gentis Anglorum: Its Contemporary Setting* (Jarrow Lecture 1992). (I am very grateful to David Pelteret for giving me a xerox of this work); Paul Remley, "Year's Work in Old English Studies," *Old English Newsletter* 25.2 (1992): 63. For Kirby's earlier comment, see D. P. Kirby, "Bede, Eddius Stephanus and the 'Life of Wilfrid,'" *English Historical Review* 98 (1983): 114.

history by comparison with those of today. Much the same relationship between the dim past and the burning present is likely to have prevailed in Bede's day. The issues relevant in, say, the 660s were necessarily remote from those of Bede's time of writing. Alan Thacker, in a commendable recent article on "Bede and the Irish," asks us to believe that Bede was "much exercised" about the dating of Easter.[18] Yet the Easter dispute, long resolved, was mere history by the time Bede wrote the *Historia ecclesiastica.* Words in books should not be confused with current emotions. Bede on Easter dating needs explanation, but it will not do to say that he "felt passionately" about a subject that had stopped being emotion-laden decades before.[19] Problems have their day. There were new issues for Bede to feel passionately about when the *Historia ecclesiastica* was being written.

One new issue stands out in the early 730s. The composition of Bede's history was somehow related to the archbishopric of Canterbury and to the elevation of Northumbria to the status of an independent ecclesiastical province. Kirby and I agree on this point, at least in principle. The reorganization was completed in the year of Bede's death, when Nothelm, a priest of London well known to him, became archbishop of Canterbury. Bede pays much attention to Canterbury; the *Historia ecclesiastica* emphasizes its contribution to the making of the English church. The harmony of the Northumbrian church with the senior bishopric in England is made entirely clear. This emphasis was a matter of choice.[20]

---

[18]Alan Thacker, "Bede and the Irish," in *Beda Venerabilis: Historian, Monk and Northumbrian,* ed. L. A. J. R. Houwen and A. A. MacDonald, Medievalia Groningana 19 (Groningen, 1996), pp. 38, 59.

[19] For agreement with Thacker that Bede's long chapter on Whitby shows how much he cared about Easter dating, see Peter Hunter Blair in n. 36, below.

[20] Goffart, *Narrators,* pp. 273–5, 287–8, 297; Kirby, *Contemporary Setting,* pp. 4–5.

Although the dealings between Canterbury and Northumbria from the 720s to 735 are less documented than we would like, the promotion of York to an ecclesiastical metropolis does shed light on the *Historia ecclesiastica*. The purpose of Bede's history was not to abase Wilfrid, or to stupefy us with the dating of Easter, or to praise Aidan, Cædmon, and Cuthbert, or to treat other particles of his subject. It was written to present the sum of these and other particulars, the aggregate that we read—an idealized, engaging, edifying account of the church of Northumbria and some of its neighbors, a glowing balance sheet of the Northumbrian past on the occasion of a great leap forward. The elevation of Northumbria to a higher ecclesiastical status was an extraordinary event. Bede could anticipate it even if his own life ran out before the change was completed. This was the future. For its guidance his history offered a vision of the past that was also a model of Christian virtue and holiness. Ultimately, the *Historia ecclesiastica* was written to sound exactly as it sounds—serene and beautiful. Bede gave it this tranquil and pleasing appearance for sturdy, level-headed, practical reasons, and he resorted to devious tactics, unavoidably, in order to attain his goal.[21]

---

[21] Here and there, I have been referred to as hostile to Bishop Wilfrid. This is a misapprehension. If I were writing about Wilfrid, I would portray him positively, as befits an important, interesting, admirable figure. (I also have a high opinion of Stephen of Ripon's *Vita Wilfridi*, whose testimony can be preferable to Bede's.) If I seem negative toward Wilfrid, it is because I try to convey how he was regarded by persons who disapproved of him either in life or, after his death, in the shape of his successors. Their hostility toward Wilfrid and Wilfridians should not be attributed to me. For a recent account of Wilfrid highly resistant to my interpretations of Bede, see Alan Thacker, "Wilfrid [St. Wilfrid] (c.634-709/10)," in *Oxford Dictionary of National Biography*, ed. H. C. G. Matthew and Brian Harrison, vol. 58 (Oxford, 2004), pp. 944–50.

What I have just said about Canterbury and York and the purpose of Bede's history is said just as clearly in *The Narrators of Barbarian History*, but placid observations attract less attention than controversial ones, such as those about Wilfrid. Wilfrid matters in my discussion—and Bede's—because his figure obstructs the horizon. Those dealing with the Northumbrian church cannot fail to see him except when Bede diverts attention to a parade of captivating substitutes. Wilfrid is not my invention. Long before I read Bede, Wilfrid had a confusing but prominent part in a survey course on church history that I took in my first year in graduate school. Political giants were familiar figures in my childhood. Winston Churchill is not too remote a parallel to Wilfrid in longevity. Equally prominent was Franklin Roosevelt, whose name, as I recall from personal experience, made rich grownups froth at the mouth. Colossi are controversial. Like them, Wilfrid was a giant bestriding his age.

Wilfrid had been dead and buried for twenty years when Bede wrote the *Historia ecclesiastica*. Emotions cool after two decades, but it was hard, nevertheless, to fit Wilfrid into a glowing, serene balance sheet of the Northumbrian past. Wilfrid stirred up enmities and earned several exiles. A realistic, factual account of "the age of Wilfrid" was incompatible with the history Bede set himself, or was asked, to write. Besides, the immediate, memorable past—the years after 705 that Bede virtually excludes from the *Historia ecclesiastica*—saw Wilfrid's successors and disciples strongly entrenched in the Northumbrian church.

Kirby's Jarrow Lecture is especially relevant here. The longest passage of arms between him and me concerns the politics of the early 700s.[22] The background to these troubles is that King Aldfrid died in 705, having exiled Wilfrid many years before. A coup d'état took place at Aldfrid's death, excluding his very young son, Osred, and making a collateral heir king. Wilfrid came running from his exile in Mercia, expecting that

---

[22] Kirby, *Contemporary Setting*, pp. 18–19, n. 51. This note is a concentrated polemic against my views.

the king who benefited from the coup d'état would receive him with open arms. Surprisingly, the intruder's reception was icy; he confirmed Wilfrid's banishment. More fool he. Wilfrid's response was to conspire with Osred's relatives. They joined forces, overthrew the intruding king in his second month, and installed little Osred after all.[23]

This set of events amounted to a full-scale reversal of alliances. Osred's family had formerly exiled Wilfrid and harassed his adherents. Now, thanks to this disputed succession, Wilfrid and his enemies made peace. Wilfrid returned to Northumbria and was able, till his death in 709, to look after his multifarious disciples and monasteries. Two of the four bishoprics in Northumbria, and heaven knows how many more churches, were in the hands of Wilfrid's followers right down to the time when Bede wrote the *Historia ecclesiastica*.[24]

Kirby rightly understands my position to be that "Wilfrid made a great comeback in 705," and he contests it with resolute minimalism. According to him, Wilfrid, a septuagenarian in failing health, returned to a kingdom in which the royal family had been implacably hostile to him. The bishops grudgingly agreed to his return, and the only churches given back to him were Hexham and Ripon. These religious communities, fearful of further vexation, remained on guard and set aside treasures for buying royal favor. Kirby corrects my use of the term "boy kings" for Aldfrid's successors; except for Osred, the kings were young, but not boys. "[T]he most influential ecclesiastical

[23] Goffart, *Narrators*, pp. 272–4. I learned most of what I know about Northumbrian politics from Kirby's writings. It is too bad that we diverge in its interpretation.

[24] Kirby, *Contemporary Setting*, pp. 18–19, n. 51. D. P. Kirby, *The Earliest English Kings* (London, 1990), p. 146, claims that "once secure in power" Osred's regime excluded Wilfrid from its liberality, but Osred was never really secure; the whole family was slipping, repeatedly ousted and sometimes restored. Its lack of generosity is an argument from silence. Is there information about its being either open-handed or stingy to anyone?

party in Northumbria" in these decades, Kirby maintains, was not Wilfrid's successors but the see of York, "judging from the way in which [Bishop John] arranged the succession to York of his fellow-monk from Whitby, Wilfrid [different from the main Wilfrid]."[25]

Kirby's objections are defensible, but inconclusive. His puffing up of the church of York omits what matters most, namely, that Bishop John arranged his succession in a thoroughly uncanonical way. Far from showing strength, John's action betrays frailty and apprehension. He was afraid that if he did not act, however illegally, outsiders—notably Wilfridians—would step in at his death and elect their candidate. There is no obstacle here to my proposal that Wilfrid's successors, such as Acca of Hexham, were in the ascendant after the great man's death. As for boy kings, I should have been more cautious, of course; but the expression is metaphorically appropriate. Boy kings do not have to be boys in age. It is uncontested that the Northumbrian kings between 705 and 729 have nothing noteworthy to their credit. None even produced an heir.

Kirby minimizes Wilfrid's comeback of 705, suggesting that Stephen's account in the *Vita Wilfridi* is rosier than called for. Kirby's own goal seems to be to make "the Contemporary Setting" of Bede's history colorless and nondescript. This is highly improbable. Bede's *Historia ecclesiastica* was not a casual, motiveless, private endeavor; the Preface to King Ceolwulf alone excludes that possibility. Nothing Kirby says diverts me from thinking that the contemporary setting of the *Historia ecclesiastica* was dramatic and stirring. Aldfrid's succession brought about an abrupt realignment of forces, one wholly in keeping with political probability. Wilfrid returned, perhaps old, but nevertheless

---

[25] Goffart, *Narrators*, pp. 258–96. Like Kirby, Alan Thacker casts the Wilfridians as underdogs: "Lindisfarne and the Origins of the Cult of St. Cuthbert," in *St. Cuthbert, His Cult and His Community to AD 1200*, ed. Gerald Bonner, David Rollason, Clare Stancliffe (Woodbridge, 1989), pp. 118–20, mainly on the tenuous grounds of the passage in my next note.

indispensable to the royal family that had formerly exiled him. Circumstances made him the adoptive father, so to speak, of little Osred. The royal family was in precipitate decline. Hostility to Wilfrid was a luxury it had every reason to forgo. The kings needed all the support they could get. Wilfrid's possession of Hexham and Ripon, which Kirby deprecates, gave him 50 percent of the bishoprics in Northumbria. Though less than 100 percent, it was not a proportion to be despised. Stephen of Ripon's reference to money for giving gifts to kings and bishops—a passage that has scandalized many commentators—should stop being taken as a sign of persecution or weakness. Even in placid, well-ordered lands, tax-free institutions find it circumspect and just to make gifts in lieu of taxes to competent authorities. We are shown an act of prudence, not of anxiety or fear. The context supplied by Stephen's *Vita* is one of normal behavior by monasteries toward kings and bishops.[26] After Wilfrid's death, his disciples could not take tranquility for granted, but the royal family needed them as much as when Wilfrid was alive, and their material condition was as opulent as ever.

The prosperity of the Wilfridians in the years before the *Historia ecclesiastica* calls for one more comment. Bede's final work, dated 734, was an open letter to Ecgberht, bishop of York, denouncing the abuses of the recent Northumbrian church. Ever

---

[26] Stephen, *Vita Wilfridi* 63 (p. 136), Wilfrid has his riches divided into four (unequal) piles, one to be distributed among a set of churches in Rome, two to be distributed among his own poor dependents (*pauperibus populi mei*), "alteram autem partem praepositi coenobiorum duorum saepe dictorum inter se dividant, ut cum muneribus regum et episcoporum amicitiam perpetrare potuerint" [the second part let the heads of the two oft-mentioned abbeys divide among themselves so that they may be able to purchase the friendship of kings and bishops]. Trans. Colgrave, *Life of Wilfrid*, p. 137. Stephen himself finds this procedure unremarkable; only modern commentators somehow forget that gifts often confirm friendship and do not have to be automatically interpreted as averting hostility.

since 705, Bede said, the church had been declining from a better past; his reference to "since 705" took in almost the whole of his adulthood. The *Historia ecclesiastica* praises Wilfrid's enemies and drastically downplays Wilfrid's achievements.[27] Because Wilfrid and company had been dominant since 705, Bede's lines to Ecgberht implicitly denounce Bede's bishop and patron, the very magnificent Acca of Hexham, who was expelled from his see late in 731. Ceolwulf, king since 729, and his cousin Ecgberht, the bishop of York, embodied a new order in Northumbria. Bede had great hopes for them. The old dynasty and its Wilfridian backers had led the church astray but were at last on the way out. The new Northumbrian leaders, with York as center of a province, offered excellent prospects of reform.[28] The *Historia ecclesiastica* would instruct and guide them.[29]

A comment of mine that has seemed very shocking is that Bede censured Bishop Acca, at least by implication, and certainly kept friendly company with the men responsible for Acca's downfall. Kirby intimates, on the contrary, that the expulsion of Acca must have made Bede anxious.

---

[27] Bede, *Epist. Ecgb.* (pp. 405–23). The best proof of Bede's success in playing down Wilfrid's achievements in Northumbria is that Alcuin, in his commemoration of the bishops of York, is aware of only Wilfrid's doings outside Northumbria.

[28] For more on Bede's concern with reform, see Alan Thacker, "Bede's Ideal of Reform," in *Ideal and Reality in Frankish and Anglo-Saxon Society: Studies Presented to J. M. Wallace-Hadrill,* ed. P. Wormald, D. Bullough, and R. Collins (Oxford, 1983), pp. 130-53; and Scott DeGregorio, "*Nostrorum socordiam temporum*: The Reforming Impulse of Bede's Later Exegesis," *Early Medieval Europe* 11 (2002): 107–22; idem, "Bede's *In Ezram et Neemiam* and the Reform of the Northumbrian Church," *Speculum* 79 (2004): 1–25.

[29] On Acca's splendid career and closeness to Wilfrid, see Goffart, *Narrators,* p. 273 with n. 177. On Bede's ties to Acca's persecutors, see ibid., pp. 273–4, 294–5.

Acca was very close to Wilfrid and succeeded him at Hexham in 709. Besides being the bishop in whose diocese Wearmouth and Jarrow were situated, he sponsored Bede's biblical commentaries. He was the equivalent to Bede of the granting agencies that foster our research with needed subsidies. Acca's eviction from Hexham in 731 came too late to fit into the *Historia ecclesiastica*. Nevertheless, Bede's letter to Ecgberht implicitly classes Acca as one of the unworthy churchmen of the recent past. No exception is made for him. Bede was on cordial terms with the dignitaries who chased him from Hexham. Kirby maintains, "[Bede] had certainly expressed great affection for Acca in the past."[30] Are we sure that he had?

The six surviving letters from Bede to Acca are all dedications of biblical commentaries. These are public, not personal documents, heading the commentaries in question and advertising Acca's sponsorship. Charles Plummer, a hero to any student of the *Historia ecclesiastica*, judged the relationship unambiguously: "Bede evidently cherished the warmest affection for [Acca]."

---

[30] Kirby, *Contemporary Setting*, p. 6. Kirby, continuing, brackets the expulsion of King Ceolwulf with that of Acca; the deposition of the king "must have been extremely disturbing [to Bede] and the expulsion of his diocesan at the very least an occasion for anxiety concerning the pastoral life of the church in Bernicia." See also Wallace-Hadrill, *Historical Commentary*, p. 207 (addenda); the editors claim that Acca's expulsion in the year of Ceolwulf's overthrow allows us to suppose "that he was a close supporter of the king." The sources tell us that King Ceolwulf was restored *before* Acca was expelled, that Acca stayed in exile till his death, and that he was replaced at Hexham while still alive (the replacement was necessarily with Ceolwulf's assent). The idea of closeness between Acca and Ceolwulf seems to be out of the question. Meanwhile, Bede praised Acca's persecutors, Ceolwulf and Ecgberht. He wrote a tract denouncing Northumbrian church life for the past twenty-five years and looking forward to improvement. These facts contradict Kirby's interpretation, and Thacker's (n. 32 below). ·

The letters embody expressions of emphatic esteem and friendship: "dearest," "dearest of prelates," "most lovable of bishops," "most loved and wished-for of all bishops there are in the world," etc. The same words, *amantissime, dilectissime,* variants of our formulaic "dearest," return again and again.[31]

Plummer read the letters as expressions of Bede's private feelings; so have others. My doubts about Bede's attachment to Acca have seemed to accuse a saint of insincerity and hypocrisy. One can only speculate about Bede's character, but the language of his letters has to be appraised in the context of the epistolary genre. His phrases are well suited to the circumstances—wholly conventional, possibly outright flattery, and in any case no measure of his feelings. Bede could not be false because no truth was asked of him, any more than it is from us when we use formulas like "Dear so-and-so," or "Sincerely yours." Good manners are in question, not feelings.[32]

Up to now, I have discussed mostly circumstances outside the *Historia ecclesiastica.* As I return to the Wilfrid problem, I shall consider at least a part of Bede's narrative.

Lovers of Bede such as Henry Mayr-Harting deplore the new harsh climate for (I believe) one particular reason: the conflicts and dissembling that certain commentators claim to detect in the *Historia ecclesiastica* contrast sharply and offensively with

---

[31] Plummer on Acca's letters: *Baedae opera historica,* pp. xxxiii, xlix ("for whom [Bede] evidently cherished a warm affection"). Bede's many addresses to Acca, ringing changes on "dearest," are listed.

[32] *Thacker, "Lindisfarne* and St. Cuthbert," p. 121, agrees with Plummer about the sincerity and depth of Bede's attachment to Acca; Wallace-Hadrill, *Historical Commentary,* p. 195, Bede was long a close friend of Acca. These opinions need at least to be qualified. It is not axiomatic that Acca's sponsorship of Bede's exegetical works generated friendship between them. Beneficiaries of patronage have to cultivate their patrons but do not necessarily have cordial feelings toward them (or, as in this case, approve of their policies as bishops). See also Goffart, "Bede's Agenda," pp. 42–43.

the sweetness and light so obvious at its surface. I allege that Bede was hostile to Wilfrid, yet nothing in the *Historia ecclesiastica* clearly attacks or disparages him. Many lines of the *Historia ecclesiastica* mention Wilfrid. In keeping with the positive and laudatory sound of the *Historia ecclesiastica*, readers are led to believe that Wilfrid was as constructive a figure in the English church as Aidan or Archbishop Theodore or the deacon James. My references to Wilfrid's ghost in Bede's history look exaggerated when balanced against these considerations. Nevertheless, a two-faced Bede existed before I said anything about him. Eric John remarked that Bede looks as though he goes out of his way more than once not to contradict the *Vita Wilfridi* "whilst conveying a totally opposed view of the same facts."[33]

Wilfrid's most memorable and popular achievement was to unburden Northumbria of its Irish clergy. "Cleansings" of this kind are not foreign to the experience of recent and earlier history. Idi Amin expels the East Asians from Uganda; Honduras evicts its Lebanese; the English drive the French *habitants* from Acadia after its conquest; Edward I bars the Jews from England. Foreign residents engage in a specialized gainful activity; by clearing them out on some pretext or other, it is expected that one's own people will be gratified by getting the jobs and the profits. The pattern repeats across the centuries (if sources allowed, it would no doubt be found in prehistory). Wilfrid succeeded in step one—getting the aliens out. Step two, taking their place and profits, eluded him. He incurred enough enmity not to be able to win a position of unassailable power in the Northumbrian church. Instead, he was exiled and had his ups and downs. His return in 705 has already been discussed. Let me backtrack to Wilfrid's initial triumph. Even as late as when Bede wrote the *Historia ecclesiastica*, Wilfrid would have remained famous and esteemed in Northumbria for ousting the Irish and making room for Northumbrians.

---

[33]Eric John, "Social and Political Problems of the Early English Church," *Agricultural History Review* 18 (1970): 44.

Irish missionaries had worked in Northumbria since about 635. At royal invitation the monastery of Iona had sent Aidan and helpers. The original Canterbury-based mission to Northumbria had been destroyed and forgotten, with the result that the Ionan Irish thought of themselves as the initiators of Northumbrian Christianity. Local disciples flocked to them. In ten years, there must have been a growing, Irish-trained English element among the clergy and monks of the Northumbrian church. Young Wilfrid spent enough time at (Irish dominated) Lindisfarne to acquire a taste for church life and a longing for travel. He soared to fame by finding the lever that eased out the Irish and delivered the church to persons like himself, native Northumbrians trained initially by Irish clergy, but then also perfected in continental church practices or adhering to them.

Expulsions of alien élites, wrapped in legality, meet with much approval in the lands where they occur and are warmly remembered. Stephen's *Vita Wilfridi* attributes a speech of justification to Wilfrid: "Was I not the first…to root out the poisonous weeds planted by the Irish? Did I not change and convert the whole Northumbrian people to the true Easter and to the tonsure in the form of a crown, in accordance with the practice of the Apostolic See?"[34] The words that Wilfrid's biographer placed in his hero's mouth were not controversial. Even in 720 Northumbrians would have recalled with pride, not the true Easter or the crown tonsure, both now routine and humdrum, but the shaking off of Irish dominance. Wilfrid's ups and downs with Northumbrian kings, his ambitions for property and power, and other aspects of his long life were open to contestation; but the cornerstone of his career, the championship of Rome against

[34] Stephen, *Vita Wilfridi* 47 (p. 98): "Necnon et ego primus…Scotticae uirulenta plantationis germina eradicarem; ad uerumque pascha et ad tonsuram in modum coronae…secundum apostolicae sedis rationem totam Ultrahumbrensium gentem permutando conuerterem." Trans. Colgrave, *Life of Wilfrid*, p. 99. This is part of a longer speech of justification at the Synod of Austerfield (date uncertain, in the earliest 700s).

Irish "poisonous weeds," was unassailable. Bede had to be aware of this.

What was he to do? He was not free to write whatever he wished. In the *Historia ecclesiastica*, the Northumbrian church had to look unfailingly rosy; and Wilfrid the extirpator of the Irish was beyond reproach. Eric John outlined how Bede escaped this dilemma: he consistently expressed simple, overt approval and just as consistently undermined it by covert maneuvers.

A salient example is Bede's account of the Synod of Whitby in 664. This was when the king of Northumbria subscribed to the Roman method of dating Easter and exiled whatever clergy clung to the Irish system. Whitby was where Wilfrid triumphed and forced the Irish out. Stephen, his biographer, conveys this message briefly and clearly; he had no need to beat about the bush. Bede, however, is anything but straightforward.

In the *Historia ecclesiastica*, the synod of Whitby is immediately followed by the onset of a terrible plague. Bede was not a slave to chronology; without taking undue liberties, he manipulates time sequences to suit his narrative. Here he behaves as though chronology forced his hand. Christian historians considered major events to be metaphysically significant; disasters were divine retribution for human misdeeds. A report of the plague in Northumbria did not *have* to be fitted in right after Whitby. Placed where it is, the plague comments tacitly on what had come before.[35]

Hunter Blair says: "In Bede's eyes, if we may judge by the length of the chapter which he devoted to it, the great Easter controversy and the decisions reached at the Synod of Whitby seemed the most important topic of the age."[36] It is hard

[35] Bede, *HE* 3.27 (p. 312). *HE* 3.26 (pp. 308–10) is an appendix to the synod of Whitby, telling in flattering terms how admirably the Irish responded to their setback.

[36] Peter Hunter Blair, *Bede's Ecclesiastical History of the English Nation and Its Importance Today* (Jarrow Lecture, 1959), p. 9. Yet the synod occurred

to see how a brief gathering of churchmen in the 660s could still be "the most important topic" of the 730s. Hunter Blair is not alone in considering chapter length a reliable measure of Bede's interest and involvement. But why should this be so? Brevity allows blunt, forthright presentations, as in Stephen's *Vita Wilfridi*. What Bede resorts to in the Whitby chapter is dilution by increase, the same thing he does when handling Gildas's *De excidio* in Book 1.[37]

A typical dilution occurs at the start of Bede's Whitby chapter. Whereas Stephen of Ripon pits the Irish bishop Colman against Wilfrid one-on-one, Bede evokes a generalized dispute involving a crowd on both sides. Wilfrid is watered down by the addition of many persons who cared about Roman Easter dating before he did, and by the attribution to him of a tedious but impeccable speech more than twice as long as the obdurate Irish reply. By heavy-duty dilution Bede succeeds in suggesting that Wilfrid was just one of a group, that the date of Easter was a serious, or at least a scholarly issue, and that expelling the Irish was not the primary objective. As plague then sets in, we infer that what happened at Whitby did not earn the blessing of Almighty God. Bede's drawn-out chapter was not concerned only with the dating of Easter.

The longer I dwell on the *Historia ecclesiastica*, the less I share Henry Mayr-Harting's view that I am hard on Bede. The climate affecting the *Historia ecclesiastica* in recent times changed from mild to harsh as soon as critical readers realized that Bede's English church could not have been so serene, lovable, and grand in reality as it was in his narrative. This realization did not occur just yesterday. I would not be surprised if Mayr-Harting

almost a decade before Bede's birth. Chapter lengths are meaningful, but they do not clearly and invariably measure an author's concern for a subject.

[37] About Bede and Gildas in Book 1 of the *HE*, see Goffart, *Narrators*, pp. 299–302.

himself, in his fine book of 1972, conceded every now and then that the whole truth about early Anglo-Saxon England does not float gently on the surface of the *Historia ecclesiastica*.[38]

The main innovation of my *Narrators of Barbarian History* concerning Bede is the contention that he was deliberate in what he wrote. Possibly, he pieced together the truth about the past out of inadequate sources, carrying out a role comparable to a midwife's. More probably the *Historia ecclesiastica* is a studied construction, a work of art, embodying sources, to be sure, but also the beliefs and calculations of its maker. Intentionalism can be disputed; the casual "just like us" that I slip in, offering today as a yardstick for measuring Bede's day, might be contested. The opposing viewpoints need to be debated; they implicate more historians than Bede.

The context in which Bede wrote the *Historia ecclesiastica* was different from the one portrayed in its pages. It is only reasonable to assume that the needs and problems of the Northumbria which Bede masks in book five are the ones that weighed on his mind when he wrote the *Historia ecclesiastica*. The history that is familiar to us from Bede's narrative—a very pleasing seventh-century Northumbrian church, all sweetness and holiness—is the image that was called for and Bede supplied, but not the one he lived in. The 730s context ranks high among subjects about which I should like to be better informed.

Today's interpreters are surprisingly wide in their disagreements. In *The Narrators of Barbarian History*, for example, I argue that Bede's account of Cædwalla, the early king of Wessex, is ironic—ostensible praise masking the portrait of a bloodthirsty upstart. The ironic Bede is a rare bird; irony mixes poorly with

---

[38] Patrick Wormald, "Bede, *Beowulf* and the Conversion of the Anglo-Saxon Aristocracy," in *Bede and Anglo-Saxon England*, ed. R. T. Farrell, British Archaeological Reports, British Series 46 (Oxford, 1978), pp. 68–69, argues that Bede had no grasp of the contemporary lay world; Mayr-Harting, *Coming of Christianity*, pp. 254–6, is similar.

the surface appearance of the *Historia ecclesiastica.*[39] Meanwhile, Kirby decides that Canterbury would have been unhappy with Bede's friendly portrayal of the Irish, and Thacker takes Bede for an Easter date fanatic.[40] The habit of reading the *Historia ecclesiastica* as a text in the mimetic mode, exactly reflecting the three-dimensional world and candidly documenting Bede's sensitivities, is still with us. The climate may be harsher for poor Bede, but the sun shines brightly on would-be critics of Bede's history. There is much for them to do.

[39] Goffart, *Narrators*, pp. 318–19. See the comment in Bede, *HE*, ed. McClure and Collins, p. 411, note to p. 244. See also on Bede's puzzling exculpation, Walter Goffart, "Bede's *Uera lex historiae* Explained," *Anglo-Saxon England* 34 (2005): 111–16.

[40] Kirby, *Contemporary Setting*, p. 15 (also p. 11): "Bede was unhappy with Aidan's failure to celebrate Easter correctly." It is paradoxical to suggest that Bede, who deeply admired the very long dead Aidan, should have personally grieved at his celebrating Easter in the only way he ever learned. Thacker, "Bede and the Irish," p. 59, alleges that Bede was even more passionate about Easter dating than his contemporaries.

Carolingian Perspectives on the Authority of Bede

JOYCE HILL

AMALARIUS OF METZ, notable as the first western scholar to make a systematic attempt to provide an exegesis of the liturgy, referred to Bede when putting forward a particular point of interpretation and made the confident assertion "his authority is sufficient for me" (*mihi sufficit ejus auctoritas*).[1] And so that settled the issue: if Bede said so, it was good enough for Amalarius, and if the assertion could be made thus baldly, it was presumably good enough for everyone else as well. The context was heavily learned—Amalarius' *magnum opus*, the *De ecclesiasticis officiis*—and although the exegesis of the liturgy was a novel undertaking, it was one that operated within the same parameters as the biblical exegesis to which the Carolingians devoted so much attention. Orthodoxy was essential and had constantly to be verified, as it was in this case. Yet the *De ecclesiasticis officiis* was written soon after Amalarius returned from Constantinople in 812, less than one hundred years after Bede's death. One might think this to be a rather short span of time in which to acquire the authoritative status attested to by Amalarius' brisk assertion, particularly when the authority context was the most exacting one of medieval exegesis, the territory of the great Doctors of the Church.

My purpose in this essay is to offer some specific examples of the ways in which the authority that Amalarius asserts was

---

[1] Amalarius, *De ecclesiasticis officiis*, IV, I (PL 105, col. 1164C). Amalarius was born, perhaps in or near Metz, c. 770x775, and died, probably at Metz, where he is buried, on 29 April 852 or 853.

rapidly established by the Carolingians who, in the process, elevated Bede to virtual patristic status, in effect co-opting him into the patristic canon, relatively modern though he was. The evidence that I shall be setting out for this will be drawn from various sources, some familiar, some less so. But amongst those sources will figure conciliar texts not previously examined for this purpose. I will be looking at the epithets applied to Bede and the ways in which his worth was acknowledged, whether by direct praise, or by citation. But before this is presented, it will be helpful to recall just why it is that Bede figured so prominently in the world of Carolingian scholarship.

He modestly defined his own activity as being that of a compiler, having made it his life's work since his ordination as priest as he puts it "for my own benefit and that of my brothers to make brief extracts from the works of the venerable Fathers on the holy Scripture, or to add notes of my own to clarify their sense and interpretation."[2] As previous chapters in this volume have emphasized, his own favored metaphor for describing the nature of his work was that he was "following the footsteps of the Fathers" (*patrum uestigia sequens*).[3] Furthermore, not only does he *say* that is what he is doing, but in his commentaries on Mark and Luke he visually *demonstrates* that he is a *compilator* by putting in the margin letters which show whose words he is using at a given point—Jerome's, Augustine's, Gregory's, etc.[4] Although Bede might be regarded the father of the modern footnote

[2] Bede, *HE* 5.24 (p. 566–7): "...in Scripturam sanctam meae meorumque necessitati ex opusculis uenerabilium patrum breuiter adnotare, siue etiam ad formam sensus et interpretationis eorum superadicere."

[3] See Paul Meyvaert, "Bede the Scholar," in *Famulus Christi: Essays in Commemoration of the Thirteenth Centenary of the Birth of the Venerable Bede*, ed. Gerald Bonner (London, 1976), pp. 62–63, n. 7.

[4] E. J. Sutcliffe, "Quotations in the Ven. Bede's Commentary on S. Mark," *Biblica* 7 (1926): 428–39. and M. L. W. Laistner, "Source-Marks in Bede Manuscripts," *Journal of Theological Studies* 34 (1933): 350–4. These marginalia—*A* signalling that a passage is taken from Augustine, *G* from

(an accolade that anyone could do without!), these marginal identifications are not footnotes in our sense, since they do not indicate where a passage comes from, textually speaking, but who was responsible for the passage. In other words, they are footprints, rather than footnotes—visible markers of the *uestigia patrum*, and thus evidence of impeccable orthodoxy. Since the Carolingian *renouatio* was about the reestablishment of a chain of authority going back to the Fathers, this was invaluable. Bede's methods gave them confidence in him, gave them models for creating their own orthodox *compilationes* even down to the practice of using marginal author identifications as visual verifiers, and provided them with handy interpretative compendia or florilegia, flowers plucked, as they were wont to say, from the fair fields of the Fathers.[5] And it was the sheer convenience of what Bede had to offer that seems first to have given him an entrée into continental Europe. The Anglo-Saxon missionary Boniface, writing from the continent only eleven or twelve years after Bede's death, asks Archbishop Ecgberht of York and

Gregory, *H* from Jerome (Hieronymus), and so on—originate with Bede, but were sometimes omitted in later manuscript copies. They are included in the modern edition of the two commentaries by Hurst in CCSL 120.

[5] It was precisely this "gathering of flowers" that Paul the Deacon was instructed to undertake by Charlemagne when he was put to work compiling an exemplary homiliary: *Capitularia Regum Francorum* (MGH: Legum Sectio II, Capitularia Regum Francorum I, p. 81). On the centrality of this intertextuality for the Carolingian *renovatio*, see John Contreni, "Carolingian Biblical Studies," in *Carolingian Essays: Andrew S. Mellon Lectures in Early Christian Studies*, ed. Uta-Renate Blumenthal (Washington, D.C., 1983), pp. 71–98; Giles Brown, "Introduction: The Carolingian Renaissance," in *Carolingian Culture: Emulation and Innovation*, ed. Rosamond McKitterick (Cambridge, 1994), pp. 1–51; and, more generally, Martin Irvine, *The Making of Textual Culture: 'Grammatica' and Literary Theory*, Cambridge Studies in Medieval Literature 19 (Cambridge, 1994).

Hwætberht abbot of Wearmouth to send him some treatises of Bede, whom he describes as a most sagacious interpreter of the Scriptures;[6] and when, only a few years later, he asks particularly for a collection of Bede's homilies, he accounts for the request by saying that they would seem to be "convenient, handy and very useful" (*habile et manuale et utillimum*).[7] The particular purpose Boniface had in mind on this occasion was preaching, and it is worth remembering that, for all their scholarship and basis in the monastic life, the later Carolingian reformers were themselves to be much concerned with extending due standards of orthodoxy to the secular church. Practicality was to remain an issue, and to be a continuing cause of Bede's usefulness.

The Boniface example brings me to the other, more down to earth reason for Bede's importance in western Europe: the existence for a couple of generations after his death of Anglo-Saxon channels of communication, such as Boniface represents. Correspondence with England, which included further requests for Bedan manuscripts, was maintained by Boniface's pupil and successor Lull until his death in 786,[8] and by then Alcuin of York was already at the court of Charlemagne. Back at home, in York, he had known a library in which Bede was on the shelves alongside the older authorities, and he eulogized Bede in the celebration of that library in his poem, *Versus de sanctis Euboricensis.* Bede is described there as "a priest of outstanding merits" (*presbyter eximius meritis*); he is celebrated as one who followed the footsteps of the Fathers, echoing Bede's own favored meta-

---

[6] Boniface, *Epistulae* 75 and 76 (MGH, Epistolae selectae I, pp. 158–9).

[7] Boniface, *Epistula* 91 (MGH, Epistolae selectae I, p. 207).

[8] Lull, *Epistula* 125 (MGH, Epistolae selectae I, p. 263), which includes a reference to Bede's commentary on Mark; *Epistula* 126 (MGH, Epistolae selectae I, p. 264); and letters to Lull from Abbot Cuthbert of Wearmouth-Jarrow which refer to Lull's requests for Bede's work, *Epistula* 116 (MGH, Epistolae selectae I, pp. 250–2), and *Epistula* 127 (MGH, Epistolae selectae I, pp. 264–5).

phor; on three occasions he is elevated to *magister*, and on one occasion he is even given the lofty title of *doctor*.[9] Alcuin was a great *compilator* himself in the Bedan patristic tradition, and he in turn taught Hrabanus Maurus, a prolific and influential Carolingian *compilator*, who also adopted the process of displaying his orthodoxy by marginal author-identifications. He explains in one commentary that he does so because he has been taught to do this by Alcuin,[10] and in his commentary on Matthew, when he refers to the practice again, he does so by deliberately using Bede's own words: "solicitous throughout lest I should be said to have stolen the words of greater men and to have put them together as if they were my own."[11]

But the emulation of Bede and his elevation as a Doctor of the Church were not confined to those with Anglo-Saxon connections at first or second hand. Obviously their influence was significant, but it was Bede's capacity to meet a need that was more significant still. His worth was quickly recognized. Paul

---

[9] Alcuin, *Versus de sanctis Euboricensis* (p. 100, line 1289; p. 102, line 1313; p. 62, line 744; p. 94, line 1207; and p. 102, line 1305, respectively).

[10] *Commentaria in libros iv regum* (PL 109, col. 10). See also J. E. Cross, "Bede's Influence at Home and Abroad," in *Beda Venerabilis: Historian, Monk and Northumbrian*, ed. L. A. J. R. Houwen and A. A. MacDonald (Groningen, 1996), pp. 17–29; and George Hardin Brown, "The Preservation and Transmission of Northumbrian Culture on the Continent: Alcuin's Debt to Bede," in *The Preservation and Transmission of Anglo-Saxon Culture*, ed. Paul E. Szarmach and Joel T. Rosenthal (Kalamazoo, Mich., 1997), pp. 159–75.

[11] *Commentarium in Mattheum* (PL 107, col. 729): "sollicitus per omnia ne majorum dicta furari et haec quasi me propria componere dicer." The phrase he is echoing here is from Bede's *In Lucam* Prol. (p. 7, lines 109–11): "sollicitus per omnia ne maiorum dicta furari et haec quasi mea propria componere dicer" [solicitous throughout lest I should be said to have stolen the words of greater men and to have put them together as if they were my own.]

the Deacon, when commissioned by Charlemagne quite early in the reform to produce an authoritative collection of suitably orthodox homilies for the benefit of the secular church, included 57 items by Bede out of a total collection of 244 items, selecting 36 of his 50 homilies, by comparison with the 34 homilies he chose from Gregory the Great's *Homilies on the Gospels*, and he supplemented these homilies of Bede with extracts from the commentaries on Luke and Mark (mainly Luke).[12] No other author was as well represented as Bede, and all authors were identified in the rubric to each item, so the homiliary—which was much copied, augmented and adapted throughout the Middle Ages—not only testifies to the standing of Bede at the time Paul made up the anthology, but also, by its circulation, contributed massively to the confirmation of Bede's stature. It is worth noting that Paul had not been directed to turn to modern authorities, but had been expressly told to collect certain flowers from the far-flung fields of the Catholic Fathers,[13] making it all the more eloquent a testimony to Bede's rapidly achieved status that he was the leading contributor to this enterprise. As I have noted, the collection was soon augmented, and still Bede remained prominent, with further extracts from the Commentary on Luke being a particularly rich source of augmentation in the period before 1100. Examples include MS 23 in Pembroke College Cambridge, and, to a greater extent,

---

[12] Cyril L. Smetana, "Paul the Deacon's Patristic Anthology," in *The Old English Homily and its Backgrounds*, ed. Paul E. Szarmach and Bernard F. Huppé (Albany, 1978), pp. 75–97. Scholars vary slightly in their count of Bedan items (53, 56 and 57 are numbers cited). The variation results from the form of identification used in the manuscripts and thus in modern schedules of contents, plus the fact that one Bedan homily occurs twice in Paul the Deacon's homiliary, once in the summer and once in the winter part. None of this alters the fact that Bede figures prominently in Paul's collection.

[13] See note 5 above.

Cambridge University Library Ii.2.19.[14] The homilies derived from the commentaries had, of course, in their original manuscripts, marginal attributions to the patristic authorities on whom Bede had drawn, but in none of the copies of Paul the Deacon is this reflected. This homiliary tradition only uses one attribution for each item, which is given in the rubric; and in all cases where the "homily" is an extract from the commentaries on Mark or Luke, the rubric attribution is to Bede alone. The augmentations thus strengthened his presence, and reinforced his stature as this essentially patristic homiliary continued to develop and circulate.

Similarly, though perhaps for a more immediately monastic context, Smaragdus of St. Mihiel, another hugely influential figure in the reformist camp, made a homiliary for the whole year and used Bede more heavily than he did any one of the older Fathers. In this case, each homily was itself a *catena* of verbal extracts but, in the very tradition of Bede, each was identified in the margin by a letter-abbreviation.[15] The manuscript closest to Smaragdus is the ninth-century Boulogne-sur-Mer Bibliothèque

[14] I am grateful to the Master and Fellows of Pembroke College and to the University Librarian for permission to consult these manuscripts.

[15] The elements in Smaragdus' homiletic *catenae* are identified by Fidel Rädle, *Studien zu Smaragd von Saint-Mihiel* (Munich, 1974). The only edition of Smaragdus' homiliary is that in PL 102, cols 14–594, under the title *Collectiones in epistolas et evangelia*, although it is more commonly known as *Expositio libri comitis*. In this edition the bracketed patristic attributions embedded in the text are expansions of the manuscript marginalia, although some are missing and some are inaccurate, so that they need to be checked against the series of articles by Alexander Souter, "Contributions to the Criticism of Zmaragdus's *Expositio libri comitis*," *Journal of Theological Studies* 9 (1908): 584–97; "Further Contributions to the Criticism of Zmaragdus's *Expositio libri comitis*," *Journal of Theological Studies* 23 (1922): 73–76; "A Further Contribution to the Criticism of Zmaragdus's *Expositio libri comitis*," *Journal of Theological Studies* 34 (1933): 46–47.

Municipale 25, and that has 513 Bedan identifications. MS Barlow 4 in the Bodleian Library Oxford is also relatively early in the transmission sequence, being from north-eastern France in the second or third quarter of the ninth century, and that has nearly 500 identifications, one in ten of which are to Bede. No other single authority comes close.[16]

Smaragdus' indebtedness to—and elevation of—Bede is striking, as is Paul the Deacon's, but neither provides any comments. Claudius of Turin does, however, in the preface to his Commentary on Genesis, written for Louis the Pious. Here we find again the metaphor of plucking the flowers, visually displayed in the body of the commentary through the practice of setting down the author identifications in the margin, a practice which, as we have noted before, is also importantly about the verification of orthodoxy. Bede is one of Claudius's identified authorities, but in the preface it is Bede's authority for the actual use of marginal identifications which is called upon:

> After studying and investigating opinions on historical events taken from mystical treasure troves of learned men, I abridged them in a brief compendium of one codex. The reader does not read my words. Instead, he reads theirs again. I have collected their words like beautiful flowers from many meadows, so my treatise is a work of theirs.[17]

---

[16] On the date and origin of the manuscript, see Helmut Gneuss, *A List of Manuscripts and Manuscript Fragments Written or Owned in England up to 1100*, Medieval and Renaissance Studies 241 (Tempe, Ariz., 2001), no. 539 (p. 91). See also Joyce Hill, "Ælfric and Smaragdus," *Anglo-Saxon England* 21 (1992): 234–5. I am grateful to Bodley's Librarian for permission to examine this manuscript.

[17] *Epistolae Karolini Ævi* II (MGH, Epistolarum Tomus IV, p. 592): "Has autem rerum gestarum sententias de mysticis thesauris sapientium inquirendo et investigando in unum codicem conpiendo brevitatis coartavi, in quibus l[ector] non mea legit, sed illorum relegit, quorum ego verba quae illi

And a few phrases later:

> And so no one will think me presumptuous and rash because
> I took arms from the cabinet of another, I have indicated the
> name of each learned authority by placing letters in the mar-
> gin, just as the blessed priest Bede did.[18]

It is hardly a wonder that an early ninth century Carolingian
poet (anonymous) called Bede "the teacher of our age" (*nostri
didascalus aevi*).[19] But what strikes me as an even more eloquent
testimony to Bede's transformation into a patristic figure is the
way in which he is used in the Carolingian ecclesiastical councils, texts which have figured little in Bedan studies. These conciliar texts, which record the impetus and the progress towards
establishing the validated orthodoxy that was the Carolingian
goal, frequently invoke the work of Gregory the Great, slightly
less but still extensively the work of Jerome and Augustine, and
to a lesser extent, but again still noticeably, the work of Ambrose, the traditional four great Doctors of the Church. But they
also cite Bede, in fact not much less frequently than Ambrose.
Bede's name is given and there is always a quotation (sometimes
in modified form), but the actual text may or may not be speci-
fied, just as with the older patristic authorities. We are dealing,

---

dixerunt veluti speciosos flores ex diversis pratis in unum collegi et meae
litterae ipsorum expositio est." The English translation is from Michael
Gorman, "The Commentary on Genesis of Claudius of Turin and Biblical
Studies under Louis the Pious," *Speculum* 72 (1997): 287.

[18] *Epistolae Karolini Ævi* II (MGH, Epistolarum Tomus IV, p. 592): "Et ne
ab aliquibus praesumptor et temerarius diiudicarer, quod [ab] alieno
armario sumpserim tela, uniuscuiusque doctoris nomen cum suis
characteribus, sicut et beatus fecit presbiter Beda, subter in paginis
adnotavi." Trans. Gorman, "Commentary on Genesis of Claudius of
Turin," p. 287.

[19] *Poetae Latini Medii Aevi Carolini* II (MGH, p. 664, poem XIX).

then, with authorization, as in the homily collections and the commentaries; we are not dealing with textual reference in a modern sense; and it is striking that in this rather abstruse and theoretical context, Bede is treated in precisely the same way as the others, even though it is solely authority that is the issue, rather than the practical value of certain of Bede's works which predisposed the *compilatores*, exegetes, and homilists to give him a prominent position. There are, in other words, no predisposing practical factors influencing his appearance in the Councils, but only his achieved stature as an authority, so that these records provide a more objective demonstration of his status than does the interpretative tradition, with its utilitarian focus.

There are five reforming councils that invoke the authority of Bede: Mainz in 813, Aachen in 816, Paris in 825, Paris again in 829, and Aachen in 836. In the Council of Mainz the text cited is the commentary on Luke, and Bede is referred to in the same breath as Jerome, who provides a parallel verification of the same point.[20] In the Council of Aachen it appears once again to be the commentary on Luke, although I shall return to that below.[21] The Council of Paris in 825 cites the *Historia ecclesiastica*,[22] which makes it unusual, since all other conciliar citations are exegetical or homiletic. But the purpose of the reference here is rather different from what we find elsewhere, since it is the citation of a narrative detail to support an extended discussion of images and signs. There is a long string of citations from various authorities (predominantly Augustine), together with the quotation from the *Historia ecclesiastica* illustrating an approved use by Augustine of Canterbury of a silver cross and Christ's image painted on a board when he first met with King Ethelbert of Kent. The Council of Paris in 829 outstrips the others in invoking Bede's authority six times. On four occasions

---

[20] *Concilia Aevi Karolini* I (MGH, Legum Sectio III, Concilia II, I p. 266).

[21] *Concilia Aevi Karolini* I (MGH, Legum Sectio III, Concilia II, I, p. 409). See below, p. 238.

[22] *Concilia Aevi Karolini* I (MGH, Legum Sectio III, Concilia II, I p. 517).

the texts quoted from are also identified: the homilies twice, the commentary on Luke once, and *De tabernaculo* once. But there are two instances where there is simply Bede's name followed by a quotation. These are identifiable as being from his commentary on the Seven Catholic Epistles (James, and the Second Epistle of Peter).[23] Finally, the Council of Aachen in 836 cites the Commentary on Mark twice,[24] and in the opening to Book 3, most interestingly of all, acknowledges Bede as "admirable teacher" (*doctor admirabilis*), while at the same time admitting that he is from modern times, "modernis temporibus"[25]—apparently not a problem, given the fundamental acceptance of his outstanding status. The tone, if one can trust oneself to capture it correctly, is more one of amazement that modern times can produce a *doctor*, than of any doubt about his standing because is he modern. The authorities with whom Bede keeps company in this chapter are Augustine and Jerome.

However, there is a puzzling turn of phrase in the Council of Aachen in 836, which misled even Werminghoff, who edited the Councils for the *Monumenta Germaniae Historica* in 1906. Just after referring to Bede as "doctor admirabilis," the Council refers to an "exposition of the gospel of John" (*expositio evangelii Iohannis*)—clearly Bede's—and then quotes from it. As we know, Bede did not write a commentary on the Gospel of John, and Werminghoff rather helplessly footnoted the quotation with the words "I have not been able to identify this Bedan quotation" (*hunc locum Bedae non inveni*), although he did point out that there was something similar in Bede's commentary on the Song of Songs.[26] The subject, in this part of the Council, is Solomon's Temple, typologically interpreted as the Church of Christ, and

---

[23] *Concilia Aevi Karolini* I (MGH, Legum Sectio III, Concilia II, I pp. 664, 666 (homilies), 662 (Luke), 620 (Tabernacle), 644, 653 (Seven Catholic Epistles).

[24] *Concilia Aevi Karolini* I (MGH, Legum Sectio III, Concilia II, I, p. 762).

[25] *Concilia Aevi Karolini* I (MGH, Legum Sectio III, Concilia II, I p. 759).

[26] *Concilia Aevi Karolini* I (MGH, Legum Sectio III, Concilia II, I pp. 759).

in fact the quotation that Werminghoff could not find is actually—in its precise wording—from one of Bede's homilies for
the Dedication of a Church.[27] But the Council had not got its
facts wrong. On the contrary, it was very accurate, because the
homily from which the quotation comes is actually an exegesis
of a Johannine lection: John 10:22–30. The author of the Council text knew precisely which work he was referring to, and so
this supposedly unidentifiable quotation increases the number
of allusions to the homilies.

So also does the quotation apparently from the commentary
on Luke in the 816 Council of Aachen. The quotation is introduced with the words "On this subject the venerable priest Bede
says thus in the exposition of the gospel of Luke" (*De qua re Beda
venerabilis presbiter in expositio evangelii Lucae ita dicit*), but what
follows is, once again, footnoted by Werminghoff as "I have
been unable to find it" (*non inveni*).[28] But the words are Bede's
and are accurately quoted from a homily which is an exposition
of the lection Luke 24:1–9.[29] Again, the reference in the Council is thus very precise, although since Bede did actually write
a commentary on Luke, which became very popular, we might
unquestioningly accept the textual identification at what might
seem to be face value.

Why did the Councils pick on these texts? Clearly, there is a
certain particularity about the narrative example drawn from
the *Historia ecclesiastica*, which could not have been furnished
by any other of Bede's writings. But as Werminghoff's footnotes
indicate, the sentiments that are supported by Bedan references could equally have been supported from other Bedan texts
and, even for the quotations themselves, there are often closely
similar turns of phrase in others of his writings, so that, if these
had been quoted instead, the point would have been just as well

[27] Bede, *Hom.* 2.24 (p. 364, lines 231–7).
[28] *Concilia Aevi Karolini*, I, ed. Werminghoff, p. 409, the Bedan quotation
being lines 8–16.
[29] *Hom.* 2.10 (pp. 248–9, lines 92–105).

made. This is not surprising, when we consider the dense intertextuality of Bede's own work: the intertextuality, that is, of its
relationship to patristic sources—themselves already intertextual—and the profound intertextuality within Bede's own corpus where, for example, the commentaries on Luke and Mark
have many passages in common.[30] Yet the selection of items for
citation or quotation in the Councils was not eclectic, since the
works drawn upon have an important feature in common: they
were among Bede's most popular and widely circulating works
in the Carolingian period. A consideration of each in turn shows
how this was so.

We tend to think of the *Historia ecclesiastica* as being of national interest, and when we look at the translations of the Alfredian
period, it seems to make sense alongside the translation of Orosius's *Historia adversum paganis libri septem*: one gives us a view of
Christian world history and the other gives us the national perspective, that is, how Anglo-Saxon England was Christianized. In
this regard, Dorothy Whitelock's study of the Old English Bede
tends to reinforce our interpretation, since the translator's selective approach makes the work more pious and less political
than the Latin original.[31] Yet the *Historia ecclesiastica* was more
popular in continental Europe than any other of Bede's works,
if we may judge from booklists and surviving manuscripts.[32] As
extant manuscript excerpts show, it was, of course, exploited for
hagiographical material (as Ælfric was also to exploit it), but it
was principally valuable as a book about mission, not simply for
the Bonifatian period on the continent, but also, as David Rollason reminded us in his Jarrow Lecture in 2001, valuable for the
kings of the Franks and their ecclesiastical advisers in the late

---

[30] The Commentary on Luke was composed between 709 and 716, with
the Commentary on Mark being one of Bede's later works.

[31] Dorothy Whitelock, "The OE Bede," *Proceedings of the British Academy* 48
(1962): 57–90.

[32] M. L. W. Laistner with H. H. King, *A Hand-List of Bede Manuscripts* (Ithaca,
N.Y., 1943), pp. 93–113.

eighth and early ninth centuries, when carrying the Christian faith to all peoples, whether abroad by conquest, or at home by teaching and church organization, was part of royal and later imperial policy.[33]

For *De tabernaculo*, there are six extant continental manuscripts from before 900, and out of the 17 biblical commentaries for which there are manuscripts of this date, only five others have as many or slightly more copies still extant.[34] This is, of course, a very imperfect test of circulation, but the list of manuscripts provided by Laistner indicates that this was a much-copied work through to the twelfth century, when interest in it seems to have tailed off. Why it was popular in the first place is that the Latin patristic tradition contained relatively little sustained exegesis of the Mosaic tabernacle, and so Bede's commentary, which is nonetheless highly respectable in drawing upon such authorities as Josephus, Jerome and Gregory the Great, filled a gap. Above all, in so doing, it actually provided a metaphoric frame of reference that was transferable to a teaching and preaching context—more so, indeed, than some of the exegesis of particular books of the Old Testament—for Bede uses the tabernacle as an image of the Church militant and stresses the practical implications of this theology for moral conduct and pastoral ministry.[35]

We have to rely on similarly imperfect manuscript evidence for the *In epistolas VII catholicas*, although it too survives in continental copies from before 900, and is very well represented in medieval library catalogues. In fact, Laistner judges it to be "the most popular of all Bede's theological expositions."[36] He sur-

---

[33] David Rollason, *Bede and Germany* (Jarrow Lecture, 2001).

[34] Laistner, *Hand-List*, pp. 5 and 70–74.

[35] For an examination of the significance of this work, see Arthur G. Holder, introduction to *Bede: On the Tabernacle*, trans. Arthur G. Holder, Translated Texts for Historians 18 (Liverpool, 1994), pp. xiii–xxvi.

[36] Laistner, *Hand-List*, pp. 5 and 30–37. The quotation is from p. 30.

mises that one reason for this may have been the lack of other commentaries on these canonical letters, but this is, of course, a reason for Bede's commentary being widely circulated and consulted. Notker of St. Gallen certainly seems to support this supposition, since his *Notatio de viris illustribus* of 885, when giving advice on which authorities to read on the epistles, cites Bede's commentary alone for this New Testament group.[37]

For the commentaries on Mark and Luke the evidence of popularity is very clear, and much of it as been alluded to already: the importance of these two texts as models for providing marginal author identifications and thus demonstrating a mode of composition that Carolingian writers adopted and acknowledged, and the sheer usefulness of these exegetical works as the source for extracts that could serve as homilies (as in Paul the Deacon's original collection and to a greater extent in subsequent augmentations), or as source-texts that could be mined by compilers such as Smaragdus, who drew on these commentaries when making up individual homilies by compiling *catenae* or chains of verbatim borrowings.[38] And of course, since the gospels were at the heart of preaching and teaching, the very subject of these two commentaries gave them an automatic prominence, once Bede was co-opted into the ranks of the authorities. There are six extant continental manuscripts of the commentary on Luke copied before 900, and nine of

[37] Dümmler, ed., *Das Formelbuch*, p. 69. The treatise was written for Salamo (later Bishop of Konstanz) when he was a newly ordained deacon. It is striking that Bede figures very prominently throughout the section offering advice on which exegetical authorities to read on the books of the Old and New Testaments. In effect, Notker offers a bibliographical definition of orthodoxy which is firmly patristic. Bede's repeated inclusion, without comment or apology, reflects a status of authority and acceptability on a par with the Fathers that was well-established by the time Notker was writing.

[38] See above, pp. 228–36.

the commentary on Mark. This puts them near the top of the list for early manuscripts, but if we take them together (as we might reasonably do in view of their extensive overlap) the total of fifteen puts them ahead of all of Bede's other biblical commentaries. In addition, they appear in 63 of the 109 booklists summarized by Laistner.[39]

As for the popularity of Bede's homilies, one only needs to refer to the position they have in Paul the Deacon's homiliary.[40] Further evidence of Bede's status is the ever-growing attribution to him of pseudonymous homilies, which continued throughout the Middle Ages, although this is at the same time the reason why Laistner's invaluable *Hand-List of Bede Manuscripts* excludes consideration of Bede's homilies: it is simply impossible to distinguish the genuine from the spurious in medieval catalogues.[41] At the same time, they confirm that Bede was a figure whose name could be used, as Augustine's was, to set an authoritative stamp on works not by him.

The range of Bedan texts drawn upon in the Councils was thus somewhat limited and not at all esoteric. Clearly, then, despite our present-day admiration of the quantity and range of Bedan material, it was not this that mattered for the Councils, but what Bede stood for. It is for this that they grant him the authority of "doctor," putting him, despite his relative modernity, firmly in the camp of the Fathers. Their references functioned as a readily recognizable confirmation, directly for the point being made but, by this very means, providing confirmation for us of the status that Bede had won.

It was an attitude which was to persist. The Anglo-Saxon homilist Ælfric, who used Carolingian homiliaries as his principal source-texts, advertised his orthodoxy, his place in the chain of

[39] Laistner, *Hand-List*, pp. 5, 44–55, and pp. 10–13 (booklists).
[40] See above, p. 232.
[41] Laistner, *Hand-List*, pp. 10, and pp. 114–18.

authority, in a Latin letter to Archbishop Sigeric of Canterbury written about 989, and explained that he drew upon Augustine, Jerome, Bede, Gregory, Smaragdus and Haymo.[42] Smaragdus and Haymo were Carolingians, the former being active in the second decade of the ninth century, and the latter in the middle years of that century. But it was Augustine, Jerome, Bede and Gregory—predominantly Bede and Gregory—that he used within the vernacular homily collection itself in order to validate the authority of his interpretations. Theirs were the names that carried weight, even amongst the less scholarly and the laity, and no distinction was made between Bede and the older Fathers, as indeed there is not in the letter to Sigeric, for Bede is contained within the list of patristic authorities, with the two Carolingians coming at the end: "Augustine of Hippo, Jerome, Bede, Gregory, Smaragdus, and sometime Haymo" (*Augustinum. ypponiensem. Hieronimum. Bedam. Gregorium. Smaragdum, et aliquando Hægmonem*).

Ælfric, in his letter to Sigeric, was doing something similar to Bede himself, and similar to Hrabanus Maurus and Claudius of Turin in commenting on their mode of composition: they were all signaling not only their impeccable orthodoxy by identifying key source-authors, but they were also making explicit their position as a link in an approved chain of authority stretching back to the Fathers themselves, a body of authorities into which Bede

---

[42] Ælfric, Praefatio to *Ælfric's Catholic Homilies: The First Series*, p. 173. On Ælfric's engagement with the Carolingian (and Bedan) intertextual *compilatio* tradition, see Joyce Hill, "Translating the Tradition: Manuscripts, Models and Methodologies in the Composition of Ælfric's Catholic Homilies," The 1996 Toller Lecture, *Bulletin of the John Rylands Library* 79 (1997): 43–65; *Bede and the Benedictine Reform*; and "Authority and Intertextuality in the Works of Ælfric," The British Academy Gollancz Lecture for 2004, *Proceedings of the British Academy* 131 (2005): 157–81.

was clearly co-opted. Within a literate context, where the manuscripts would actually be read, it was possible to go on to signal
the links in the chain as they occurred in the main body of the
text through the visual means of marginal letter-abbreviations—
or attributions in the rubrics in the case of Paul the Deacon's
homiliary, where single-authored discrete items or extracts were
presented. But in Ælfric's case, where a listening audience is
imagined, and where the ultimate, if not the immediate audience is conceived of as laity, this method would have been use-
less—literally invisible to an audience that would not actually
see the written text. As an alternative method, therefore, attribution was presented through the aural means of embedding it
as part of the phraseology of the homily itself. For example, "the
expositor Gregory said…" ("Gregorius se trahtnere cwæð"),
"the teacher Bede said….," ("se lareow Beda cwæð"), and so on.
The method of signaling the attribution necessarily differs from
that found in literate contexts, but the purpose is exactly the
same, and while it is true that Ælfric does twice cite Haymo as an
authoritative name in the Catholic Homilies, all other attributions are to earlier authorities, the Fathers, as we would recognize them, and Bede. Yet no distinction is made. Bede is cited
in exactly the same way as the traditional Fathers of the Church:
very frequently, very confidently, and with no explanation or
apology. More telling still, in relation to the status that Bede had
achieved, is the fact that it is his name that is cited even when
this particular attribution is demonstrably taken second-hand
from a Carolingian intermediary, such as Ælfric's manuscripts
of the homiliaries of Paul the Deacon or Smaragdus. He thus
accords to Bede the same status as is presented to him in these
source-materials, recognizing that his is the powerful name to
use— on a par with Gregory's, Augustine's and Jerome's.

This co-option of Bede into the patristic canon is a measure of
his importance to the Carolingians. My focus thus far has been
on evidence in which Bede is, as it were, "on display." But for a
full appreciation of his practical importance we need to look a
little farther than this and consider how Bede was, at the same

time, a hidden link in the chain of authority. In other words, although there are innumerable references to him as an authority, he was actually used more often than he was acknowledged. Two examples from the homily tradition will illustrate the point.[43]

In one part of the *catena* for his homily on Sexagesima Sunday, Smaragdus gives a marginal attribution to Gregory.[44] This is technically accurate since the words are in origin those of Gregory, although in fact Smaragdus's immediate source was Bede's *In Lucam*. We can be sure of this because Smaragdus's version of Gregory's text at this point is modified in precisely the way found in Bede's commentary, which we know, in any case, was one of Smaragdus's major sources. It is consequently reasonable to suppose that he also took from Bede the patristic attribution, which would have been in the manuscript's margin. Ælfric, in his Second Series homily for Sexagesima Sunday, can be shown to have used Smaragdus, yet again the attribution is to Gregory.[45] In this sequence of textual transmission, therefore, it is the ultimate source that remains visible in each successive transmission: Bede is invisible in Smaragdus's text, and Smaragdus and Bede are both invisible in Ælfric's. Gregory's name acts as the guarantor of orthodox interpretation in each instance, although the modification that both Smaragdus and Ælfric used was introduced by Bede. Ælfric's Second Series homily for

[43] The two examples that follow are discussed in more detail and in a broader context in Hill, "Authority and Intertextuality in the Works of Ælfric."

[44] Smaragdus's homily is at PL 102, cols. 109-12. Rädle, *Studien zu Smaragd*, p. 214, identifies Bede's commentary as Smaragdus's immediate source.

[45] Ælfric, *Hom.* 6, in *Ælfric's Catholic Homilies. The Second Series*, pp. 52–59. It is analysed in relation to its immediate sources by Hill, "Ælfric and Smaragdus," pp. 225–8.

[46] Ælfric, *Hom.* 23, in *Ælfric's Catholic Homilies. The Second Series*, pp. 213–17. My comments relate only the main body of the homily in Godden's edition (i.e. lines 1–125). Thorpe's numbering of the homilies at this point differs from that of Godden, but the number is provided here so

the Third Sunday after Pentecost provides a similar example.[46] Gregory is named as the source, and the homily in question, identified by Förster,[47] was shown by Smetana to be available in Paul the Deacon's homiliary.[48] However, the pattern of textual abbreviation and omission allows us to see that Ælfric's immediate source was actually Smaragdus's homily for the same day, and since Smaragdus's attribution at this point was to Gregory, Ælfric was able to adopt this as the authorizing name, at the same time as he was working with this portion of the text.[49] Yet within the dense intertextual tradition that we are dealing with here, the situation is even more complicated than this summary indicates, because close textual analysis shows that Smaragdus did not work directly from Gregory but from Bede's *In Lucam*, from which he took both the modifications and the patristic attribution.[50]

These examples show that, in a straight competition between Bede (his immediate source) and Gregory (the available attribution), Smaragdus may be inclined to choose Gregory as the attribution. For Ælfric, however, the competition in these two

that connections can be made with earlier scholarship: *Ælfric Sermones Catholici*, ed. Thorpe, 2: 370–8 (homily XXVI). The Stilling of the Storm and the Gadarene Swine, which are edited by Godden as a confirmatory appendix (lines 126–98, pp. 217–20), are separately numbered in Thorpe's edition as homily XXVII.

[47] Max Förster, "Über die Quellen von Ælfrics exegetischen Homiliae Catholicae," *Anglia* 16 (1894): p. 5, § 49.

[48] Cyril L. Smetana, "Ælfric and the Early Medieval Homiliary," *Traditio* 15 (1959): 198.

[49] Smaragdus's homily is at PL 102, cols 355–8. On the relationship between Smaragdus's text and that of Ælfric, see Joyce Hill, "Ælfric's Sources Reconsidered: Some Case Studies from the *Catholic Homilies*," in *Studies in English Language and Literature, 'Doubt wisely': Papers in Honour of E. G. Stanley*, ed. M. J. Toswell and E. M. Tyler (London, 1996), pp. 372–7.

[50] See Rädle, *Studien zu Smaragd*, p. 214 for Bede's commentary being Smaragdus's immediate source.

examples was between Smaragdus (the manuscript-homiliary that he was working from) and Gregory (the available marginal attribution)—and that was no competition at all.[51] He never cites Smaragdus by name in the body of his homilies—there would have been no point since his was not a universally recognized "great name," important though he was in Benedictine Reform circles—and Ælfric would not have known that Bede was the transmitter, standing between Gregory and Smaragdus. Who would Ælfric have chosen as the authority-name had he known? Probably Gregory since, as Smaragdus indicates, there was a hierarchy even within the patristic canon, although we recall that Paul the Deacon's homiliary, in its original and augmented form, simplifies the intertextual complexity of Bede's commentaries on Luke and Mark by attributing extracts drawn from these solely to Bede, when the originals had many different marginal attributions to antecedent authorities.[52]

We are thus brought face-to-face with Bede's anomalous position. On the one hand, he is unambiguously in the patristic camp, co-opted by the Carolingians into the patristic canon and thus honored by successive writers, both in the way he is referred to and the way he is used. Yet, on the other, he is like the Carolingians, self-consciously writing as a *compilator* and cre-

---

[51] In discussing the sources of the two homilies given here as examples of process of text and attribution, Godden discounts Smaragdus on the grounds that he is derivative: Malcolm Godden, *Ælfric's Catholic Homilies: Introduction, Commentary and Glossary*, Early English Texts Society SS 18 (Oxford, 2000), pp. 388–94 (Sexagesima Sunday) and 549–55 (Third Sunday after Pentecost). However, Bede is derivative in precisely the same way; and to discuss Ælfric's homilies in relation to the initiating or ultimate source without paying attention to the evidence we have for his use of an immediate source tends to misrepresent Ælfric's working methods. In addition, source-study which does not attend to the intertextual complexity of the exegetical tradition fails to penetrate the mindset of those working within it—of whom Bede is a pivotal figure.

[52] See above, pp. 231–33.

ating textual *catenae* which, in some works are visually signaled by marginal letter-abbreviations. Generally, in analyzing textual transmission, that is to say, in source-study, we tend to accede to the authority ascribed to Bede by the scholars of the early middle ages, and we follow them, as Ælfric did, in accepting him as an authority grouped with the Fathers themselves. Yet there is no logical reason why, on the basis of modern perceptions of the derivative text, he should not be grouped with the Carolingian *compilatores*, and so be treated in modern scholarship, as they are, as a "mere" transmitter. Of course, it is important to understand how the transmission takes place, and Bede's anomalous and yet pivotal position is in fact an important point of access for those of us interested in studying how textual transmission took place, and in penetrating the mindset of those who worked within a dense intertextual tradition. To put it in simple terms, we might say that he is, at one and the same time, a *de facto* compilator and a *de jure* "adopted" Father of the Church. But if we use him, in source study scholarship, as if he is a primary source, rather than as an intermediate transmitter, we need to remember that we do so within terms of reference that may be artificially constructed: in his case the early medieval construction of him as a member of the patristic textual community when, objectively, his intellectual and compositional approaches are closer to those of the Carolingian compilatores than to the Fathers with whom he is bracketed. That, however, opens up a whole host of questions about the intertextuality of early medieval exegesis and how we deal with it in modern scholarship, questions which go beyond the scope of this paper, and which I have explored in greater detail elsewhere.[53]

As Rosamond McKitterick has pointed out in her recent book on *History and Memory in the Carolingian World*, the act of writing in itself created authoritative knowledge and, for the Carolin-

[53] See Hill, "Authority and Intertextuality in the Works of Ælfric."

[54] Rosamund McKitterick, *History and Memory in the Carolingian World* (Cambridge, 2004), in particular chapter 10, pp. 218–44.

gians, the more that wisdom rested on the wisdom of others, the greater was its power.[54] Alcuin, in his *De Rhetorica*, put into Charlemagne's mouth the question, "How can our speech attain the authority which that of the ancients had?," to which Alcuin's answer was "Their books ought to be read and their words well impressed upon our memory."[55] What attracted the Carolingians to Bede was that they could see in him this very process being undertaken in a textual and thus transmittable context, and it showed them how to do it for themselves. Since he was not quite of their time, and since the scale and scope of his work gave them access to the patristic tradition in what, at least in the late eighth and early ninth century, was an incomparable—and indeed highly convenient—fashion, they took him as the teacher of their age, and recognized him as "magister" and "doctor." Bede might have demurred, but they were in no doubt. It was the Carolingians who thus incorporated him into the canon of required knowledge, making his work accessible, shaping his reputation, and validating his authority in ways which meant that he in turn became as powerful a validator of interpretative orthodoxy as the great Fathers themselves.[56]

[55] Cited by McKitterick, *History and Memory*, p. 243. Alcuin, *Disputatio de rhetorica*, pp. 132–3.

[56] Some years ago Professor Pfaff looked at the evidence for Bede's status within the liturgical tradition: see Richard W. Pfaff, "Bede Among the Fathers: The Evidence of Liturgical Commemoration," *Studia Patristica* 28 (1993): 225–9. On the whole, that evidence points to a rather later date for his commemoration as a "doctor," but perhaps this apparent difference can be accounted for by the nature of the evidence. The material examined by Pfaff enshrines recognition after the event; that examined in the present paper shows the recognition in process of being established and exploited within a renewed and self-conscious tradition of authority. One might reasonably expect a time-lag before there could be recognition in the form of liturgical commemoration with appropriate "patristic" epithets—although, as Pfaff explains, Bede is commemorated liturgically with a different class of epithets from quite an early date.

Bibliography

PRIMARY SOURCES

Abelard, Peter. *Historia calamitatum.* Translated by Betty Radice and M. T. Clanchy, *The Letters of Abelard and Heloise.* New York, 2003.

Ælfric. Catholic Homilies. Edited by Peter Clemoes, *Ælfric's Catholic Homilies: The First Series.* Early English Text Society, SS 17. Oxford, 1997. Edited by Malcolm Godden, *Ælfric's Catholic Homilies. The Second Series: Text.* Early English Text Society, SS 5 London, 1979.

_____. *Ælfric Sermones Catholici.* Edited by Benjamin Thorpe. 2 vols. London, 1844–46.

Alcuin. *Alcuini sive Albini Epistolae.* Edited by Ernst Dümmler. MGH Epistulae 4. Berlin, 1896.

_____. *Disputatio de rhetorica et de virtutibus sapientissimi regis Karli et Albini magistri.* Edited with English translation by W. S. Howell. Princeton, 1941.

_____. *Versus de sanctis Euboricensis.* Edited and translated by Peter Godman, *The Bishops, Kings and Saints of York.* Oxford, 1982.

Amalarius. *De ecclesiasticis officiis.* Edited in PL 105.

Ambrose. *Hexaemeron.* Edited by C. Schenkl. CSEL 32.1. Vienna, 1897.

Apponius. *In Canticum Canticorum expositio.* Edited by B. De Vregilli and L. Neyrand. CCSL 19. Turnhout, 1986.

Bibliography

Augustine. *Contra Faustum Manichaeum.* Edited by Joseph Zycha. CSEL 25.1. Vienna, 1891.

_____. *De civitate Dei.* Edited by Bernard Dombart and Alphonse Kalb. CCSL 47 and 48. Turnout, 1955. Translated by Henry Bettenson, *The City of God.* Revised edition. Harmondsworth, 2004.

_____. *De consensu Euangelistarum.* Edited by F. Weihrich, CSEL 43. Vienna, 1904.

_____. *De diversis quaestionibus ad Simplicianum.* Edited by Almut Mutzen-bacher. CCSL 44. Turnhout, 1970.

_____. *De doctrina christiana.* Edited by J. Martin. CCSL 32. Turnhout, 1962. Translated by D. W. Robertson, Jr., *On Christian Doctrine.* Indianapo-lis, 1958.

_____. *Enarrationes in Psalmos.* Edited by D. E. Dekkers and J. Fraipont. CCSL 40. Turnhout, 1956.

_____. *Tractatus in euangelium Ioannis.* Edited by R. Willems. CCSL 36. Turnhout, 1954.

Bede. *Collectio ex opusculis sancti Augustini in epistulas Pauli apostoli.* Trans-lated by David Hurst, *Bede the Venerable: Excerpts from the Works of St. Augus-tine on the Letters of the Blessed Apostle Paul.* Cistercian Studies Series 183. Kalamazoo, Mich., 1999.

_____. *Collectio Psalterii Bedae Venerabili adscripta.* Edited by Gerald M. Browne. Bibliotheca Teubneriana. Munich and Leipzig, 2001. Translated by Browne, *The Abbreviated Psalter of the Venerable Bede.* Grand Rapids, Mich., 2002.

_____. *De arte metrica et de schematibus et tropis.* Edited by Calvin B. Kendall. CCSL 123A. Turnhout, 1975. Translated by Calvin B. Kendall, *Bede: The*

Art of Poetry and Rhetoric. Bibliotheca Germanica Series Nova. Volume 2. Saarbrücken, 1991.

_____. *De octo quaestionibus.* Edited in PL 93. Translated by Arthur Holder, *Bede: A Biblical Miscellany.* Translated Texts for Historians 28. Liverpool, 1999.

_____. *De natura rerum liber.* Edited by C. W. Jones. CCSL 123A. Turnhout, 1975.

_____. *De tabernaculo.* Edited by David Hurst. CCSL 119A. Turnhout, 1969. Translated by Arthur G. Holder, *Bede: On the Tabernacle.* Translated Texts for Historians 18. Liverpool, 1994.

_____. *De templo.* Edited by David Hurst. CCSL 119A. Turnhout, 1969. Translated by Seán Connolly, *Bede: On the Temple.* Translated Texts for Historians 21. Liverpool, 1995.

_____. *De temporum ratione.* Edited by Charles W. Jones. CCSL 123B. Turnhout, 1977. Translated by Faith Wallis, *Bede: The Reckoning of Time.* Translated Texts for Historians 29. Liverpool, 1999.

_____. *Epistola ad Ecgbertum Episcopum.* Edited by Charles Plummer in *Venerabilis Baedae opera historica.* 2 vols. 1896. Reprinted, 2 vols. in 1, Oxford, 1946. Translated by Judith McClure and Roger Collins in *Bede: Ecclesiastical History of the English People.* Oxford, 1994.

_____. *Epistola ad Pleguinam.* Edited by Charles W. Jones. CCSL 123C. Turnout, 1980. Translated by Faith Wallis, *Bede: The Reckoning of Time.* Translated Texts for Historians 29. Liverpool, 1999.

_____. *Epistola ad Wichthedum.* Edited by Charles W. Jones. CCSL 123C. Turnout, 1980. Translated by Faith Wallis, *Bede: The Reckoning of Time.* Translated Texts for Historians 29. Liverpool, 1999.

Bibliography

——. *Explanatio Apocalypseos.* Edited by Roger Gyrson. CCSL 121A. Turnhout, 2001. Translated Rev. Edward Marshall, *The Explanation of the Apocalypse by Venerable Beda.* Oxford, 1878.

——. *Expositio Actuum Apostolorum.* Edited by M. L. W. Laistner. CCSL 121. Turnhout, 1960. Translated by Lawrence T. Martin, *The Venerable Bede: Commentary on the Acts of the Apostles,* Cistercian Studies Series 117. Kalamazoo, Mich., 1989.

——. *Historia ecclesiastica gentis Anglorum.* Edited and translated by Bertram Colgrave and R. A. B. Mynors. Oxford, 1969. Reprinted with corrections, 1991.

——. *Historia abbatum auctore Baeda.* Edited by Charles Plummer in *Venerabilis Baedae opera historica.* 1896. Reprinted, 2 vols. in 1, Oxford, 1946. Translated by D. H. Farmer in *The Age of Bede.* Harmondsworth, 1998.

——. *Homiliae euangelii.* Edited by David Hurst. CCSL 122. Turnhout, 1965. Translated by Lawrence T. Martin and David Hurst, *Bede the Venerable: Homilies on the Gospels.* 2 vols. Cistercian Studies Series, 110 and 111. Kalamazoo, Mich., 1991.

——. *In Cantica Canticorum.* Edited by David Hurst. CCSL 119B. Turnhout, 1983.

——. *In epistolas VII catholicas.* Edited by David Hurst. CCSL 121. Turnhout, 1983. Translated by David Hurst, *Commentary on the Seven Catholic Epistles of the Venerable Bede.* Cistercian Studies Series 82. Kalamazoo, Mich., 1985.

——. *In Ezram et Neemiam.* Edited by David Hurst. CCSL 119A. Turnhout, 1969. Translated by Scott DeGregorio, *Bede: On Ezra and Nehemiah,* Translated Texts for Historians 47. Liverpool, 2006.

——. *In Habacuc.* Edited by J. E. Hudson. CCSL 119B. Turnhout, 1972. Translated by Seán Connolly, *Bede: On Tobit and On the Canticle of Habakkuk.* Dublin, 1997.

_____. *In Lucae euangelium expositio.* Edited by David Hurst. CCSL 120. Turnhout, 1960.

_____. *In Marci euangelium expositio.* Edited by David Hurst. CCSL 120. Turnhout, 1960.

_____. *In primam partem Samuhelis libri IIII.* Edited by David Hurst. CCSL 119. Turnhout, 1962.

_____. *In principium Genesis.* Edited by C. W. Jones. CCSL 118. Turnhout, 1967.

_____. *In prouerbia Salomonis.* Edited by David Hurst. CCSL 119B. Turnhout, 1983.

_____. *In Regum librum XXX quaestiones.* Edited by David Hurst. CCSL 119. Turnhout, 1972. Translated by W. Trent Foley and Arthur G. Holder, *Bede: A Biblical Miscellany.* Translated Texts for Historians 28. Liverpool, 1999.

_____. *In Tobiam.* Edited by David Hurst. CCSL 119B. Turnhout, 1983. Translated by W. Trent Foley and Arthur G. Holder, *Bede: A Biblical Miscellany.* Translated Texts for Historians 28. Liverpool, 1999.

_____. *Nomina locorum ex Beati Hieronimi et Flaui Iosephi collecta opusculis.* Edited by David Hurst. CCSL 119. Turnhout, 1972.

_____. *Retractatio in Actus Apostolorum.* Edited by M. L. W. Laistner. CCSL 121. Turnhout, 1960.

_____. *Vita sancti Cuthberti.* Edited and translated by Bertram Colgrave, *Two Lives of Saint Cuthbert.* 1940. Reprinted, Cambridge 1985.

Benedict. *Regula sancti Benedicti.* In *La Règle de saint Benoît.* Edited by A. de Vogüé. Paris, 1971–77.

Bibliography

Biblia sacra iuxta Latinam Vulgatam versionem ad codicem fidem. 17 vols. Rome, 1944.

Biblia Latina cum Glossa Ordinaria: Facsimile Reprint of the Editio Princeps 1480/81. Edited by K. Froehlich and M. T. Gibson. 4 vols. Turnhout, 1992.

Boethius. *Contra Eutychen.* Edited and translated by H. F. Stewart, E. K. Rand and S. J. Tester, *Boethius: the Theological Tractates.* LCL. 1918. Reprinted, Cambridge, Mass., 1990.

_____. *De consolatione philosophiae.* Edited and translated by S. J. Tester. LCL. 1918. Reprinted, Cambridge, Mass., 1990.

_____. *De institutione arithmetica.* Edited by G. Friedlein. Leipzig, 1867.

Boniface. *Epistolae.* In *Die Briefe des heiligen Bonfatius et Lullus.* Edited by Michael Tangl. MGH, Epistolae selectae I. Berlin, 1916.

Capitularia Regum Francorum. Edited by A. Boretius. MGH: Legum Sectio II. Capitularia Regum Francorum I. Hannover, 1883.

Cassiodorus. *Institutiones.* Edited by R. A. B. Mynors. Oxford, 1937.

Claudius of Turin. *Claudius Taurinensis Espiscopi Epistolae.* In *Epistolae Karolini Ævi.* Edited by E. Dümmler. MGH, Epistolarum Tomus IV. Berlin, 1895.

Concilia Aevi Karolini. Edited by A. Werminghoff. MGH, Legum Sectio III, Concilia II, I. Hannover and Leipzig, 1906.

Cuthbert. *Epistolae.* In *Die Briefe des heiligen Bonfatius et Lullus.* Edited by Michael Tangl. MGH, Epistolae selectae I. Berlin, 1916.

Eugippius. *Eugipii excerpta ex operibus Sancti Augustini.* Edited by P. Knoll. CSEL 9. Vienna, 1885.

Eusebius. *Historia ecclesiastica.* Edited and translated by Gustave Bardy. *Histoire ecclésiastique.* SC 31, 41, 55, and 73. Paris, 1952–60.

Gregory the Great. *Moralia in Job.* Edited by Marc Adriaen. CCSL 143, 143A and 143B. Turnout, 1979–85.

Hincmar of Rheims. *De divortio Lotharii Regis.* Edited in PL 125.

Holy Bible Translated from the Latin Vulgate: The Old Testament first published by the English College at Douay, A.D. 1609, and the New Testament, first published by the English College at Rheims, A.D. 1582. Rockford, Ill., 1971.

Hrabanus Maurus. *Commentaria in libros iv regum.* Edited in PL 109.

_____. *Commentarium in Mattheum.* Edited in PL 107.

Hugh of Fouilloy. *De claustro animae.* Edited in PL 176.

Isidore of Seville. *De natura rerum.* Edited with a French translation by Jacques Fontaine, *Traité de la nature.* Bordeaux, 1960.

_____. *Etymologiae.* Edited by W. M. Lindsay. 2 vols. Oxford, 1911.

Jerome. *Epistulae I–LXX.* Edited by I. Hilberg. CSEL 54. Vienna, 1910.

_____. *Prologus sancti Hieronymi in libro Regum.* In *Biblia sacra iuxta Latinam Vulgatam versionem ad codicem fidem.* Vol. 5, pp. 3–11. Rome, 1944.

_____. *Praefatio sancti Hieronymi in libro Ezrae.* In *Biblia sacra iuxta Latinam Vulgatam versionem ad codicem fidem.* Vol. 8, pp. 2–7. Rome, 1950.

_____. *Liber interpretationis hebraicorum nominum.* Edited by Paul de Lagarde. CCSL 72. Turnhout, 1959.

_____. *In Esaiam.* Edited by M. Adriaen. CCSL 73 and 73A. Turnhout, 1963.

Bibliography

Liber Vitae Ecclesiae Dunelmensis. Edited by J. Stevenson. Surtees Society 13 (1841).

"Liber Vitae Ecclesiae Dunelmensis, BL MS Cotton Domitian A. vii." Edited by D. Dumville and P. Stokes. Trial version, Dept. Anglo-Saxon, Norse and Celtic, Cambridge 2001.

Lull. *Epistolae.* In *Die Briefe des heiligen Bonfatius et Lullus.* Edited by Michael Tangl. MGH, Epistolae selectae I. Berlin, 1916.

Notker of St. Gallen. *Notatio de viris illustribus.* In *Das Formelbuch des Bischofs Salamo III von Konstanz.* Edited by Ernst Dümmler. 1857. Reprinted, Osnabrück, 1964.

Origen. *Commentarius in Canticum.* In *Origenes Werke.* Edited by W. A. Baehrens. GCS 33. Leipzig, 1899.

_____. *Homélies sur Samuel.* Edited and translated by Pierre and Marie Thérèse Nautin. SC 328. Paris, 1986.

Paul the Deacon. *Homiliarium.* Edited in PL 95.

Pliny. *Historia Naturalis.* Edited by H. Rackham. Cambridge, Mass., 1929.

Poetae Latini Medii Aevi Carolini. Edited by E. Dümmler. MGH. Berlin, 1884.

Prudentius. *Contra orationem Symmachi.* Edited and translated by H. J. Thompson. Cambridge, Mass., 1969.

Smaragdus. *Collectiones in epistolas et evangelia.* Edited in PL 102.

Stephen of Ripon. *Vita Wilfridi.* Edited and translated by Bertram Colgrave, *The Life of Bishop Wilfrid by Eddius Stephanus.* 1927. Reprinted, Cambridge, 1985.

Vita Ceolfridi. Edited by C. Plummer as *Historia abbatum auctore Anonymo.* In *Venerabilis Baedae opera historica.* 2 vols. 1896. Reprinted 2 vols. in 1, Oxford, 1946.

Vita sancti Cuthberti auctore anonymo. Edited and translated by Bertram Colgrave, *Two Lives of Saint Cuthbert.* 1940. Reprinted, Cambridge, 1985.

William of Malmesbury. *Gesta Regum Anglorum.* Edited by R. A. B. Mynors, R. M. Thompson, and M. Winterbottom. Oxford, 1998.

SECONDARY SOURCES

Anderson, George W. *A Critical Introduction to the Old Testament.* London, 1964.

Atkinson, Clarissa W. *The Oldest Vocation: Christian Motherhood in the Middle Ages.* Ithaca, N.Y., 1991.

Auerbach, Erich. "'Figura'." Translated by Ralph Manheim, pp. 11–76. In *Scenes from the Drama of European Literature: Six Essays.* 1959. Reprinted, Gloucester, Mass., 1973.

Bell, David N., ed. *The Libraries of the Cistercians, Gilbertines, and Premonstratensians.* Corpus of British Medieval Library Catalogues 3. London, 1992.

Bischoff, Bernhard and Michael Lapidge. *Biblical Commentaries from the Canterbury School of Theodore and Hadrian.* Cambridge Studies in Anglo-Saxon England 10. Cambridge, 1994.

Blair, John. *The Church in Anglo-Saxon Society.* Oxford, 2005.

Blair, Peter Hunter. *The World of Bede.* London, 1970.

Bibliography

———. *Bede's Ecclesiastical History of the English Nation and Its Importance Today.* Jarrow Lecture, 1959. Reprinted in Lapidge, *Bede and His World*, pp. 19–33.

Bogaert, Pierre-Maurice. "Les livres d'Esdras et leur numérotation dans l'histoire du canon de la Bible latine." *Revue Bénédictine* 110 (2000): 5–26.

Bonner, Gerald. "Bedan Studies in 1973." *The Clergy Review* 53 (1973): 689–96.

———. *Saint Bede in the Tradition of Western Apocalyptic Commentary.* Jarrow Lecture, 1966. Reprinted in Lapidge, *Bede and His World*, 2:154–83.

———. "Bede and his Legacy." *Durham University Journal* 78.2 (1986): 219–30.

Bonner, Gerald, ed. *Famulus Christi: Essays in Commemoration of the Thirteenth Centenary of the Birth of the Venerable Bede.* London, 1976.

Borst, Arno. *Das Buch der Naturgeschichte: Plinius und seine Leser im Zeitalter des Pergaments.* 2nd edn. Heidelberg, 1995.

Bradley, Ritamary. "Patristic Background of the Motherhood Similitude in Julian of Norwich." *Christian Scholar's Review* 8 (1978): 101–13.

Briggs, E. "Nothing but Names: the Original Core of the Durham *Liber Vitae*." In Rollason, *The Durham Liber Vitae and its Context*, pp. 45–61.

Brown, George Hardin. *Bede the Venerable.* Boston, 1987.

———. "Aldhelm(640?–709/10)." In Szarmach, *Medieval England*, pp. 5-17.

———. "The Preservation and Transmission of Northumbrian Culture on the Continent: Alcuin's Debt to Bede." In *The Preservation and Transmission of Anglo-Saxon Culture*, Edited by Paul E. Szarmach and Joel T. Rosenthal, pp. 159–75. Kalamazoo, Mich., 1997.

_____. *Bede the Educator.* Jarrow Lecture, 1996.

_____. "Bede's Commentary on 1 Samuel." In *Biblical Studies in the Early Middle Ages: Proceedings of the Conference on Biblical Studies in the Early Middle Ages, Gargnano on Lake Garda, 24–27 June 2001,* pp. 77–90. Edited by Claudio Leonardi and Giovanni Orlandi. Florence, 2005.

Brown, Giles. "Introduction: The Carolingian Renaissance." In *Carolingian Culture: Emulation and Innovation.* Edited by Rosamond McKitterick, pp. 1–51. Cambridge, 1994.

Bynum, Caroline Walker. *Jesus as Mother: Studies in the Spirituality of the High Middle Ages.* Berkeley, 1982.

Campbell, James. *Essays in Anglo-Saxon History.* London, 1986. Originally published in *Latin Historians.* Edited by T. A. Dorsey, (London, 1966), pp. 159-90.

_____. "Bede." In *The Oxford Dictionary of National Biography.* Edited by H. C. G. Matthew and Brian Harrison. Vol. 4, pp. 758–65. Oxford, 2004.

Cameron, Averil. Review of Goffart, *Narrators of Barbarian History.* In *American Historical Review* 95 (1990): 1172–3.

Cameron, M. L. *Anglo-Saxon Medicine.* Cambridge, 1993.

Caplan, Harry. "The Four Senses of scriptural Interpretation and the Medieval Theory of Preaching." *Speculum* 4 (1929): 282–90.

Carroll, Sr. Mary Thomas Aquinas. *The Venerable Bede: His Spiritual Teachings.* Catholic University of America Studies in Medieval History 9. Washington, D.C., 1946.

Casey, Michael. *Sacred Reading: The Ancient Art of Lectio Divina.* Liguori, Mont., 1996.

Bibliography

Coates, Simon J. "The Bishop as Pastor and Solitary: Bede and the Spiritual Authority of the Monk-Bishop." *Journal of Ecclesiastical History* 47 (1996): 601–19.

Contreni, John J. "Carolingian Biblical Studies." In *Carolingian Essays: Andrew S. Mellon Lectures in Early Christian Studies.* Edited by Uta-Renate Blumenthal, pp. 71–98. Washington, D.C., 1983.

Cross, Frank and Elizabeth A. Livingstone, eds. *The Oxford Dictionary of the Christian Church.* 2nd edn. Oxford, 1974.

Cross, J. E. "Bede's Influence at Home and Abroad." In Houwen, *Beda Venerabilis,* pp. 17–29.

Daniélou, Jean. *From Shadows to Reality: Studies in the Biblical Typology of the Fathers.* Translated by Wulstan Hibberd. Westminster, Md., 1960.

Dargan, Edwin Charles. *A History of Preaching.* 2 vols. 1905. Reprinted, New York, 1968.

Davidse, Jan. "The Sense of History in the Works of the Venerable Bede." *Studi medievali* 23 (1982): 647–95.

_____. "On Bede as Christian Historian." In Houwen, *Beda Venerabilis,* pp. 1–15.

Davy, Marie-Madeleine. *Initiation à la symbolique romane (xiie siècle).* 2nd edn. Paris, 1973.

de Ghellinck, Joseph. *Littérature latine au Moyen Age.* Paris, 1939.

DeGregorio, Scott. "The Venerable Bede on Prayer and Contemplation." *Traditio* 54 (1999): 1–39.

_____. "*Nostrorum socordiam temporum:* The Reforming Impulse of Bede's Later Exegesis." *Early Medieval Europe* 11 (2002): 107–22.

_____. "Bede's *In Ezram et Neemiam* and the Reform of the Northumbrian Church." *Speculum* 79 (2004): 1–25.

_____. Bede's *In Ezram et Neemiam*: A Document in Church Reform?" In Lebecq, *Bède le Vénérable*, pp. 97–107.

_____. "Bede, the Monk, as Exegete: Evidence from the Commentary on Ezra- Nehemiah." *Revue Bénédictine* 115 (2005): 343–69.

_____. Introduction to *Bede: On Ezra and Nehemiah*. Translated by Scott DeGregorio. Translated Texts for Historians 47. Liverpool, 2006.

Dekkers, Eligius and Aemilius Gaar, eds. *Clavis patrum latinorum.* 3rd edn. Brepols, 1956.

de Lubac, Henri. *Exégèse médiévale: les quatre sens de l'Écriture.* 2 vols. Paris, 1959.

Denter, Thomas. *Die Stellung der Bücher Esdras im Kanon des Alten Testamentes. Eine kanon- geschichtliche Untersuchung.* Diss. Freiburg. Marienstatt, 1962.

de Vogüé, Adalbert. "Les plus anciens exégèses du Premier Livre des Rois: Origène, Augustin et leur epigones." *Sacris Erudiri* 29 (1986): 5–24.

Dionisotti, Anna Carlotta. "On Bede, Grammars, and Greek." *Revue Bénédictine* 92 (1982): 11– 41.

Dockray-Miller, Mary. *Motherhood and Mothering in Anglo-Saxon England.* New York, 2000.

Druhan, David Ross. *The Syntax of Bede's Historia ecclesiastica.* Catholic University of America Studies in Medieval and Renaissance Latin 8. Washington, D.C., 1938.

Eby, John C. "Bringing the *Vita* to Life: Bede's Symbolic Structure of the Life of St. Cuthbert." *American Benedictine Review* 48 (1997): 316–38.

Bibliography

Eckenrode, Thomas R. "Original Aspects in Venerable Bede's Tidal Theories with Relation to Prior Tidal Observations." Ph.D. diss., St. Louis University, 1970.

_____. "Venerable Bede as a Scientist." *American Benedictine Review* 22 (1971): 486–507.

_____. "Venerable Bede's Theory of Ocean Tides." *American Benedictine Review* 25 (1974): 56–74.

_____. "The Growth of a Scientific Mind: Bede's Early and Late Scientific Writings." *Downside Review* 94 (1976): 197–212.

_____. "The Venerable Bede and the Pastoral Affirmation of the Christian Message in Anglo-Saxon England." *The Downside Review* 99 (1981): 258–78.

Economou, George. *The Goddess Natura in Medieval Literature.* Cambridge, Mass., 1972.

Edwards, Jr., O. C. *A History of Preaching.* Nashville, Tenn., 2004.

Englisch, Brigitte. *Die Artes liberales im frühen Mittelalter (5.–9. Jh.): Das Quadrivium und der Komputus als Inidikatoren für der exacten Wissenschaften zwischen Antike und Mittelalter.* Sudhoffs Archiv, Beiheft 33. Stuttgart, 1994.

_____. "Realitätsorientierte Wissenschaft oder praxisferne Traditionswissen? Inhalte und Probleme mittelalterliche Wissenschaftsvorstellungen am Beispiel von *De temporum ratione* des Beda Venerabilis." In *Dilettanten und Wissenschaft. Zur Geschichte und Aktualität eines wechselvollen Verhältnisses.* Edited by Elisabeth Strauss, pp. 11–34. Philosophie und Repräsentation/ Philosophy and Representation 4. Amsterdam, 1996.

Farrell, Robert T. *Bede and Anglo-Saxon England: Papers in Honour of the 1300th Anniversary of the Birth of Bede, given at Cornell University in 1973 and 1974.* British Archaeological Reports 46. London, 1978.

Foley, William Trent. *Images of Sanctity in Eddius Stephanus'* Life of Bishop Wilfrid, *an Early English Saint's Life*. Lewiston, N.Y., 1992.

Fontaine, Jacques. *Isidore de Séville et la culture classique dans l'Espagne visigothique*. 2nd edn. Paris, 1983.

————. *Isidore de Séville: genèse et originalité de la culture hispanique au temps des Wisigoths*. Turnhout, 2000.

Foot, Sarah. "Parochial Ministry in Early Anglo-Saxon England: The Role of the Monastic Communities." In *The Ministry: Clerical and Lay. Papers read at the 1988 Summer Meeting and the 1989 Winter Meeting of the Ecclesiastical History Society*. Edited by W. J. Sheils and Diana Wood, pp. 43–54. Studies in Church History 26. Oxford, 1989.

Förster, Max. "Über die Quellen von Ælfrics exegetischen Homiliae Catholicae." *Anglia* 16 (1894): 1–61.

Fransen, P. –I. "Description de la collection de Bède le Vénérable sur l'Apôtre." *Revue Bénédictine* 71 (1961): 22–70.

————. "D'Eugippius à Bède le Vénérable." *Revue Bénédictine* 97 (1987): 187–94.

French, Roger and Andrew Cunningham. *Before Science: the Invention of the Friars' Natural Philosophy*. Aldershot, 1996.

Fry, Donald K. "The Art of Bede: Edwin's Council." In *Saints, Scholars and Heroes: Studies in Medieval Culture in Honour of Charles W. Jones*. Edited by Margot H. King and Wesley M. Stevens. Vol. 1., pp. 191–207. Collegeville, Minn., 1979.

Gerchow, Jan. "The Origins of the Durham *Liber Vitae*." In Rollason, *The Durham Liber Vitae and its Context*, pp. 63–85.

Bibliography

Giles, J. A. *The Complete Works of the Venerable Bede.* 12 vols. London, 1843–44.

Gneuss, Helmut. *Handlist of Anglo-Saxon Manuscripts: A List of Manuscripts and Manuscript Fragments Written or Owned in England up to 1100.* Medieval and Renaissance Studies 241. Tempe, Ariz., 2001.

Godden, Malcolm. *Ælfric's Catholic Homilies: Introduction, Commentary and Glossary.* Early English Text Society, SS 18. Oxford, 2000.

Goffart, Walter. *The Narrators of Barbarian History (A.D. 550–800): Jordanes, Gregory of Tours, Bede, and Paul the Deacon.* Princeton, 1988. Reprinted, Notre Dame, Ind., 2005.

———. "The *Historia ecclesiastica*: Bede's Agenda and Ours." *The Haskins Society Journal* 2 (1990): 29–45.

———. "Bede's *Uera lex historiae* Explained." *Anglo-Saxon England* 34 (2005): 111–16.

Gorman, Michael. "The Commentary on the Pentateuch Attributed to Bede in PL 91.189–208." Revue *Bénédictine* 106 (1996): 61–108, 255–307.

———. "Bede's *VIII Quaestiones* and Carolingian Biblical Scholarship." *Revue Bénédictine* 109 (1999): 32–74.

———. "The Commentary on Genesis of Claudius of Turin and Biblical Studies under Louis the Pious." *Speculum* 72 (1997): 279–329.

———. "The Canon of Bede's Works and the World of Ps. Bede." *Revue Bénédictine* 111 (2001): 399–445.

———. "Source Marks and Chapter Divisions in Bede's Commentary on Luke." *Revue Bénédictine* 112 (2002): 246–90.

Grabbe, Lester. *Ezra-Nehemiah.* Old Testament Readings. London, 1998.

Guglielmetti, Rosanna. "'Super Cantica canticorum': Nota sulla tradizione dei commenti di Ruperto di Deutz, Bernardo di Clairvaux, Guglielmo di Saint-Thierry, Beda e Alcuino." *Studi Medievali* 43 (2002): 277–86.

Hanning, Robert. *The Vision of History in Early Britain.* New York, 1966.

Harris, Stephen. "Bede and Gregory's Allusive Angels." *Criticism* 44.3 (2002): 271–89.

Harrison, Kenneth. "Easter Cycles and the Equinox in the British Isles." *Anglo-Saxon England* 7 (1978): 1–8.

Hart-Hasler, J. N. "*Vestigia patrum sequens*: The Venerable Bede's Use of Patristic Sources in his Commentary on the Gospel of Luke." Unpublished Ph.D. diss. Cambridge, 1999.

_____. "Bede's Use of Patristic Sources: The Transfiguration." *Studia Patristica* 28 (1993): 197–204.

Haskins, Charles Homer. *Studies in the History of Mediaeval Science*, 2nd edn. Cambridge, Mass., 1927.

Hawkes, Jane and Susan Mills, eds. *Northumbria's Golden Age.* Stroud, 1999.

Hill, Joyce. "Ælfric and Smaragdus." *Anglo-Saxon England* 21 (1992): 203–37.

_____. "Ælfric's Sources Reconsidered: Some Case Studies from the *Catholic Homilies.*" In *Studies in English Language and Literature, 'Doubt wisely': Papers in Honour of E. G. Stanley.* Edited by M. J. Toswell and E. M. Tyler, pp. 362–86. London, 1996.

_____. "Translating the Tradition: Manuscripts, Models and Methodologies in the Composition of Ælfric's Catholic Homilies." The 1996 Toller Lecture. *Bulletin of the John Rylands Library* 79 (1997): 43–65.

Bibliography

_____. *Bede and the Benedictine Reform.* Jarrow Lecture 1998.

_____. "Authority and Intertextuality in the Works of Ælfric." The British Academy Gollancz Lecture for 2004, *Proceedings of the British Academy* 131 (2005): 157–81.

Holder, Arthur G. "New Treasures for Old in Bede's *De tabernaculo* and *De templo.*" *Revue Bénédictine* 99 (1989): 237–49.

_____. "Allegory and History in Bede's Interpretation of Sacred Architecture." *American Benedictine Review* 40 (1989): 115–31.

_____. "Bede and the Tradition of Patristic Exegesis." *Anglican Theological Review* 72 (1990): 399–411.

_____. "The Venerable Bede on the Mysteries of Our Salvation." *American Benedictine Review* 42 (1991): 140–62.

_____. Introduction to *Bede: On the Tabernacle.* Translated by Arthur G. Holder. Translated Texts for Historians 18. Liverpool, 1994.

_____. "(Un)Dating Bede's *De Arte Metrica.*" In *Northumbria's Golden Age,* pp. 390–95.

_____. "The Patristic Sources of Bede's Commentary on the Song of Songs." *Studia Patristica* 34 (2001): 370–5.

Hollis, Stephanie. *Anglo-Saxon Women and the Church: Sharing a Common Fate.* Woodbridge, 1992.

Houwen, L. A. J. R. and A. A. MacDonald, eds. *Beda Venerabilis: Historian, Monk and Northumbrian.* Groningen, 1996.

Irvine, Martin. "Bede the Grammarian and the Scope of Grammatical Studies in Eighth-Century Northumbria." *Anglo-Saxon England* 15 (1986): 15–44.

_____. *The Making of Textual Culture: 'Grammatica' and Literary Theory.* Cambridge Studies in Medieval Literature 19. Cambridge, 1994.

Jay, Pierre. *L'exégèse de Saint Jérôme, d'après son Commentaire sur Isaïe.* Paris, 1985.

Jenkins, Claude. "Bede as Exegete and Theologian." In Thompson, *Bede: His Life, Times, and Writings,* pp. 152–200.

John, Eric. "Social and Political Problems of the Early English Church." *Agricultural History Review* 18 (1970): 39–63. Reprinted in *Anglo-Saxon History: Basic Readings.* Edited by David A. E. Pelteret, pp. 21–53. New York, 2000.

Jones, Charles W. "The 'Lost' Sirmond Manuscript of Bede's computus." *English Historical Review* 51 (1937): 204–19.

_____. *Baedae Opera de Temporibus.* Medieval Academy of America 41. Cambridge, Mass, 1943.

_____. *Saints' Lives and Chronicles in Early England.* Ithaca, N.Y., 1947.

_____. "Bede." In *Dictionary of Scientific Biography.* Edited by Charles C. Gillispie. Vol. 1, pp. 564–6. New York, 1970.

_____. "Some Introductory Remarks on Bede's *Commentary on Genesis.*" *Sacris Erudiri* 19 (1970): 115–98.

_____. "Bede's Place in the Medieval Schools." In Bonner, *Famulus Christi,* pp. 261–85.

Kaczynski, Bernice M. "Bede's Commentaries on Luke and Mark and the Formation of a Patristic Canon." In *Anglo-Latin Literature and Its Heritage: Essays in Honour of A. G. Rigg on His 64th Birthday.* Edited by Siân Echard and Gernot R. Wieland, pp. 17–26. Publications of the Journal of Medieval Latin 4. Turnhout, 2001.

Bibliography

Karkov, Catherine E. "Whitby, Jarrow and the Commemoration of Death in Northumbria." In *Northumbria's Golden Age*, pp. 126–35.

Kelly, J. N. D. *Jerome: His Life, Writings, and Controversies*. London, 1975.

Kelly, Joseph F. "Bede on the Brink." *Journal of Early Christian Studies* 5 (1997): 85–103.

Kendall, Calvin B. "Imitation and Bede's *Historia ecclesiastica*." In *Saints, Scholars, and Heroes: Studies in Medieval Culture Presented to Charles W. Jones*. Edited by Margot H. King and W. M. Stevens. Vol. 1, pp. 161–90. Collegeville, Minn., 1979.

―――. "Bede's *Historia ecclesiastica*: The Rhetoric of Faith." In *Medieval Eloquence*. Edited by James J. Murphy, pp. 145–72. Berkeley, 1987.

―――. "'The Manifest Truth of History': Method and Meaning in Bede's Triple Narrative of the Conversion of King Edwin." Paper presented at the conference on "Bede as Writer and Thinker," Center for Medieval Studies, University of Minnesota, April 1998.

Ker, W. P. *The Dark Ages*. London, 1958.

Kirby, David P. "Bede's Native Sources for the *Historia ecclesiastica*." *Bulletin of the John Rylands Library* 48 (1965–66): 341–71.

―――. "Bede, Eddius Stephanus and the 'Life of Wilfrid'." *English Historical Review* 98 (1983): 101–14.

―――. *The Earliest English Kings*. London, 1990.

―――. *Bede's Historia ecclesiastica gentis Anglorum: Its Contemporary Setting*. Jarrow Lecture 1992. Reprinted in Lapidge, *Bede and His World*, 2:903–26.

Knappe, Gabriele. *Traditionen der klassichen Rhetorik in angelsächsischen England*. Anglistische Forschungen 236. Heidelberg, 1996.

_____. "Classical Rhetoric in Anglo-Saxon England." *Anglo-Saxon England* 27 (1999): 5– 29.

Knibbs, Erik. "Exegetical Hagiography: Bede's Prose *Vita Sancti Cuthberti.*" *Revue Bénédictine* 114 (2004): 233–52.

Knowles, David. *Saints and Scholars: Twenty-Five Medieval Portraits.* Cambridge, 1962.

Kugel, James L. *The Bible as It Was.* Cambridge, 1997.

Laistner, M. L. W. "Source-Marks in Bede Manuscripts." *Journal of Theological Studies* 34 (1933): 350–4.

_____. "Bede as a Classical and a Patristic Scholar." *Transactions of the Royal Historical Society.* 4th Series 16 (1933): 69–94. Reprinted in *Intellectual Heritage,* pp. 93–116.

_____. "The Library of the Venerable Bede." In Thomson, *Bede,* pp. 237–66.

_____. *The Intellectual Heritage of the Middle Ages: Selected Essays by M. L. W. Laistner.* Edited by Chester G. Starr. Ithaca, N.Y., 1957

Laistner. M. L. W. with H. H. King, *A Hand-List of Bede Manuscripts.* Ithaca, N.Y., 1943.

Lapidge, Michael, ed. *Bede and his World: The Jarrow Lectures.* 2 vols. Aldershot, 1994.

Lapidge, Michael. *The Anglo-Saxon Library* (Oxford, 2006).

Lapidge, Michael, with John Blair, Simon Keynes, and Donald Scragg, eds. *The Blackwell Encyclopaedia of Anglo-Saxon England.* Oxford, 1999.

Lebecq, Stéphane, Michel Perrin, and Olivier Szerwiniack, eds. *Bède le Vénérable: entre tradition et postérité.* Lille, 2005.

Leclercq, Jean. *The Love of Learning and the Desire for God.* Translated by Catharine Misrahi. New York, 1962.

Lees, Clare and Gillian Overing. "Birthing Bishops and Fathering Poets: Bede, Hild, and the Relations of Cultural Production." *Exemplaria* 6 (1994): 35–65.

Leonardi, Claudio. "Il venerabile Beda e la culura del secolo VIII." *Settimana di studi* 20 (1973): 603-58.

Mâle, Émile. *Religious Art in France, The Thirteenth Century: A Study of Medieval Iconography and Its Sources.* Bollingen Series 90.2. Edited by Harry Bober. Translated by Marthiel Mathews. Princeton, 1984.

Markus, Robert A. *Bede and the Tradition of Ecclesiastical Historiography.* Jarrow Lecture, 1975. Reprinted in Lapidge, *Bede and His World*, 1:385–403.

Marsden, Richard. *The Text of the Old Testament in Anglo-Saxon England.* Cambridge Studies in Anglo-Saxon England 15. Cambridge, 1995.

Martin, Lawrence T. "Bede's Structural Use of Wordplay as a Way to Teach." In *From Cloister to Classroom: Monastic and Scholastic Approaches to Truth.* Edited by E. Rozanne Elder, pp. 145–72. Kalamazoo, Mich., 1986.

_____. "The Two Worlds in Bede's Homilies: The Biblical Event and the Listeners' Experience." In *De Ore Domini: Preacher and Word in the Middle Ages.* Edited by Thomas L. Amos, Eugene A. Green, and Beverly Mayne Kienzle, pp. 27–40. Kalamazoo, Mich., 1989.

_____. Introduction to *The Venerable Bede: Commentary on the Acts of the Apostles.* Cistercian Studies Series, 117. Kalamazoo, Mich., 1989.

Matter, E. Ann. *The Voice of My Beloved: The Song of Songs in Western Medieval Christianity.* Philadelphia, 1990.

Mayr-Harting, Henry. *The Coming of Christianity to Anglo-Saxon England.* London, 1972.

_____. *The Venerable Bede, the Rule of St. Benedict, and Social Class.* Jarrow Lecture 1976. Reprinted in Lapidge, *Bede and His World,* 1:404–34.

_____. "Bede's Patristic Thinking as an Historian." In *Historiographie im frühen Mittelalter.* Edited by Anton Scharer and Georg Scheibelreiter, pp. 367–74. Veröffentlichungen des Instituts fur Österreichische Geschichtsforschung. Vienna, 1994.

McClure, Judith. "Bede's Old Testament Kings." In *Ideal and Reality in Frankish and Anglo- Saxon Society. Studies Presented to J. M. Wallace-Hadrill,* Edited by Patrick Wormald, pp. 76–98. Oxford, 1983.

_____. "Bede's *Notes on Genesis* and the Training of the Anglo-Saxon Clergy." In *The Bible in the Medieval World: Essays in Memory of Beryl Smalley.* Edited by Katherine Walsh and Diana Wood, pp. 17–30. Studies in Church History, *Subsidia* 4. Oxford, 1985.

McClure, Judith and Roger Collins, eds. Introduction to *The Ecclesiastical History of the English People. The Greater Chronicle. Bede's Letter to Egbert.* Oxford World's Classics. Oxford, 1994.

McCready, William D. *Miracles and the Venerable Bede.* Texts and Studies 118. Toronto, 1994.

_____. "Bede and the Isidorian Legacy." *Mediaeval Studies* 57 (1995): 43–73.

_____. "Bede, Isidore, and the *Epistola Cuthberti.*" *Traditio* 50 (1995): 75–94.

McKitterick, Rosamond. *History and Memory in the Carolingian World.* Cambridge, 2004.

Metzger, Bruce M. and Roland E. Murphy, eds. *The New Oxford Annotated Bible, New Revised Standard Version.* New York, 1994.

Meyvaert, Paul. "Bede and Gregory the Great." Jarrow Lecture, 1966. Reprinted in Lapidge, *Bede and His World*, pp. 107–32.

_____. "Bede the Scholar." In Bonner, *Famulus Christi*, pp. 40–69.

_____. "In the Footsteps of the Fathers: The Date of Bede's *Thirty Questions on the Book of Kings* to Nothelm." In *The Limits of Ancient Christianity: Essays in Honour of R. A, Markus.* Edited by William F. Klingshirn and Mark Vessey, pp. 267–86. Ann Arbor, Mich., 1999.

_____. "The Date of Bede's In Ezram and His Image in the Codex Amiatinus," Speculum 80 (2005): 1087–1133.

Neville, Jennifer. *Representations of the Natural World in Old English Poetry.* Cambridge Studies in Anglo-Saxon England 27. Cambridge, 1999.

Nie, Giselle de. *Views from a Many-Windowed Tower.* Amsterdam, 1987.

Ogilvy, J. D. A. *The Place of Wearmouth-Jarrow in Western Culture History.* Jarrow Lecture, 1968. Reprinted in Lapidge, *Bede and his World*, pp. 235–46.

Olsen, Glen. "Bede as Historian: the Evidence from his Observations on the Life of the First Christian Community at Jerusalem." *Journal of Ecclesiastical History* 33 (1982): 519–30.

Orchard, Andy. *The Poetic Art of Aldhelm.* Cambridge Studies in Anglo-Saxon England 8. Cambridge, 1998.

O'Reilly, Jennifer. Introduction to *Bede: On the Temple.* Translated Seán Connolly. Translated Texts for Historians 21. Liverpool, 1995.

_____. "Islands and Idols at the End of the Earth: Exegesis and Conversion in Bede's *Historia ecclesiastica*." In Lebecq, *Bède le Vénérable*, pp. 119–45.

Parkes, Michael B. *The Scriptorium of Wearmouth Jarrow*. Jarrow Lecture 1982. Reprinted in *Bede and his World*, 2:555–86

Pelikan, Jaroslav. *What Has Athens to Do with Jerusalem? Timaeus and Genesis in Counterpoint.* Jerome Lectures, 21. Ann Arbor, Mich., 1997.

Pelteret, David. "Year's Work in Old English Studies 1988: History and Culture." *Old English Newsletter* 23.1 (1989): 81–98.

Pépin, Jean *Théologie cosmique et théologies chrétiennes*. Paris, 1964.

Pfaff, Richard W. "Bede among the Fathers: The Evidence of Liturgical Commemoration." *Studia Patristica* 28 (1993): 225–9.

Plummer, Charles. *Venerabilis Baedae opera historica*. 2 vols. 1896. Reprinted, 2 vols. in 1, Oxford, 1946.

Rädle, Fidel. *Studien zu Smaragd von Saint-Mihiel*. Munich, 1974.

Ray, Roger. "Bede, the Exegete, as Historian." In Bonner, *Famulus Christi*, pp. 125–40.

———. "Bede's *Vera Lex Historiae*." *Speculum* 55 (1980): 1–21.

———. "What Do We Know about Bede's Commentaries?" *Recherches de théologie ancienne et médiévale* 49 (1982): 1–20.

———. "The Triumph of Pagan Rhetorical Assumptions in Pre-Carolingian Historiography." In *The Inheritance of Historiography, 300–900*. Edited by Christopher J. Holdsworth and Timothy P. Wiseman, pp. 66–84. Exeter, 1986.

———. "Bede and Cicero." *Anglo-Saxon England* 16 (1987): 1–15.

———. *Bede, Rhetoric, and the Creation of Christian Latin Culture*. Jarrow Lecture 1997.

Bibliography

Reese, James M. "Wisdom of Solomon." In *The Oxford Companion to the Bible*, pp. 803–5. Edited by Bruce M. Metzger and Michael D. Coogan, pp. 803–5. Oxford, 1993.

Remley, Paul. "Year's Work in Old English Studies." *Old English Newsletter* 25.2 (1992): 59–67.

Ritson, G. Joy. "Eros, Allegory and Spirituality: The Development of Heavenly Bridegroom Imagery in the Western Christian Church from Origen to Gregory the Great." 2 vols. Ph.D. diss., Graduate Theological Union. Berkeley, 1997.

Robertson, Jr., D. W. Introduction to *Saint Augustine: On Christian Doctrine.* New York, 1958.

Robinson, Bernard. "The Venerable Bede as Exegete." *Downside Review* 112 (1994): 201–26.

Rollason, David. *Bede and Germany.* Jarrow Lecture, 2001.

Rollason, David, A. J. Piper, Margaret Harvey, and Linda Rollason, eds. *The Durham Liber Vitae and its Context.* Woodbridge, 2004.

Rouse, Richard H. and Mary A. Rouse. *Registrum Anglie de libris doctorum et auctorum veterum.* Corpus of British Medieval Library Catalogues 2. London, 1991.

Scully, Diarmuid. Introduction to *Bede: On Tobit and On the Canticle of Habakkuk.* Translated by Seán Connolly. Dublin, 1997.

———. "The Atlantic Archipelago from Antiquity to Bede: The Transformation of an Image." Unpublished Ph.D. diss., University College, Cork, 2000.

Smalley, Beryl. *The Study of the Bible in the Middle Ages.* 1959. Reprinted, Notre Dame, 1964.

Smetana, Cyril L. "Ælfric and the Early Medieval Homiliary." *Traditio* 15 (1959): 163–204.

_____. "Paul the Deacon's Patristic Anthology." In *The Old English Homily and its Backgrounds.* Edited by Paul E. Szarmach and Bernard F. Huppé, pp. 75–97. Albany, 1978.

Smyth, Marina. *Understanding the Universe in Seventh-Century Ireland.* Studies in Celtic History 15. Woodbridge, 1996.

Souter, Alexander. "Contributions to the Criticism of Zmaragdus's *Expositio libri comitis.*" *Journal of Theological Studies* 9 (1908): 584–97.

_____. "Further Contributions to the Criticism of Zmaragdus's *Expositio libri comitis.*" *Journal of Theological Studies* 23 (1922): 73–76.

_____. "A Further Contribution to the Criticism of Zmaragdus's *Expositio libri comitis.*" *Journal of Theological Studies* 34 (1933): 46–47.

_____. *A Glossary of Later Latin to 600 A.D.* Oxford, 1949.

Southern, R. W. "Bede." In *Medieval Humanism and Other Studies,* pp. 1–8. 1970. Reprinted Oxford, 1984

_____. *Robert Grosseteste: the Growth of an English Mind in Medieval Europe.* Oxford, 1986.

Stancliffe, Clare. "Cuthbert and the Polarity between Pastor and Solitary." In *Saint Cuthbert: His Cult and His Community to A.D. 1200.* Edited by Gerald Bonner, David Rollason, and Clare Stancliffe, pp. 21–44. Woodbridge, 1989.

Stevens, Wesley. *Bede's Scientific Achievement.* Jarrow Lecture, 1985. Reprinted in Lapidge, *Bede and his World,* 2:645–88.

Stock, Brian. *The Implications of Literacy: Written Language and Models of Interpretation in the Eleventh and Twelfth Centuries.* Princeton, 1983.Strunz,

Bibliography

Franz. "Beda Venerabilis in der Geschichte der Naturbetrachtung und Na turforschung," *Zeitschrift für deutsche Geschichte* 1 (1935): 311–32. Reprinted in *Scientia* 66 (1939): 57–70, with French translation in its Supplementum (1939): 37–49

Sutcliffe, E. J. "Quotations in the Ven. Bede's Commentary on S. Mark." *Biblica* 7 (1926): 428–39.

Szarmach, Paul, M. Teresa Tavormina and Joel T. Rosenthal, eds. *Medieval England: An Encyclopedia.* New York, 1998.

Thacker, Alan. "Bede's Ideal of Reform." In *Ideal and Reality in Frankish and Anglo-Saxon Society: Studies Presented to John Michael Wallace-Hadrill.* Edited by Patrick Wormald, Donald Bullough, and Roger Collins, pp. 103–22. Oxford, 1983.

_____. "Lindisfarne and the Origins of the Cult of St. Cuthbert." In *St. Cuthbert, His Cult and His Community to AD 1200.* Edited by Gerald Bonner, David Rollason, Clare Stancliffe, pp. 103–22. Woodbridge, 1989.

_____. "Monks, Preaching and Pastoral Care." In *Pastoral Care Before the Parish.* Edited by John Blair and Richard Sharpe, pp. 137–70. Leicester, 1992.

_____. "Bede and the Irish." In Houwen, *Beda Venerabilis,* pp. 31–59.

_____. "Wilfrid [St. Wilfrid] (c. 634-709/10)." In *Oxford Dictionary of National Biography.* Edited by H. C. G. Matthew and Brian Harrison. Vol. 58, pp. 944–50. Oxford, 2004.

_____. *Bede and Augustine: History and Figure in Sacred Text.* Jarrow Lecture, 2005, forthcoming.

Thompson, A. Hamilton, ed. *Bede, His Life, Times, and Writings: Essays in Commemoration of the Twelfth Centenary of his Death.* Oxford, 1935.

Thum, Beda. "Beda Venerabilis in der Geschichte der Naturwissenschaften." *Studia Anselmiana* 6 (1936): 57–71.

Tugene, Georges. "L'histoire 'ecclesiastique' du peuple anglais: Réflexions sur le particularisme et l'universalisme chez Béde." *Recherches Augustiniennes* 17 (1982): 129–72.

———. *L'idée de nation chez Bède le Vénérable.* Collection des Études Augustiniennes. Série Moyen Âge et Temps Modernes 37. Paris, 2001.

Wallace-Hadrill. D. S. *The Greek Patristic View of Nature.* Manchester, 1968.

Wallace-Hadrill, J. M. *Bede's Ecclesiastical History of the English People: A Historical Commentary.* 1988. Reprinted Oxford, 1991.

Wallis, Faith. Introduction to *Bede: The Reckoning of Time.* Translated by Faith Wallis. Translated Texts for Historians 29. Liverpool, 1999.

Ward, Benedicta. *The Venerable Bede.* London, 1990.

———. *Bede and the Psalter.* Jarrow Lecture, 1991. Reprinted in Lapidge, *Bede and His World,* 2:868–902.

———. "'In medium duorum animalium': Bede and Jerome on the Canticle of Habakkuk." *Studia Patristica* 25 (1993): 189–93.

West. Philip. "Liturgical Style and Structure in Bede's Christmas Homilies." *American Benedictine Review* 23 (1972): 424–38.

Whitelock, Dorothy. *After Bede.* Jarrow Lecture 1960. Reprinted in Lapidge, *Bede and His World,* 1:35–49.

———. "The OE Bede." *Proceedings of the British Academy* 48 (1962): 57–90.

Willmes, Ansgar. "Bedas Bibelauslegung." *Archiv für Kulturgeschichte* 44 (1963): 281–314.

Bibliography

Wiseman, Timothy P. "Practice and Theory in Roman Historiography." *History* 28 (1981): 375–393

Wood, Ian. *The Most Holy Abbot Ceolfrid.* Jarrow Lecture, 1995.

Wood, Leon. *A Survey of Israel's History.* Revised by David O'Brien. Grand Rapids, Mich., 1986.

Wormald, Patrick. "Bede and Benedict Biscop." In Bonner, *Famulus Christi*, pp. 141–69.

_____. "Bede, *Beowulf* and the Conversion of the Anglo-Saxon Aristocracy." In Farrell, *Bede and Anglo-Saxon England*, pp. 32–90.

Wright, Addison G. "Wisdom." In *The New Jerome Biblical Commentary.* Edited by Raymond E. Brown, Joseph A. Fitzmyer, and Roland E. Murphy, pp. 76–98. Englewood Cliffs, N.J., 1990.

Wright, Neil R. "Bede and Virgil." *Romanobarbarica* 6 (1981): 361–79.

Contributors

GEORGE HARDIN BROWN, Professor Emeritus of English, Stanford University

SCOTT DEGREGORIO, Assistant Professor of English Language and Literature, University of Michigan–Dearborn

WALTER GOFFART, Professor Emeritus of History, University of Toronto and Senior Research Scholar and Lecturer, Yale University

JOYCE HILL, Professor of Old and Middle English, University of Leeds

ARTHUR G. HOLDER, Dean and Professor of Christian Spirituality, Graduate Theological Union, Berkeley, California

CALVIN B. KENDALL, Morse Alumni Distinguished Teaching Professor Emeritus of English, University of Minnesota

LAWRENCE T. MARTIN, Professor of English and Director of American Indian Studies, University of Wisconsin–Eau Claire

ROGER RAY, Professor of History and Director of the Humanities Institute, University of Toledo

ALAN THACKER, Reader in Medieval History and Executive Editor of the Victoria County History, Institute of Historical Research London, University of London

FAITH WALLIS, Associate Professor in the Department of History and of Social Studies of Medicine, McGill University, Montreal

Index

Abelard, Peter, 14

Acca, bishop, 42, 52–54, 129, 216, 218–20

Ælfric of Eynsham, 239, 242–8

Æthelfrith, king, 56

Aidan, bishop, 213, 221–2, 226n

Alcuin, 13, 139, 141, 218n, 230–1, 249

Aldfrid, king, 214–16

Aldhelm, 41, 139

Amalarius of Metz, 227

Ambrose, St, 12–13, 53, 77, 123, 139, 176, 235

Anselm of Bec, St, 11, 176

Apocrypha, 47, 193

Aquinas, Thomas, St 14

Arator, 20, 52

Atilius Fortunatianus, 141

Augustine, author of *De mirabilibus sacrae scripturae*, 69, 78

Augustine of Canterbury, St, 236

Augustine of Hippo, St 11–13, 20–24, 45, 48, 53, 57, 63, 76n, 78, 95n, 103–4, 106, 112n, 113, 117–18, 123–6, 130, 139, 141, 176, 178, 191, 198, 228, 235–7, 242–4

Basil of Caesarea, 30

Bede:

accused of heresy: 20–21

as *doctor*: 14, 43–46

as hagiographer: 92–97, 181–4

as historian: 29–32, 179–88, 203–226

as innovator: 19–26, 46, 52, 60, 62, 138, 143–5, 156–68, 190–1

as reformer: 58–59, 156–65, 181, 218n

concern with pastoral care: 54–57, 156–65

exegetical technique: 52–60, 101–119, 122–4, 127–40, 147–65, 171–5

latinity of: 26–27, 29, 136–9

knowledge of Greek, 20

reputation as Church Father: 11–14, 167, 227–249

use of classical rhetoric: 17–18, 21–24, 28–32, 38

Works of:

CPE, 53–54

DAM, 49

De oct. quest., 58

De tab., 14, 47, 51, 54n, 55, 58, 122, 143n, 148–9, 154n, 166n, 237, 240

De templ., 14, 47, 50–51, 54n, 55, 58, 122, 143n, 148–9, 154n, 187

DNR, 48–49, 65, 71–79, 81n, 88, 90n, 96

Printed in the United States
48377LVS00004B/79-273